NEEPA MAJUMDAR

Wanted Cultured Ladies Only!

FEMALE STARDOM
AND CINEMA IN INDIA,
1930S–1950S

UNIVERSITY OF ILLINOIS PRESS
URBANA AND CHICAGO

All photos are courtesy of the National Film Archive of India unless otherwise indicated.

Manufactured in the United States of America
1 2 3 4 5 C P 5 4 3 2 1
∞ This book is printed on acid-free paper.

Library of Congress Cataloging-in-Publication Data
Majumdar, Neepa.
Wanted cultured ladies only! : female stardom and cinema in India, 1930s–1950s / Neepa Majumdar.
p. cm.
Includes bibliographical references and index.
ISBN 978-0-252-03432-9 (cloth : alk. paper)
ISBN 978-0-252-07628-2 (pbk. : alk. paper)
1. Motion pictures—India—History.
2. Motion picture actors and actresses—India—Biography.
3. Actresses—India—Biography.
4. Women in motion pictures.
I. Title.
PN1993.5.I8M34 2009
791.4302'8092291411—dc22 2008035896

WANTED CULTURED LADIES ONLY!

Contents

Illustrations

Acknowledgments

I am grateful to the many institutions and individuals without whose generous support this book could not have been written. A Junior Research Fellowship from the American Institute of Indian Studies enabled me to conduct initial research at the National Film Archive of India, and a grant-in-aid of research from Indiana University allowed me to view the Library of Congress's collection of early Indian films. I am also thankful to the Film Studies Program at Indiana University for a dissertation fellowship and to the University of Pittsburgh for its Third Term Research Stipend, which enabled me to return for further research to the NFAI. The generous assistance of Mr. Suresh Chabria during my first visit to the NFAI, and of Mr. K. Shashidharan during my second visit, enabled me to use my limited time at the archive efficiently. I extend grateful thanks also to the librarians at NFAI, especially Ms. Eyer, Ms. Joshi, and Ms. Kshirsagar, for their helpful suggestions during the research process, and to Mr. Kiran A. Dhiwar for his help in arranging video screenings for me. Mr. M. D. Bhandare and Bhagyashree Bhandare of the American Institute of Indian Studies provided indispensable logistical help in Pune.

During the time I have spent working on this book, James Naremore has been unfailing in his support and encouragement. Without his example and direction, I would not be the scholar I am today. Jim's course on stars and his scholarship on stardom and acting strongly influenced my own thinking on film stars and performance. It was in a class on theories of mass culture taught by him and Patrick Brantlinger that I first encountered the heady excitement of engaging what might otherwise be viewed as culturally debased texts. This was at a time when Indian commercial films were not yet fashionable, instead epitomizing lowbrow culture, and this class gave me my first opportunity to write on my own guilty pleasures. Similarly, if I am in film studies today, it is entirely thanks to Barbara Klinger's energizing film courses, which enticed me into film studies against my original intentions. At Indiana University, Purnima Bose was one of my earliest readers, and conversations with her helped shape the direction of my research. I thank her and Radhika Parameswaran for their friendship and their suggestions on the earliest draft of chapter 4, which I presented at the "Materializing India" conference they organized at Indiana University.

My colleagues at the University of Pittsburgh have provided a supportive and intellectually engaging environment, and I thank Lucy Fischer and Marcia Landy for their feedback on my work. I am grateful to Shalini Puri for giving up precious time from her leave to read every word of the first full draft of this book. Her meticulous comments and suggestions helped me rethink key areas of my argument. Corey Creekmur has been equally important to the final shape of this book, and I thank him for his insightful reading of many incarnations of my manuscript and for his generosity in sending me films and other materials that I did not have access to. Corey and Philip Lutgendorf were the original instigators of what eventually became chapter 7 of this book, and over the years they have been important interlocutors on various portions of the book that I have presented at conferences in Iowa and Wisconsin.

During the finishing stages of this book, I have been the grateful recipient of generous suggestions and feedback from colleagues working in Indian cinema, including Manishita Dass, Sangita Gopal, and Priya Jaikumar. I thank Rashmi Bhatnagar for always being ready to give up her time to read any fragment I needed a second pair of eyes for. Gayatri Chatterjee, Rosie Thomas, and Ravi Vasudevan generously shared hard-to-find films with me, and Ranjani Mazumdar took it upon herself to obtain most of the photographs for this book. Without her help and the efficiency of NFAI in finding most of the images I wanted, this would have been a dull book indeed! I thank my students Ben Herstrom, for his research assistance with microfilms of *Bombay Chronicle,* and Usha Iyer, for bringing me some of the book's images. For their support over the course of writing this book, I thank Pravu Mazumdar, Deepa Majumdar, Yifen Beus, Katrina Boyd, Millie Elliot, and Arti Mehta.

This book would quite simply not exist without the support of Mark Best, Ila Majumdar, and Maya Best. I thank Mark for his patient hours of reading and rereading pages that even I could no longer bear to look at, and for being perhaps the only person who would watch Indian silent movies with me for entertainment. I thank my mother for her calm presence in the home, which made it possible for me to juggle teaching, writing, and parenting. Perhaps the person who gave up the most for this book is Maya, and for that the two words "thank you" can never be enough.

Introduction

TRANSLOCATING HOLLYWOOD STARDOM IN INDIA

Cinema arrived in India on 7 July 1896, just six months after the first public screening by the Lumière brothers in Paris. By the 1930s, alongside the material technology of filmmaking, such as raw film stock, cameras, projectors, lighting equipment, and, most recently, sound systems, Indian cinema had imported the less material but no less powerful cultural apparatus of the Hollywood *mode* of filmmaking, which was then, in varying accents, grafted onto existing Indian forms of entertainment. A stock-taking account of the history of Indian cinema written for the 1933 annual issue of *Rangbhoomi,* a Hindi weekly film magazine which had started the previous year, described the cultural complications associated with the entry of this new medium into India: since cinema had spent its infancy and youth in another country before coming to India, "that is why its limbs, its color, its appearance, its mentality, and its instincts have all become foreign." The author used the allegory of hospitality to a stranger to raise the question of compatibility: how does one offer food on a leaf-plate to one who is used to Western-style plates; Indian clothing to one who wears suits; or the Devanagiri script to one used to foreign accents?[1] Against this concern with translation, consider a 1937 *filmindia* editorial titled "India Has No Stars": "In India we never had real stars, and will probably never have any for a long time to come."[2]

By the 1930s, Indian journalistic discourse on cinema was already historicizing itself and was obsessively engaged in asserting Indian cinematic identity and measuring it against international norms. Contrary

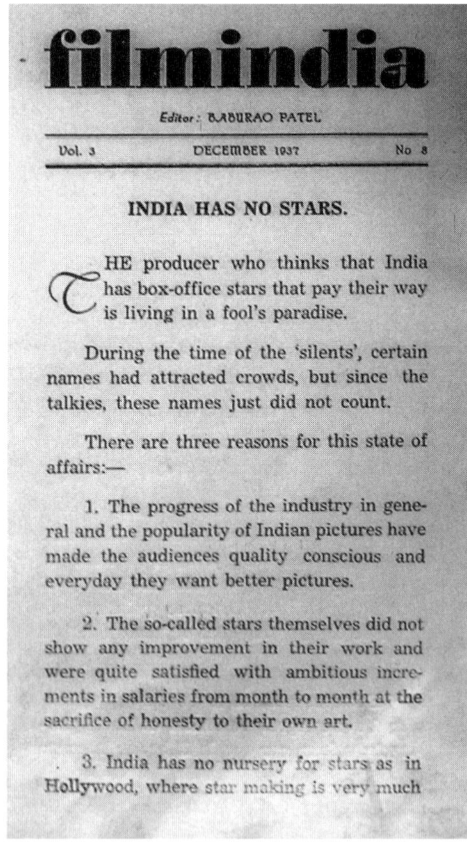

filmindia

Editor: BABURAO PATEL

Vol. 3 DECEMBER 1937 No 8

INDIA HAS NO STARS.

THE producer who thinks that India has box-office stars that pay their way is living in a fool's paradise.

During the time of the 'silents', certain names had attracted crowds, but since the talkies, these names just did not count.

There are three reasons for this state of affairs:—

1. The progress of the industry in general and the popularity of Indian pictures have made the audiences quality conscious and everyday they want better pictures.

2. The so-called stars themselves did not show any improvement in their work and were quite satisfied with ambitious increments in salaries from month to month at the sacrifice of honesty to their own art.

3. India has no nursery for stars as in Hollywood, where star making is very much

"India Has No Stars," *filmindia* editorial, December 1937.

to the proclamations of editors and journalists, a "star system" existed in India, but without a printed discourse on the private lives of Indian stars, even though gossip about the sexual liaisons, marriage, divorce, and other scandals of Hollywood stars was routine. In the case of Indian stars, private information was regularly deflected back to a professional context. Rather than the on- and off-screen activities of individual stars, stardom itself was more regularly the subject of fascination and discussion.

Technology is never culturally neutral, and the importation of cinema technology into India was always accompanied by its products. Motion-picture cameras, sound, and color arrived in conjunction with the films themselves, and the material technology and its cultural products became inseparable in the public mind. Thus, it is likely that the first motion-picture cameras, for instance, became inseparable from their production of very specific images, as the Lumière cameramen who traveled around the world to sell the cinematograph screened films to demonstrate the capabilities of their new technology. The Lumière production, *Train Arriving at the Station* (1895), for example, almost immediately gave rise to its Indian counterpart (albeit produced by a foreign production company, Andersonoscopograph), in a Bombay variant, *Train Arriving at Churchgate Station* (1898). Similarly, as American, British, French, and other films circulated in India, they advertised both the new technologies and their cultural and representational possibilities in the form of advertising methods, exhibition venues, technical journals, genres, and stars. Thus, alongside film equipment, film genres, and narrative forms, stardom itself may be regarded as one of the cultural technologies imported from Hollywood. This "technology" included not only Hollywood films starring popular actors and actresses, but perhaps more important, the paraphernalia of publicity, such as photography and film magazines, and the ideologies underlying stardom.

The translocation of the cultural apparatus of narrative forms and film culture into India is far more complex than a simple imported/indigenous dichotomy can hope to suggest. Stephen Hughes, for instance, cautions against a purist lineage of Indian cinematic forms because "the cultural genealogies involving Hindu mythological traditions are insufficient for understanding the pre-history of cinema in India." Rather, the visual and narrative forms of early Indian cinema must be placed in the wider context of parallel transcultural negotiations in other popular forms of representation. Cultural practices such as Indian popular painting, photography, and early cinema emerge through "intricate, dynamic processes implicated in strategies of containment, subjugation, accommodation," and their reuse of specifically traditional ways of arranging spatial relations and of seeing or *darsana*.[3] Indian popular painting from the late nineteenth century, exemplified by the work of Raja Ravi Varma, shifted the meaning of conventions of British "academic" art, such as symmetry and perspective, to combine illusionism with strategies of "frontality," producing what Ashish Rajadhyaksha calls a neo-traditionalist style.[4] Judith Mara Gutman makes a similar point regarding the language of frontality in early Indian photography, which produced photographs "that are puzzling at first to the Westerner" because they draw in unfamiliar ways on "a history of Indian tradition and visual pattern-making." Christopher Pinney reads the translocation of Western techniques in Indian photography, lithography, and early cinema in terms of a diverse set of possibilities in which Western representational techniques "became one among many tools."[5]

The complex issue of translocation is also exemplified, in the case of cinema, in the oft-repeated story of the impulse behind the films of

D. G. Phalke, the maker of *Raja Harishchandra* (1913), long considered to be one of the first feature films in India.[6] While the mythological genre, Phalke's "invention," has been regarded as unique to India, its original cinematic model, as Phalke describes it, was a foreign film, *The Life of Christ.*[7] Yet reading the relation between *The Life of Christ* and Phalke's mythologicals, such as *Lanka Dahan,* through the lens of colonial mimicry neglects the complex cultural space in which *both* films circulated. It is not simply a matter of Indianization of a cultural text originating in the West, but of complex and ultimately commercially driven negotiations of popular taste and critical canons. The stunt and costume film genres, popular in the 1920s, provide further evidence of the complex rewriting of specifically Hollywood technologies of entertainment onto existing Indian forms. A genre that was singlehandedly launched in India by the wild success of Douglas Fairbanks in *The Thief of Bagdad* (Raoul Walsh, 1924), the Indian stunt or action film also drew on "India's own popular visual and performing arts (especially the folk and company theatre form) [which] remained the chief stylistic source of inspiration."[8]

In considering some of the analytical problems posed by the transcultural relocation of the star concept in the early decades of Indian cinema, this book participates in the recent turn to a feminist film history that has reanimated early cinema studies with a project of radically restoring historical and local specificity to multiple "vernacular" cinemas, relativizing and thus expanding the variable and sometimes anachronistic local meanings of the "early" in "early cinema" and the "star" in "stardom."[9] More than merely a project of recovery of marginalized (female) figures or (non-Western) cultural spaces, this new history has also forced a reappraisal of basic disciplinary questions, such as the nature of historical evidence, the relation of film history and theory, and Hollywood's status as the normative popular cinema. Yet, paradoxically, the study of early cinema stars in any national context remains in some ways plagued with the burden of the seemingly always already known, as the regulatory and gendered discourses of cinema and stardom in locations as different as China, Japan, and Britain appear to share a familiar terrain. In this shared global discourse of stardom, we find early film actresses as the object of both fascination and moral censure, taking on the burden of a more generalized anxiety regarding increased female participation and visibility in the public sphere.

Studies of early star discourse in non–U.S. spaces are compelled also to consider their subject in relation to the unquestionable status of Hollywood stars as paradigmatic of stardom itself.[10] Within this terrain, certain repeated topoi present themselves, such as the "New Woman" and her negotiations with modernity, social and technological mobility, and new configurations of domesticity, leisure, and public space. In many recent studies, the predominant model concerning the relation of global and local idioms of cinema has been Miriam Hansen's influential formulation of Hollywood's global impact in mediating "a sensory-reflexive discourse of the experience of modernity and modernization, a matrix for the articulation of fantasies, uncertainties, and anxieties." Hansen's argument is primarily that Hollywood cinema's hegemony as the "first global vernacular" is to be seen not merely as the economic practice it undoubtedly was, but also as a mediation of modernity at the level of the *senses* rather than in terms of representative strategies or narrative form. As Catherine Russell puts it, "the concept of vernacular modernism enables us to recognize the different values attached to cultural forms beyond a formalist model that assigns meaning to technical effects outside their specific contexts of production and reception." To explain why *Hollywood* products, rather than, say, the films produced by Pathé, became the global vernacular, without resorting to arguments about economics, Hansen places the emphasis on local practices of *consumption.* But since localized modes of consumption might apply equally to, say, Pathé, Hansen returns us to the notion of an "Americanization from below," which she explains as a "powerful matrix for modernity's liberatory impulses—its moments of abundance, play, and radical possibility, its glimpses of collectivity and gender equality." If we consider the anxieties surrounding cinema and stardom in multiple national contexts, we find that local debates on cinema were shaped not only by the encounter with Hollywood, but also by older contexts of performance predating Hollywood and often drawing on similarly vernacularized idioms of negotiated global and local performative modes. The concept of vernacular modernism has enabled a productive shift from the focus on national identity in cinema studies toward a flexible and porous understanding of the experience of local film culture, and has opened itself up to new meanings in specific, historically grounded contexts. Both Manishita Dass and William Gardner, for example, writing on Indian and Japanese cinema respectively, turn to the linguistic meaning of *vernacular* to amplify its resonance for the particular cinematic cultures they are studying. Zhang Zhen and Weihong Bao likewise explore multiple resonances of the vernacular, the modern, and the modernist in the context of early cinema in Shanghai.[11]

The reformulation of local cinematic practices as vernacular has also brought a tendency to flatten distinctions among the different ways in which local cinematic discourses functioned outside the context of

Hollywood as a technological, cultural, and economic model. This returns us again to the always already known, the "Modern Girl" and the "New Woman," body-oriented "lower" genres such as stunt films and their spectators, and technologies of speed associated with urbanization, so that modernity has become the new paradigm replacing national identity.[12] In my work, I have found vernacular modernism to be a useful paradigm precisely because it clarifies the ways in which dominant Indian star discourse was *not* in alignment with it. I engage the concept of vernacular modernism in my chapter on the hierarchies of stardom, where the object of study, stunt films, invites its usage. In the dominant discourse of Indian stardom in the 1930s, Hollywood provided a technological model, but emphatically not a model "for modernity's liberatory impulses."[13] Rather, Indian cinema found its model for liberatory, modern (female) identities in nationalist discourses. These identities were aligned with a new urge for respectability, and replaced a more cosmopolitan model of female identity in films of the late 1920s. In the 1930s, although Hollywood embodied technical competency (in producing and innovatively promoting stars), it was not regarded as a model on which Indian star desires could be mapped. Ideologies of Hollywood stardom, with their emphasis on conspicuous consumption, material culture, consumer products, and visible lifestyles, were antithetical to the project of nationalism. If cinema was to insert itself into national debates, it had to refashion its norms of identification and desire as embodied in stars. The result, of course, was a somewhat predictable realignment of star virtue with normative Hindu womanhood. In its broadest outline, one might say that early star culture in India is also always already known. Some of the clichés regarding this period include the social taboo on acting (for both men and women); the recruitment first of prostitutes and then of Anglo-Indians for female roles in silent cinema, and only later the gradual participation of "respectable" Hindu and Muslim women; and the moral taint of cinema as an institution. Most such accounts of early Indian stars make little or no distinction between stars and actors, or between stardom and popularity. Fussy distinctions such as these returned me to the realization that the question "what is a star?" is inextricably tied to theoretical questions of methodology and to other basic questions: How was the idea of the "star," both cinematic and precinematic, understood in India? How was knowledge about stars promoted, shaped, and controlled? What ideologies of gender and subjectivity were inscribed in competing models of stardom?

In analyzing early Indian cinema, one senses overwhelmingly an absent object of study. While this situation is endemic to early cinema studies in many countries, it raises important questions regarding historiographic method.[14] Those of us who work on early Indian cinema, both silent and early sound, tend to envy our colleagues working in other national spaces who can draw on what seems to us like a wealth of surviving materials. At the same time, we are compelled to be more speculative in our assertions, given that the complexity of grounded realities anchored in material cultures becomes skewed by the accidental resurfacing of this or that piece of material or textual "evidence." In areas of research where primary materials are no longer available in their obvious sites (such as films and film magazines), the accidental takes on a new importance in historiographical method—not only the accidentally surviving film text, but also the accidental find of the researcher.[15] My historiographic methodology in this book has to be framed in terms of this caveat.

In film studies, theorizations of the star have been implicated from the start in the actual practice of star analysis. Through individual case studies, Richard Dyer's work on stars implicitly proposed a methodology for star analysis that went beyond screen roles and biography. Drawing from his work, the star was understood as a highly visible social icon constituted out of film roles, biographical information, and extra-cinematic discourses. In this model, derived from the practices of Hollywood cinema, the definition of the star text also implied the appropriate sources for research on stars. Already in American cinema of the 1920s, we see some of these attributes of stardom that became a blueprint for research materials: "Stars became complex creatures with 'textual identities' created by the popular press and Hollywood's promotion machines. . . . Myriad film-related mechanisms—including newspaper interviews and film reviews, trade magazine articles and fan magazines, press agent stunts and theater exhibition displays, publicity photographs and advertising for consumable tie-in products—all formed a discourse of stardom that guaranteed the widest possible circulation of a star's image."[16] What had happened historically was now being replicated in cinema studies: Hollywood provided the global paradigm for cinematic stardom worldwide, and now its modes of functioning were also providing a blueprint for research methodology. That such a blueprint *is* to an extent universal can be seen in a pioneering study of three Indian star texts by Behroze Gandhy and Rosie Thomas, the first to go beyond a biographical and anecdotal approach to Indian stars. Their analysis of Fearless Nadia, Nargis, and Smita Patil relies on the following underlying premises, drawn ultimately from Dyer's important work: that the star image derives from a complex relation between multiple personae constructed through film texts and extra-filmic discourses; that the composite star "text" thus produced is often incoherent; that its incoherences and contradictions can then be read as saying something about the social and cultural context in which the star text is consumed; and that important source materials or building blocks for such a study are rumor, gossip, public revelations about private lives, and multiple exposures of the "real" person behind the role to be found in extra-cinematic sources.[17]

When I approached the subject of stardom in early Indian cinema with a similar blueprint, I found that many of the basic premises underlying such an approach were immediately challenged.[18] India clearly had a functioning star system in the 1930s, but it was not understood in terms of a discourse on private life, that essential staple of star studies, and the textual sites where stardom was articulated were dominated by what I have come to designate as a discourse of surfaces, as opposed to concerns about the "inner essence of the performer."[19] Even though the term *star* was used readily and frequently in relation to Indian players, its connotations did not match my assumptions that there would be a dense extra-textual discourse surrounding individual stars, with private "revelation" of the sort that was readily available in Hollywood or Shanghai at the time. Challenged by the realities of historically situated practices, I found, instead, that "stars" and "stardom" demanded theoretical defamiliarization in the same way that there is a "need to infuse a plurality into the word 'imagination' . . . to make it usefully global" and to avoid bringing "the heterogeneous practices of seeing under the jurisdiction of this one European word 'imagination.'" Dipesh Chakrabarty observes that the "political subject of modernity" always comes up against "the resistance that embodied practices put up against the project of historicization."[20] Even in the United States, Arthur Knight's study shows that a different set of embodied practices produces a need for "both broadening and specializing the meanings of 'star' and 'stardom'" so that these terms could adequately accommodate African American experiences of Hollywood stars. In the context of British cinema stars, too, Bruce Babington notes Richard Dyer's acknowledgment of "the problematics of applying a theory based on Hollywood stars to other cinemas," and he derives a locally specific concept of stars from fifteen "microdiscourses" in *Picturegoer*'s discussion of Violet Hopson. More recent approaches to star study have expanded the textual horizon of what star analysis means, marking surprising interfaces between stardom and other sites of culture.[21] Jennifer Bean's work retheorizes Hollywood's early female stunt stardom as parallel to and competing with cinema's own discourse of referential and psychological realism. Like Bean's, Lucy Fischer's work also presents a way in which stars can make meaning not only through a construction of subjectivity, but also through their surface design.[22]

My overarching argument in this book is rooted in the consequences of Indian commercial cinema's historical status as a guilty pleasure, an unacknowledged cultural force in public life, and a site of public and governmental disavowal. The Indian government's very belated recognition of the film industry *as* industry (with its attendant tax break and financing options) in 1998, and its development as an industry, despite the absence of state support, indicates the ambivalence with which it has been regarded until the end of the twentieth century.[23] This ambivalence toward cinema began in the 1930s, when a desire to participate in the cultural mainstream, which was informed at the time by predominantly nationalist concerns, reshaped cinematic discourse from the cosmopolitan mode of the 1920s to an increasingly bourgeois-nationalist mode beginning in the 1930s.[24]

Commercial cinema's ambivalence toward its own cultural status and the female gendering of stardom that this book argues for are fundamentally connected. It is crucial here to distinguish between cinema and mass culture in India. Although shaped by the technologies of mass reproduction and circulation, Indian cinema previously had nothing like the mass presence it gained from the mid-1940s onward; the film industry more than doubled its production between 1945 and 1951.[25] In the cultural mainstream of both urban and rural India, cinema played a relatively minor role. An easy gauge of this marginalization is the refusal of the bourgeoisie and certainly of the political leadership of the freedom movement to engage with or discuss cinema's social role. In contrast to the public debate among intellectuals about the value of cinema in other parts of the world, such as Germany, where Hollywood's hegemony was stronger and where cinema had more of a status as mass culture, in India we find that, with few exceptions, the discussions about cinema in the 1930s and 1940s were restricted to those involved in some way in its production and circulation. Outside the insular world of cinema and film journalism at this time, with rare exceptions, cinema was referenced only in the form of memoirs and other "informal" modes of writing, as a guilty pleasure that had no place in mainstream cultural discourse. This is why I argue that the female gendering of stardom in India, which is connected to the disavowal of cinema, is not to be understood in terms of Andreas Huyssen's formulation of mass culture as woman in Western discourses.[26] The cultural status of cinema and stardom in India had less to do with fear of the masses and the feminization of the crowd than with the place of cinema in a cultural mainstream that systematically ignored it. Thus, in emphasizing female stardom in this book, I take my cue from star discourse in the 1930s in which the gender of stardom was implicitly understood to be female, and implicit equivalences were made between cinema, stardom, femininity, and nation. Although my book does not discuss popular male stars such as K. L. Saigal, my argument is that their status as stars would have been understood as feminized via the equivalences I have suggested. I understand *femininity* here as a relational, rather than biological, term that structures a set of oppositions in which we can see cinema itself as feminized in relation to the more masculine activities of nationalist politics, and stardom as feminized in relation to production studios.[27] In addition to the axis of gender, cinema stardom at this time was mapped on the axis of class as well, with the "cultured lady" emerging as the touchstone by which cinema was to be brought to the attention of the cultural elite. This book argues that the 1930s saw film discourse delinking stardom from the ideological underpinnings of Hollywood star appeal, which centered on the American dream, as the repeated calls for the improvement of the educational status of its performers aligned "culture" with the new public role of women in the national movement.

Cinema's status as guilty pleasure in India was mirrored not only in its relative absence from mainstream intellectual discourse but also in its absence as a respectable field of study. In the era of transnational capital, with the opening of India's economy in 1991 and the increased blurring of national boundaries, it is no coincidence that the emergence of "Bollywood" as a resented but increasingly visible category and commercial cinema's recently conferred industry status occurred in tandem with the burgeoning scholarly work on Indian cinema in the last decade. While much of the work on Indian cinema continues to focus overwhelmingly on post-Independence and contemporary cinema, it is now less burdened by the need to repeatedly reintroduce the basics in each new book and article. New work on Indian cinema is crucially invested in contesting and enlarging the rather dehistoricized critical vocabulary that still permeates public discussion, with terms such as "Bollywood," the "masala" film, the "song and dance sequence," or the "star system" taken as "enduring, traditional, structural" rather than "contingent, syncretic, historical."[28] Two events in 1994 significantly shaped Indian film study's own turn to history, and especially to pre-Independence cinema: the Pordenone silent film festival showcasing India's silent cinema, and the publication of *The Encyclopaedia of Indian Cinema,* now in its second (1999) edition. The *Encyclopaedia* provided a starting point for the recovery and documentation of the early years of film culture in India, while also pointing to the irretrievable gaps in our knowledge of India's cinematic past and the need to develop methodologies of scholarship that take into account the absence of the basic object of study, the films themselves. Recent work by a cadre of scholar-detectives has begun the task of creatively filling in some of these gaps, taking on the challenge of writing about silent cinema even in the absence of the films themselves.[29]

This book participates in these efforts to historicize specific cultural contexts for the study of Indian cinema by focusing on stardom, one of the least theorized and most visible areas of popular culture in India. Dominating the cinema at all levels, from the economic structuring of the film industry to the formulaic nuances of textual strategies, stardom is a crucial area of study for Indian cinema because it came to take over, almost exclusively, the function of product identification that genres have had in Hollywood cinema. While straddling the gap between academic and popular writing, stardom as a subject of inquiry in Indian cinema is better represented in popular discourse than in scholarly work. In this already attenuated field of study, certain stars, such as Amitabh Bachchan, Nargis, and Fearless Nadia, have received more scholarly attention than others.[30] My goal in this book is to go beyond individual case studies to provide a modest starting point for theorizing Indian stardom in historically grounded ways. One such starting point that this book proposes is the centrality of innuendo as a particular rhetorical form of accessing and engaging stars. What was understood in the 1930s as gossipy journalism was a specific style, relying on double entendre, literalized meanings, knowing misdirections, nonspecificity, and, more generally, what might be called the literary wink. The widespread use of innuendo enabled specific screen stories and biographical details to make sense, even without full amplification, because of a generalized discourse of unspecific but salacious knowledge.

This book, then, is as much about stardom as it is about specific stars, and the distinction between the two matters very much for understanding early cinema culture in India. In Part I of the book, chapters 1 and 2 attempt a history of the idea of stardom in India, taking apart and separating its assumed equivalence with "fame" and "popularity," on the one hand, and its economic importance, on the other. I have chosen to start this book with a discussion of the Indian star discourse of the 1930s, rather than earlier, because the notion of stardom became consolidated with the coming of sound and its wider association with cinema itself, rather than with specific genres. This consolidation was the result of a growing professionalization of cinema, including the burgeoning of film journalism and the establishment of film studios. But in detailing the contours of star discourse in the 1930s, I also look back to earlier forms of precinematic and noncinematic fame, and to the forms of film stardom dominant in the last years of the 1920s, basing my account on a reading of surviving and available material, such as film titles, film advertisements, and the 1927–28 hearings set up by the Indian Cinematograph Committee (ICC).[31] Given that most silent-era films have not survived, while those of the 1930s and 1940s have only patchily survived or are unavailable for viewing, I have relied equally on print discourse in film magazines and newspapers, which, too, have survived in an incomplete and haphazard manner. Throughout my discussion, I have tried to keep in mind that the newspapers and magazines I have used represent a predominantly middle-class, literate viewpoint, which is hardly representative of the entire film-viewing population. Even though film audiences in the silent era included male migrants to urban areas, who worked in factories and in menial jobs, the film magazines themselves worked hard to convey a sense of their readership as made up of the educated, "cultured" classes.[32] During the war years, magazines like *filmindia* and *Sound* also emphasized their popularity with soldiers. Aware that the "real" story of Indian film culture of the period must emphasize the lost oral discourse surrounding cinema, my attempt has been to gather indirect evidence for an understanding of the contours of oral culture, particularly the gossip surrounding cinema as an institution. I theorize gossip and its absence from print culture in the context of the attenuated discourse of private lives of stars, arguing that the question of the public's access to, or desire for, a star's "true" self is rearticulated in a variety of displacements. Private discourse about stars, understood ultimately as a site of potentially scandalous and titillating revelation, is displaced onto the institution of cinema itself, with generalized gossip constituting the "star persona" of *cinema* rather than of the individual star. With this context in mind, I turn in chapter 3 to a variety of sites in which fictitious and intertextual star identities appear, demonstrating possible methodologies of star analysis even in the absence of extratextual materials that constitute star texts. In short stories, reports about court cases, and intertextual star references in film texts, I locate some of the ways in which star gossip circulated, without being attached to specific names. Continuing my analysis of the margins of written discourse, in chapter 4 I turn to questions of spectatorship as they pertain to two popular stars, Sulochana and Fearless Nadia, who occupied the high-brow and low-brow ends of the spectrum of stardom in the 1930s. In this chapter, I examine the relationship between popularity and stardom, looking for traces of the very different fan responses to Sulochana and Nadia in the rhetorical forms they took.

Part II of the book focuses on the period from the mid-1940s to the 1950s. Chapter 5 examines new configurations of stardom in the context of changes in star discourse instituted by the breakdown of the studio system in the mid-1940s and the establishment of the "stardom racket," as one magazine puts it.[33] With a shift to a star-based production system came changes in the meaning and uses of the word *star* and its association with a rhetoric of excess. I analyze the close relationship between stardom and melodramatic conventions, arguing that star identities shared in an aesthetics of "frontality," which dominated a wide range of Indian cultural practices. When stars began to economically dominate the institution of cinema, private identities became displaced onto various forms of doubling in which the star identity replicated itself, whether through multiple roles in the same film or through a split between the body and voice of screen actress and playback singer. Chapter 6 reads the 1950s star Nargis in terms of the function of double roles in "repairing" her off-screen identity, while chapter 7 analyzes the half-century-long vocal stardom of Lata Mangeshkar in terms of the dual identifications of aural and visual stardom. The two forms of doubling presented in Part II represent new ways of containing and managing anxieties about the circulation of female bodies and private identities in the burgeoning mass-culture status of cinema.

To suggest some of the multiple models of female stardom and performance that I discuss in this book, I shall briefly discuss a sequence in the film *Jagte Raho* (*Stay Awake,* Shombhu Mitra, 1956). *Jagte Raho* is an obvious allegory of the nation, structured around vignettes, as a thirsty peasant, searching for water, finds himself lost in the nightmarish urban landscape of an apartment building. As he enters various apartments and witnesses the degenerate lifestyles of the urban upper classes, each apartment provides a microcosmic and critical view, mediated through the gaze of the "unsophisticated" peasant, of the alienation of modern India from its traditional roots. Through its contrast between the innocent, traditional, rural figure of the peasant, and the decadent, Westernized, urban, modern occupants of the apartment building, *Jagte Raho* encapsulates many of the binary oppositions that have structured Indian cinema's construction of national identity.

In one sequence, the hidden peasant watches a drunken man force his wife to entertain him with a song. Not satisfied with her sober rendition of a "traditional" song, he plays a recording of a more upbeat, "modern" song. In a drunken haze, he sees, in place of the peasant, his wife dressed as a courtesan and performing a seductive dance, while singing the recorded song. This visualization of the courtesan-wife is structured as a point-of-view shot, as the "objective" shots of the peasant and the "subjective" shots of the courtesan-wife, signaled through an initial blurred effect, are intercut with shots of the husband looking. It is important to note that in this spectacle, which is the performative center of the sequence, the woman occupies an imaginary space of the ideal female body constructed by the desire of the husband and framed by a moral commentary constituted by his drunken state and the contrast with his actual wife. As this book demonstrates, the connotations of public performance and, thus, of visual availability, shared by the female star, the stage actress, and the courtesan, make them all occupy an analogous space in the public imagination, a space that is morally defined in opposition to the domestic space of the wife. In this sequence in *Jagte Raho,* the only way to legitimize the viewer's pleasure in this song and dance performance is to provide the good wife with an imagined double, with both roles played by the same actress. The lyrics of the song that the wife-as-imagined-courtesan sings—"I am the heartthrob of millions"—also emphasize that the closest cultural equivalent to the female star in India was the courtesan. This sequence sets up an opposition between film music/star and traditional music/wife, clearly aligning itself morally *against* film music by making the man who enjoys it both drunk and lecherous. The distinction between the two types of song hinges on the figure of the woman, whose moral standing is defined by her refusal to participate in the "low" performance of film songs. The figure of the wife functions as a strong visual and narrative index of the film's notion of authentic Indian values. Yet by placing both types of women within the same cinematic performance context, the film actually deftly undercuts its own critique and successfully showcases the ease with which it is able to play with different models of femininity. Thus commercial cinema has often displayed an ambivalence toward its own cultural status; the disavowal of cinema and the guilty pleasure in female performance are themes that unify this book.

If cinema has been a particularly intense site of contestation over issues of cultural authenticity, film stardom, imagined as inherently female, has been passed over as an even more unspeakable area of cultural expression. There is, thus, a close alignment between concerns over national identity, the disavowal of cinema, and the negative discourse on female stardom, all of which this sequence from *Jagte Raho* aptly illustrates. The man's imaginary replacement of the peasant with the wife-as-courtesan suggests the connection between woman and nation, as a morally questionable female identity blurs and obscures that repository of the nation's "true" identity, the earthy peasant.

PART I

"India Has No Stars"

1. *The Split Discourse of Indian Stardom*

In our country the feelings in the star's heart remain in the heart.

—Ibrahim Haji Mohammad Mistri, "America's Arrogant Stars," *Rangbhoomi,* 24 June 1933, 9–12 (quote on 11; my translation)

In the 1932 annual Puja issue of the English-language film weekly, *Filmland,* director Charu Roy complains that in nearly fifteen to twenty years of filmmaking in Bengal, "there was never a film whose market value was mainly due to its feature player." This, he says, is unlike Hollywood, where "generally we find that the public cares more for the featuring star than for the producing company." He unfavorably compares Bengali cinema's inability to profit from its stars not only to Hollywood but also, more immediately, to Bombay cinema. Even though he says that "most of us [in Bengal] have [a] great aversion for Bombay pictures for cheap stunts," he cannot help but name Bombay's "successful" stars and their films in order to demonstrate his point about the state of Bengali cinema.[1] By the end of the decade, the need to create an Indian cinematic identity still continued to be seen in terms of the absence of, or the need to redefine, Indian stars. In 1937 the Bombay magazine *filmindia* made exactly the same point as Charu Roy and about the very same performers who had appeared in his list of successful Bombay stars: Sulochana, Gohar, Sabita Devi, and Durga Khote.[2] As in Charu Roy's article, the *filmindia* author, Baburao Patel, negatively defined India's stars in relation to Hollywood stars who functioned as the exemplary products of a rationally ordered and efficiently operating star system. In both of these articles, as in a host of others from the same decade voicing similar concerns, there is the sense that stardom is always the already understood, instantly available concept whose best examples are inevitably Hollywood names.

Film stardom or, more broadly speaking, cinematic and mass-mediated modes of circulation of fame, similarly drew simultaneously from Hollywood and diverse local practices. As a practice of celebrity, stardom belongs in a longer history of fame in India, understood both as forms of public presentation of the self and as modes of circulation and exchange of knowledge about individuals. But while sharing in a longer history of fame, cinematic stardom also marks a rupture of sorts because of radical forms of intimacy and distance associated with the new medium that changed the very terms by which individual selves were circulated in the public sphere. While stars were closer and more "present" in terms of sheer scale, if one were to compare the size of human figures on stage and on screen, they no longer shared a physical space with their audience. Thus, shaped by mechanical reproduction and its attendant proliferation of images of the self, film stardom entered a much wider sphere of cultural practice that now included an anonymous mass audience and reconfigured the relation between public and private identities.

Working from the argument that the discourse of stardom in India was deeply divided between the dual imperatives of matching a Hollywood-style discourse and responding to Indian cultural needs and constraints, this chapter situates "stardom" in a broader history of fame, examining non- or precinematic forms of celebrity in India that were akin to the dynamics of film stardom as understood in its Hollywood context.[3] Earlier contexts of fame explain the link between the social genre and the emergence of "stars" in Indian cinema. At the same time, a dual discourse on Hollywood and Indian stars circulated in Indian film magazines of the 1930s, emphasizing different ways of managing gossip and private information. The cultural apparatus of Hollywood cinema that accompanied the technology of filmmaking included the institution of stardom in all its aspects. From the format of film magazines to the look of stars and star photographs, the entire mise-en-scène of stardom as practiced in Hollywood became a ready-made model of stardom, which was widely discussed and circulated in film magazines. Yet there was a deep contradiction between the impulse to discuss Indian stars in Hollywood terms (hence the use of titles like "the Indian Douglas Fairbanks") and the reality of a very different set of constraints and desires pertaining to the reception of Indian celebrities, involving issues such as the construction of private identities, the social status of female stars, the management of sexuality, nationalist politics, and the social relevance of stars. Several competing models of cinematic stardom circulated simultaneously, even as the question most often discussed in film journalism was whether the players in Indian cinema were "real" stars in relation to Hollywood stars.

If language is a signpost of reality, then the notion of stardom certainly predated the cinema in India as it did in the West, through its regular use in urban Indian theater, for example, in the name of nineteenth-century Calcutta's Star Theatre. The English word *star* was more often transliterated than translated into Bengali and Hindi.[4] But even in its precinematic usage in India, the term *star* seemed to have been borrowed with the implicit understanding that its meaning was transparently self-evident, that it needed no explanation in its new setting in India, and that its "real" referent was to be found in English theater practices. *Star* became a word that conjured far more than a celebrated performer, and as a widespread naming practice, it became so overdetermined that its referent no longer carried any specificity. A *Times of India* report on the film actress Ermeline in 1927, for example, says that she "had been employed as a star in the Shri Krishna Film Co., of Bombay." In other words, "star" is a salaried profession like any other. It is not the product of publicity, charisma, or sheer luck. Such uses of the term *star* continue even today in writings about stars of that period, as in this example: "Most of the studios maintained a permanent staff of technicians and stars. The female stars were still largely drawn from among 'dancing girls' and Jewesses [*sic*] or Anglo-Indians like Sulochana (Ruby Myers), Ermeline and Patience Cooper."[5]

Yet the casual mention of "stars" in Indian cinema of the 1930s was also complicated by knowledge and consumption of American cinema and its stars. An early example of this complication is the Calcutta-based production company Madan, which self-consciously emulated the Hollywood-style star system and ambitiously targeted Western markets though an alliance with Italian producers.[6] In its advertising, Madan used Hollywood star names along with the promise of "beauties from Bengal." For example, the company's 1920 advertisement for the mythological film *Shakuntala* promised "European acting" from the "eminent American star Miss Dorothy Kingdon, the celebrated Gohar from Calcutta, and several other beautiful Indian ladies."[7] Madan was known and criticized for not being "Indian" enough because of its perceived tendency to cater to Westernized tastes and a foreign market: "in Bengal Madans . . . are looked upon more as birds of passage than the bonafide children of the soil."[8] Hostility to Madan arose, in no small part, from its growing monopoly.[9] Such a view of Madan as being "un-Indian" would actually fit with its attempt to practice and promote a Hollywood-like star system. The question remains, however, of the extent to which there was a disjunction between Madan's desire to practice a rhetoric of Hollywood-style stardom and the actual nature of the journalistic discourse around its stars. In recent histories of Indian cinema, the ready usage of the term *star* to refer to players in the first three decades of cinema in India functions similarly to obliterate questions about the redefinition of stardom in a different historical and social setting.

A closer look at the public discourse on film stardom in popular journalism of the time, in the films themselves, and in the publicity machinery surrounding stars (however imperfect) reveals that the term *star* and the concept of stardom by no means have a fixed referent until at least the late 1930s. Rather, there is a fluid coexistence of multiple and often competing notions of what *star* signifies. Discussions in film magazines of the 1930s suggest that the concept of stardom was invested with highly contested meanings arising from a crucial dissonance between the cultural imperatives of India at that time and the desire to import wholesale from Hollywood a "finished" concept of stardom as a technology of publicity—but without all its underlying assumptions about individuality, sincerity, the ideology of democracy (understood to mean the idea that anyone can become a star), and a specifically "modern" relationship between the public and the private. We thus find a disjunction between the practice and rhetoric of Indian stardom and the knowledge of stardom in America, but these two types of discourses coexisted on the pages of the same magazines and their differences were not foregrounded. The result was the tendency in the Indian discourse to stage *stardom* itself, with the enactment and management of stardom assuming greater significance than the construction of individual star personae through multiple filmic and extra-filmic avenues.

A Brief History of Fame

Despite its ready and common usage even in the context of nineteenth-century Bengali theater and early cinema, it is doubtful that the term *star* had, in practice, the same connotations in India as in Britain or the United States.[10] In the U.S. context, the term *star* by itself conjures up the kind of sexualized image evoked in Richard deCordova's description of the theater star Harry Montague being "hounded by hundreds of female fans." How would such expressions of public (and gendered) enthusiasm translate in the context of nineteenth-century Bengali and Marathi theater or in the context of silent cinema in India? We know, for example, that "thousands of people became captivated and went mad over [the] beautiful beardless youths" who performed female roles in the play *Indar Sabha.*[11] While passion for individual performers certainly marked spectatorial responses to the theater, the word *star,* though in circulation, was not specifically identified with the relation between audience and performer. In very early Hollywood cinema, the idea of the "star" was coupled with that of the "fan," with fandom becoming gendered as female.[12] In India, the "star" was not typically coupled with the "fan" until the early 1940s, and even then the construct was used awkwardly and sparingly.[13]

The precinematic forms of Indian fame that are relevant to a history of cinematic stardom are those that were themselves the product of mass culture, with its attendant separation between the anonymous masses and the well-known figure, knowledge about whom was circulated through various mass-produced and folk media. In the context of new forms of public culture shaped, in part, by print media, oral discourse continued to play an important role in constituting fame, and distinctions between "mass," "folk," and "oral" became blurred in street culture.[14] At the risk of simplification, I would place noncinematic modes of celebrity in nineteenth-century India in a hierarchical continuum from renown to notoriety or infamy, whether seen in terms of social respectability (e.g., national leaders versus dancing girls) or, in the colonial context, in terms of censorship (e.g., "terrorists" were both renowned and infamous, depending on one's position in the colonial establishment). Within the hierarchical arrangement of these categories, there are certain consistent parameters, such as gender and the mode of circulation of knowledge about the celebrity. The more respectable celebrity tended to be male, and knowledge about him was likely to be circulated in the print media, while the notoriety of female celebrities was usually circulated through oral gossip. At one end of the spectrum, we might start with older modes of renown, such as written hagiographic traditions. The hagiographic tradition continued to some extent in the modern autobiographical and biographical literatures of nineteenth-century Bengal, particularly in the usage of the term *atmacarit* (autobiography) with its "allusion to the entire body of *carita* literature . . . in which the lives of kings and saints were recorded." It is important to note, as Partha Chatterjee does, that "women's life stories were not given the status of *carit*" but were called *smrtikatha* (memoirs). Rather, as a mode of circulation of renown, the "modern" version of hagiographic traditions, such as the *atmacarit,* is dominated by male figures ranging from nationalists of the nineteenth-century Bengal "renaissance," such as Raja Rammohan Roy, to contemporary figures like Gandhi. Over and above the official circulation of men's public selves, mainly through print journalism, one can speculate that there was an oral aspect to their fame as well.[15] A less official category of celebrity would include popular national heroes, both male and female, ranging from the Rani of Jhansi, made heroic in the anti-British uprising of 1857, to the more recent "terrorists" of the 1910s and 1920s, such as Bhagat Singh and Khudiram Bose. Since information about them, unlike news about national leaders, was censored, their renown had a more oral and visual basis, passed along in folk songs, doggerel, and popular lithographs.[16]

Another category of celebrity that brushes against notoriety was to be found in the medium of Kalighat *pats,* anonymous paintings sold on the streets of nineteenth-century Calcutta. One of its popular subjects was the new relationship between men and women, which differed from earlier iconographic traditions in Indian art and represented anxieties about contemporary altered gender relations.[17] Through the presentation of new character types, such as the *Babu* and the Westernized woman, and well-known scandals of the time, the *pats* circulated notoriety in drawings that were popular and marketable, and that disseminated multiple versions of contemporary scandals. The most famous of these scandals was the affair between the head priest at the temple at Tarakeshwar and a married woman, Elokeshi, whose husband eventually murdered her. This crime was a sensational event involving a prolonged court case, and besides its representation in *pats,* also became the subject of stage plays.[18] Kalighat paintings were a site of generalized gossip about Westernized women and their dominance over decadent and foppish *babus,* as just one instance of this medium's "intense aversion from [*sic*] the kind of society created by the modern age." They participated in a broader street culture where similar forms of gossip and critique formed a dense oral culture targeting well-known *babus* and their goings-on.[19]

For the purposes of this study, a more significant category of celebrity is that of the performing woman, ranging from stage actresses (such as Binodini of the nineteenth-century Calcutta stage) to courtesans of all classes, who were uniformly considered to be prostitutes. Rimli Bhattacharya notes the need to distinguish between the "emergent group of theatre actresses who, in the first decades of public theatre, were for the most part first-generation, and the existing professionalised class of baijis (used here in the generic sense for courtesan singer-dancers)."[20] Although both groups of women were sometimes extremely celebrated, their popularity was always framed within a discourse of respectability in which they were strictly marginalized. Thus one cannot talk about their stardom or fame in the same terms as that of Western theater stars such as Harry Montague. In general, rumor, gossip, and scandal, as modes of circulating knowledge about celebrities, were attached to "low" art forms and tended to be gendered as female. A tenuous link may be drawn between such preexisting sites of gossip in India and the status of gossip surrounding early Indian cinema, with its attachment to female stars. We find that links between aesthetics and social class, and other recurrent tropes in discussions of celebrity or notoriety in Indian entertainment—specifically, celebrity that is based upon forms of female performance—appear again in discussions of cinematic stardom.

The Calcutta stage actress Binodini, who was both a celebrated performer and a memoirist, offers some insight into the link between fame and the word *star.* From Rimli Bhattacharya's introduction to Binodini's writings, we can infer that her stardom took the form of word-of-mouth fame (or notoriety, depending on the person's point of view), reviews in magazines and newspapers, magazine photographs (usually with complimentary captions), and her own writings serialized in magazines.[21] But there was clearly then, as later with silent and early sound cinema, a sense of the unspeakable when it came to nonprofessional information about her and other actresses. Instead, Bhattacharya says, "while actresses did write from time to time and the theatre magazines almost always carried their photographs, the bulk of the writings were by male writers who not infrequently wrote fictitious first-person women's lives, usually of *actress-like* figures." The prevalence of photographs and fiction, together with the dearth of personal information on actresses, denied them agency and suggests, rather, their primary status as objects of spectacle and speculation. Despite the circulation of photographs and popular paintings of actresses, in Bengal there was no real consumer culture selling products associated with actresses' names. This would, in any case, have been impossible because of the massive anxieties caused by the advent of women on the public stage in Bengal.[22] Stardom was enunciated in a much more consumerist context in Marathi theater, which had no women performers until the 1920s and whose male actors playing female roles, such as Bal Gandharva, "became models for women offstage." Kathryn Hansen mentions "medicinal tonic, soap, keychain, Gandharva cap, and toilet powder" as some of the "products advertised with Bal Gandharva's image."[23]

One event in the history of nineteenth-century Bengali theater is particularly relevant to understanding the usage of the term *star* in India. Rimli Bhattacharya says: "The events leading up to the building and naming of the Star Theatre, subsequently a landmark in the city [Calcutta] and in the history of Bengali theatre, offer a paradigmatic tale of the precise place of the actress in visible monuments of cultural production."[24] In her now-famous autobiography, the actress Binodini wrote: "While the theatre was being built, they had all told me, 'The theatre house that is coming up is going to be linked with your name, so that your name will continue to live, even after your death. That is to say, the theatre is to be called the "B Theatre."' This had only added to my enthusiasm. . . . But when they came back after the registration . . . I asked them anxiously what name they had given the new theatre. 'The Star,' Dasu-Babu had said with some satisfaction. I was so affected by this news that I sat down and was incapable of speech for the next two minutes. A little later, controlling myself, I said, 'Alright.' . . . I wondered afterwards, was all their love and affection only a show of words in order to get some work out of me?" In the reading of Bhattacharya and others, this event is paradigmatic of the low status of actresses and of Binodini's deep sense of betrayal that the theater she had helped build was not named "B Theatre" after her as promised, but was named, instead, the Star Theatre after the Calcutta Star Theatre Company, founded in 1883. But this raises the question of who or what was the referent of *star* in Star Theatre and the Calcutta Star Theatre Company. Clearly, Binodini's sense of betrayal indicates that she did not consider herself to have been even indirectly or discreetly referred to by the title, though such discretion was quite possible, considering the indirect reference contained in the planned reduction of "Binodini" to "B" in "B Theatre." Yet if Binodini was not the star of the Calcutta Star Company, who was?[25] In the naming of this theater, *star* seems to have been used less for its connotation of celebrity performance than for its function as an instant signifier of the standards of international (English) theater.

Early Film Genres and the Emergence of Cinematic Stardom

The star system, unlike cinema itself, may be said to have arrived in India not six months but fifteen years after it was "established" in Hollywood.[26] If the Hollywood star system emerged and developed in the 1910s, in India it was only in the mid-1920s that identifiable and popular stars emerged. In the absence of a well-narrated originary story like that of Florence Lawrence's "death," I propose the mid-1920s as the beginnings of a functioning discourse on stardom in India, for until then both the number of films produced and their genres prevented a wide circulation of cinematic fame.[27] For the emergence of cinematic fame, there is, at the very least, the need for repetition of the player's presence across different film vehicles.[28] The number of Indian feature-length films produced took off only in the 1920s. From a mere two films in 1912, the annual production of films in India rose to 61 in 1924.[29]

There is also a close link between film genres at this time and the specific type of recognition and identification, similar to star dynamics, that they elicited. In the 1910s, players in films were drawn from family members and friends of filmmakers, and the "stars" (if defined as public figures who draw audiences to the movies) were arguably not the actors but the roles or well-known characters in the mythological, historical, literary, and legendary stories that cinema was drawing upon. From a family-based production system in the 1910s, by the end of the 1920s filmmaking in India had shifted to a more formalized studio system, which was to last until the mid-1940s. Cinema production in the 1930s was not as thoroughly centralized in Bombay as it was to become over the next decades. Although production companies came and went, there were several major regional studios, such as Kohinoor and Krishna; by the mid-1930s the three most prestigious studios were Prabhat Studios in Poona, Bombay Talkies in Bombay, and New Theatres in Calcutta. Most studios produced films that were strongly marked by their regional identity, even while they attempted to address an all-India market. One indication of their strong regional affiliation is that Prabhat and New Theatres routinely produced two versions of each film, one in the regional language (Marathi and Bengali, respectively) and the other in Hindi, often with different actors in each version.

Even in the context of Indian silent cinema, which identified its films in terms of genres, "it is notoriously difficult to ascribe genres to Indian films in the Hollywood sense, given the fact that films routinely combine a variety of genres, and there has never been a Hollywood-type inscription of distinct budgets into genre-productions."[30] However, this is not to say that the concept was entirely absent, since genre was one of the terms by which producers advertised films. Many of the early cinema genres in India were derived from urban theater traditions and can be divided into two groups, which, based on the sources of their stories, I will refer to as extra-cinematic and cinematic genres. The mythological, the historical, the devotional, and the literary adaptation were all genres whose stories and characters were already well known and derived from sources outside of cinema. Genres that presented new characters and stories written specifically for cinema included the social, the crime film, the stunt film, and the comedy, many of which had significant overlap.[31] The costume genre arguably straddled both extra-cinematic and cinematic categories because it could partake of both the historical and the more fantasy-oriented stunt film genres.[32]

Genre certainly had an effect on the nature and development of stardom in India. Until the early 1920s, stars were not so much the lure as familiar Indian stories, the demand for which was greater than the supply. According to the 1928 *Report of the Indian Cinematograph Committee,* "as regards the relative popularity of Indian and Western films, there is no doubt that the great majority of the Indian audiences prefer Indian films," and this was particularly true of the "less cultured classes."[33] Film production until the mid-1920s was almost exclusively dominated by the extra-cinematic genres, which drew upon preexisting sources of fame through their main characters, who would already have been celebrated in other contexts, such as mythology, literature, history, and legend. This is not unlike the choice of subject in pre-1910s American cinema. According to Richard deCordova, celebrity in early American cinema was "caught up in a circulation of events exterior to the cinema as an institution." Cinema's function was "merely to represent" people already famous. Of course, in the case of American cinema, unlike the Indian mythological, such people and events were usually of contemporary and topical fame. In the Indian extra-cinematic genres, the two types of fame, of the player and of the character, were conflated. Even when a recognized "star" such as Patience Cooper (already a well-known stage actress) played in mythologicals and historicals, one can speculate that the original source of her fame might have been her embodiment of characters who were already known to audiences.[34] We see similar mechanisms at work in the fame of actors in urban and folk theater traditions that relied on familiar stories. Sudipto Chatterjee mentions an example from nineteenth-century Bengali theater: "Gopalsundari [Bengali stage actress playing mythological roles] was so successful in the role that thereafter she adopted the name [of the character] that shot her to fame—Sukumari—as her social name." In Marathi and Parsi theater, too, stardom was often attached to specific roles: "Success in a role led to the public affixing the name of the character to the actor's name or nickname." Balwant Gargi cites similar examples from the current annual folk theater tradition of Ramlila, where the actors, who play the same character year in and year out, become known by their character names; their identity, and hence fame, is entirely subsumed within that of a well-known character.[35]

All but one of the approximately twenty-one films produced in 1920 belonged to the extra-cinematic genres with their preexisting sources of fame.[36] But by 1924, only twenty-seven out of sixty-one films belonged to these genres, the rest being made up mainly of socials and "costume" films.[37] After 1925, cinematic genres, such as socials, stunt films, and costume dramas, became dominant. Since the social genre was set in contemporary times and dealt with issues relevant to the present, it lent itself more easily to specifically cinematic modes of fame. Richard deCordova notes that, unlike films of the first decade of American cinema that drew upon noncinematic sources for their subject matter, "stars such as Florence Lawrence . . . emerged out of an explicitly fictional mode of film production. The spectator did not pay to see a record of Mary Pickford's movements, but paid, rather, to see her activity in the enunciation of a *fiction.*" While the distinction in Hollywood is between nonfiction (Mary Pickford's movements) and fiction or between spectacle and narrative, the distinction I am referring to is based on the status of the *character* played by an actress. In mythological and other extra-cinematic genres, such as the devotional and the historical, all of which used previously known stories and characters, the narrative would have had something other than the status of a fiction as deCordova uses it here, with myth and legend inhabiting a space somewhere between fiction and nonfiction. For example, Patience Cooper's enunciation of the familiar character of Damayanti in *Nala Damayanti* would have had less the effect of fiction than that of a documentation of a familiar and preexisting event. Further layers of references to well-known personages were also possible in mythological films, such as *Bhakta Vidur* (Kanjibhai Rathod, 1921), where the *Mahabharata* character Vidur was also layered with more contemporary references to Gandhi. Only socials and other cinematic genres provided a new filmic space for the enunciation of a fiction and of characters constituted entirely in the medium of cinema and incarnated solely by its stars. We see a similar effect of the social genre in nineteenth-century Bengali theater. Sudipto Chatterjee observes that in Bengali mythological and historical plays, "characterization, in general, was thinner in psychological complexity" than in social plays "where the subjects were closer to contemporary reality." The implication here is that the cinematic genres required more "acting" and hence were more conducive to the production of stars. A further linkage between stardom and the social genre is to be found in the observation in a 1935 magazine editorial that "the social talkies do not become popular unless there is some good and well-known player in it."[38] The social genre, then, is key to the emergence of cinematic stardom in India, but the relation between the social genre and stardom was a circular one: without social films, no identifiable stars could emerge, and without stars, a social film could not be successful.

Judging by their titles, the majority of socials were about the domestic sphere or were female-centered.[39] The social film may be compared to the popular social romance genre of Hindi novels at this time, which Francesca Orsini defines as "a corpus of novels, mainly focusing on women, which consisted of a love-story while ostensibly arguing in favour of some aspect of social reform" and providing "racy entertainment." The increase in the number of socials at the end of the silent era—in other words, the willingness to present "new" or unknown stories—suggests a greater confidence in the inherent appeal of this new medium.[40] Some socials, such as *Cinema Queen* (Mohan Bhavnani, 1925), *Cinema Girl* (Bhagwati Prasad Mishra, 1930), and *Daily Mail* (N. G. Devare, 1930), were about the world of cinema itself, suggesting that producers believed the public to be interested in "inside stories" about this institution, an interest easily channeled into, or derivative of, star fascination.[41] *Cinema Queen* was meant to be a star vehicle, "exploiting the autobiographical ambiguities generated by a star [Sulochana] playing a star." This type of social film also drew on its audience's parallel interest in Hollywood stars. In the late 1920s, Hollywood functioned as the preeminent model of modernity, with films such as Imperial Film Company's *Indira* (1928) being advertised thus: "Don't miss this picture because it presents an enchanting story revealing the social life of a Cinema Actress."[42] The glamorous associations of Hollywood-style stardom are clearly on offer in this "enchanting story," so that the idea of stardom comes attached to Hollywood ideologies.[43] By the 1930s, as I will argue, star ideologies became separated from Hollywood's function as a model of a scientifically run star machine, and Indian social films now rarely, if ever, referred to the glamorous world of cinema in this self-referential way.

It is not surprising that the earliest sound films tried to diminish the risk of the new technology by briefly returning to the safety of mythological and historical genres.[44] Once again, the appeal of these films had to be based on the fame of personages belonging to a noncinematic arena of fame, even when they were played by popular silent stars. A 1932 *Rangbhoomi* article on the "three ages" of Indian cinema critiques the "third age" of sound cinema on the grounds that "once again religious pictures are back." Clearly, the extra-cinematic genres were considered to be a throwback to more "primitive" times. However, the 1930s very quickly saw a return in the popularity of the social and a greater interest in Indian stars as the addition of sound made Indian films even more popular than foreign films. Although the first sound film, *Alam Ara,* was made in 1931, silent film production still exceeded sound films until 1933.[45] This is why film magazines of the early 1930s were still profiling stars such as Sulochana, Ermeline, and Patience Cooper, who had dominated the silent cinema of the late 1920s, focusing now on their transition to sound.

Did India Have Stars?

One way to read the early decades of cinematic stardom in India would be in terms of Richard deCordova's statement that "the emergence of the star system [in America] can perhaps best be seen as the emergence of a knowledge and analyzed in these terms." In deCordova's usage, "knowledge" refers to the degree to which personal details about actors and actresses became public. However, in the Indian context, it is more useful to modify deCordova's argument to include the *concept* of stardom itself as another emergent knowledge being negotiated. In speaking of American cinema, deCordova distinguishes between the types of knowledge that produced the "picture personality" and the "star," and assigns "the emergence of the former to 1909 and the latter to 1914."[46] According to deCordova's analysis, picture personalities were constituted out of three forms of knowledge. The first and most basic was a knowledge of their names; the second was knowledge of their personalities as revealed intertextually through multiple film roles. Such intertextuality, however, "restricted knowledge about the players to the textuality of the films they were in." The third form of knowledge concerned their professional careers, which might include information about other, nonfilmic experience and qualifications. Paralleling these distinctions in conceptualizing the picture personality, we might consider the difference between "fame," or name recognition, and "achievements," or acting talent, across multiple films in star discourse in Shanghai. Unlike the predominantly professional focus of the picture personality, the "star," according to deCordova's reading, was produced by the additional knowledge of personal information and through a "fairly thoroughgoing articulation of the paradigm professional life/private life. With the emergence of the star, the question of the player's existence outside his/her work in films entered discourse." Now "the private lives of the players were constituted as a site of knowledge and truth." In the case of both picture personality and star, the knowledge was produced through a dialectic of withholding and revealing information often coded as "secret." This privileged information then served to invest the figure thus produced with greater allure. "And yet the content of the secret was different" in the case of the star "because it had very little if anything to do with the actor's appearance in films. With the star the actor became a character in a narrative quite separable from his or her work in any film." In the case of the Hollywood star, "the journalistic apparatus that supported the star system became geared towards producing an endless stream of information about the private lives of the stars," and this is the type of Hollywood star discourse circulating in India in the 1920s and 1930s. Geoffrey Macnab claims that in early British cinema, there was no such intermediary phase of picture personalities, and that "when actors were mentioned, it was usually because they had done damage to a farmer's field or broken the peace," suggesting that extra-filmic information was constitutive of actors' public image from the start.[47]

DeCordova's distinction between the picture personality and the star is pertinent to understanding the emergence of new configurations of private and public, and the boundaries between the speakable and the unspeakable with respect to film stardom in India. Inflected through knowledge about Hollywood modes of star circulation, the picture personality and the star existed not in chronological order but simultaneously, in the form of two parallel systems of circulation of fame, which I designate the "official" and "unofficial" discourses of stardom. Until the early 1940s, the characteristics of the picture personality fit the official discourse, or the circulation of information about stars in mainstream journalism, with the bulk of extra-cinematic knowledge about stars confined exclusively to professional and career details. The unofficial discourse of Indian stardom, by contrast, was more in keeping with deCordova's notion of the star. But in its curiosity about private lives, especially focusing on sexuality, it existed on the margins of respectability, its primary mode of circulation being oral gossip and "yellow journalism," which was designated as such by mainstream magazines. No longer empirically available, the unofficial discourse has to be inferred from references in the mainstream press, which only vaguely alluded to it in the form of innuendos and censure. Alongside the official and unofficial modes of circulation of fame pertaining to Indian film personalities, there was also a third form constituted by Indian participation in a full-blown Hollywood discourse of stardom, which matched deCordova's notion of the star and coexisted alongside the official Indian star discourse on the pages of mainstream journalism. All three modes of stardom existed in a complex interrelationship with one another during the studio era of the 1930s.

The Hollywood Star Discourse in India

By 1925, the star system was already fully in place in Hollywood and had a strong presence in India through the films themselves and through the pages of Indian film magazines, which devoted considerable space to news and gossip about Hollywood stars.[48] According to Baburao Patel, the editor of *filmindia, Photoplay* was the only American fan magazine available in India during the 1930s, but it was not widely read because of its cost. Older Hollywood film journals such as *Moving Picture World* were probably also in circulation, though not necessarily as current issues.[49] Journalistic discussion of Indian stars in the 1930s was thin compared to the star discourse in American magazines such as *Photoplay,* the majority of whose articles were about actors and actresses. In Indian film magazines, articles about stars constituted a much smaller fraction of the entire magazine, and that fraction, too, did not usually vary beyond star profiles, interviews, photographs and "color plates" (rarely having anything to do with the printed matter on the page), articles on acting, film reviews that mentioned stars, and the occasional news item about a star. The majority of the ads at this time were for filmmaking technology (addressed to film professionals) and publicity material (not necessarily focusing on stars) supplied by producers and addressed to a more literate film-going public. In *Photoplay,* by contrast, the range of article topics that referenced stars included reports on star rivalries and fights, beauty, cosmetic and fashion tips and ads, recipes from stars, childhood photographs, and lists of addresses of stars: in other words, not only information about the private lives of stars, but also star-related consumer products, whose range dictated an entire way of living and contributed to the overall glamor of stardom.

Hollywood functioned not only as a model that was written about as if it were "over there," but also as a machine that operated "here," on the pages of these magazines, appearing alongside discussion of Indian stars. Indian film magazines and newspapers included various forms of extra-filmic circulation of information on Hollywood stars. In addition to printed articles revealing privileged information ("the truth about . . .") about stars, items of a visual nature were also available, such as signed photographs and color plates. Through autographed photographs, there was a fetishization of the star image, which the autograph intensified through its assumed indexical link to the star. In a film magazine, the autographed photo also serves as an example of the dynamic of absence/presence and intimacy/distance characterizing the experience of stardom as analyzed by John Ellis: "The star is at once ordinary and extraordinary, available for desire and unattainable. This paradox is repeated and intensified in cinema by the regime of presence-yet-absence that is the filmic image." The photo is mass-produced and available to many readers simultaneously, yet each reader/subscriber gets a "personal" autographed photo, often a full-blown close-up of the face. According to Mitsuyo Wada-Marciano, film magazines of the silent era in Japan also provided parallel coverage of Japanese and Hollywood stars, sometimes on the same page, evoking "both a desire oriented to the West, and a desire for national identity," and a distinct sense of "here and there" that extended beyond the magazines to film genres such as the women's film. Her discussion of the actress Okada Yoshiko draws on scandals concerning her behavior during productions and her numerous affairs to show how her off-screen persona, while coinciding with the modern women in sensationalist novels of the time, created a "noticeable gap, a counterpoint" with her on-screen roles as "dispirited, financially insecure, even doomed women." Scandals such as these, which are associated specifically with *this* actress, are, in Indian cinema of the 1930s, associated with the generalized figure of the actress, rather than with named individuals. When individuals are named, it is to assert their *difference* from this image.[50]

Parallel coverage produced significant overlap between Hollywood and Japanese star ideologies. But in Indian film magazines, such as *The Cinema,* despite dual coverage, there was no such overlap. Thus, even while there was knowledge of, and participation in, a fully functioning star discourse from Hollywood, with interest in the private lives of stars, that interest was not to be seen in the pages on Indian stars in the same magazine. The range of articles about Hollywood stars in *The Cinema* included star profiles, hobbies of Hollywood stars, two separate pieces about near-miss accidents during a shoot, recommendations for a star career in Hollywood, speculative pieces about stars, and articles celebrating events designed to showcase stars.[51] Some of these pieces were written by Indians from a Hollywood "insider's" point of view. For example, "Screen Beauties I Have Known" was penned by Sheikh Iftikhar Rasool, himself the "star of the East" and interviewed in the August 1931 issue. It described exclusively Hollywood "beauties," such as Pola Negri, Maria Corda, Lya de Puti, and Anna May Wong.[52] In contrast to the range of subjects through which Hollywood stars could be encountered in *The Cinema,* Indian stars were featured mainly in interviews; for example, the August 1931 issue had interviews with Raja Sandow, Gohar, and Sheikh Iftikhar Rasool.

The type of information in profiles of Hollywood film stars and Indian stars similarly matched deCordova's distinction between the "star" and the "picture personality." An article on Alice White presented, in addition to information about her biography and filmography, more "private" details about her lovers, her hobbies, her "real" hair color, and her previous jobs.[53] Even titles emphasized the private. "The Tragic End to the Love of Two Famous Actors" was about Douglas Fairbanks and Joan Crawford, and was couched in terms of an exclusive revelation of the "true" story about these stars.[54] There were other articles in a similar vein, promising a look at the "real" person behind the star, as in "The Truth about the Stars" and "The Truth about Greta Garbo."[55]

In their construction of Hollywood stars, Indian film magazines also participated in ideologies of stardom specific to Hollywood. Essays about the secrets of stardom and star profiles emphasizing the humble origins of the star articulated the democratic promise underlying Hollywood stardom by implying that knowledge about the secrets of stardom might potentially enable any reader to become a star, even though this was clearly not applicable to readers in India.[56] Ideologies of individualism and "authenticity" were to be found in articles promising the "truth" about a star, even if the truth inevitably disappointed because the titles of articles were far more extravagant than the actual truth revealed. Nevertheless, in all these pieces there was a general emphasis on private information and the "inner" identity of the star. Some of the contradictions of circulating Hollywood star ideologies in Indian magazines became clear in an article in *Cinema Sansar* that laid out more explicitly the democratic basis of Hollywood stardom. In this piece, as in most writings at this time, no distinction was made between "good actor" and "star." It argued that the basis of Hollywood stardom is real-life experience in ordinary jobs, such as typist, dancer, and telephone girl, and related the life stories of Ann Harding, Barbara Stanwyck, and others to prove the point that there is no better school for acting than "real" jobs.[57] This is the exact opposite of the equally explicit, class-based argument made most frequently about Indian stars. A prior career as dancer, in the Indian context, was precisely what was unacceptable in the Indian discourse on female performance. As I discuss more fully in chapter 4, only in the late 1920s, with the earliest articulation of the idea of the film star, did a prior career as telephone girl become acceptable and even glamorized in the film *Telephone Ni Taruni/Telephone Girl* (Homi Master, 1926), in which actresses already coded as other, such as the Anglo-Indian Sulochana, could play with the Hollywood-derived links between extra-cinematic and cinematic careers for women.

The function of private-life discourse in Hollywood cinema of the 1910s, according to Richard deCordova, was "to convince the public that film actors lived healthy, conventional lives behind the screen." In the 1920s, however, private-life discourse in Hollywood shifted to an interest in star scandals, which "became a site for the representation of moral transgression and social unconventionality."[58] In India, Hollywood star discourse was put to different uses than in America. There was avoidance of explicit scandals, and the private lives of Hollywood stars remained firmly within the discourses of family and romance; in other words, it had more in common with the American star discourse of the 1910s. Moreover, the emphasis was on the hard work done by stars rather than on the conspicuous consumption of their lifestyles, probably because the consumer goods with which they were identified in the United States were not in circulation in colonial India. A consumer culture surrounding stars did not appear in India until much later. For example, although cosmetics advertisements were routine in newspapers, stars were never linked to such products in the 1930s.

The "Official" Discourse on Indian Stars: Profiling the Face

According to Y. A. Fazalbhoy's *Indian Film,* published in 1939, the English-language press dominated "not only from the point of view of absolute circulation . . . but also in respect of moral influence. The opinion of the average English daily carries far more weight than its vernacular counterpart," mainly because it is not regionally confined as vernacular newspapers are. Fazalbhoy divides the press into English-language and vernacular newspapers, on the one hand, and, on the other, that "very vociferous group of periodicals which devotes itself entirely to the Film Industry." Around a core of "well-established papers" in many languages "has grown up a number of far less respectable publications" which use "methods not very different from blackmail." Fazalbhoy accuses these periodicals of using the extortionist practice of writing negative reviews unless film producers increase their advertising quota. The institutional difference from Hollywood was that most film magazines got advertising only from film producers and studios, which meant that it was impossible for them to be even marginally independent of the industry they were critiquing and reviewing.[59] The interests of film journalists were perhaps more closely tied to the film industry in India than in Hollywood. A newspaper editor from Bombay said to the Indian Cinematograph Committee: "all newspapers get critique paragraphs type-written from the exhibitors themselves." Even in the case of foreign films, they get it "readymade, cut and dry, only to be sent to the printer." In answer to the question of whether it was possible to "criticise a picture honestly," he replies, "Our trade is so closely interwoven with the interests of the producers and exhibitors that we cannot possibly think of doing so."[60]

The "official" discourse of Indian stardom, which appeared in the "respectable" mainstream press, was aligned with deCordova's notion of the picture personality, with its emphasis on professional rather than private information about players. Gossip, where it did exist, tended to be professional gossip. What I have designated the "unofficial" discourse of stardom in India appeared in oral gossip and also in the "less respectable publications," whose very existence can only be inferred from references such as the following in Fazalbhoy's account: "Over and above this, many journals try to make a reputation by personal attacks on all and sundry connected with the Film Industry and by the revelation, real or fictitious, of the details of their private lives."[61]

Indian star profiles, though appearing alongside Hollywood-related material in the same magazines, thus differed conspicuously from Hollywood star profiles, mainly in their avoidance of private details and overt gossip, and were more or less formulaic in structure. A brief biographical section would focus on early childhood and education (when it existed); the rest was usually an extended filmography and other career-related information. Many articles featuring female stars in the early 1930s seemed to have a stock format, which, in addition to the bare-bones biography and filmography, also included a paragraph describing the actress's face (often with an accompanying photo featuring a close-up of her face). Reading exactly like the description of a still, such paragraphs always identified one primary emotion as the actress's forte and explored its manifestation in her facial expression. The focus on a typography of emotion and the description of an arrested emotion, divorced from references to any specific film, may be seen as "colloquial" expressions of Indian aesthetics.[62] In effect, each star served as the conveyor of one of the *rasas*.[63] Likewise, such descriptions of beauty may be seen as versions of the *roopa varnana* tradition of description of the heroine's beauty in Indian poetry. An example from *Varieties Weekly:* "She is at her best while depicting an attitude of sorrow. Her dishevelled hair falling in clusters over her superb countenance, her bright forehead, wrinkled due to care and sorrow stamped on her countenance, her eyes filled with tears, but being prevented in their overflow by the tense and rigid control that pervades over her entire form and gives an expression of loftiness to the sorrow she is enshrouded in, is one of her tense postures that expresses her original talents."[64]

Other star profiles in *Varieties Weekly* have identical passages: Enaxi Rama Rau "is at her best while depicting the sentiment of love"; Miss Rampyari "is at her best while depicting the sentiment of anger." The need to find more and more unique emotions to fit different stars obviously puts a strain on the author's imagination, as, for example, when he describes Miss Sultana "at her best when depicting an affected pose" and Miss Ermeline "at her best when depicting an attitude of arrogant defiance." It is clear from similar descriptions in other magazines that this mode of writing about female stars is not the personal quirk of one writer. The choice of "at her best" as a recurrent expression seems startlingly similar to the language of Hollywood star discourse more than a decade earlier. *Moving Picture World* used similar wording, for example, in "Miss Weber is at her best in the role of the young matron—the womanly woman who makes a home. She radiates domesticity."[65] It is notable that, although the linguistic format of star profiles, like the actual format of magazines, may have been borrowed from Hollywood, the terms of description are vernacularized from the character types and womanly virtues, in the case of *Moving Picture World*, to absolute emotions aligned with *rasas* in the Indian star profiles.

An article reporting an interview with the actress Durga Khote in *Rangbhoomi* similarly discusses her acting in *Ayodhya ka Raja* (V. Shantaram, 1932) in *rasa* terms, focusing on the emotion of pity (*karuna*): "The expression on Khote's face was filled with karuna and her voice had a sharp and mysterious effect which left a deep impression on my heart."[66] The same magazine carried an essay on film acting, which recommended that aspiring actors practice a variety of emotions, such as "grief, fear, happiness, anger, surprise, [and] love," in front of a mirror.[67] Such a practice of pure emotional expression, divorced from any specific narrative context, suggests the propensity to regard acting as a series of still moments. This is not unlike the approach to acting as "posing" in very early American cinema, where a similar typography of facial expression emerged from Delsartian and other precinematic acting styles.[68]

In her discussion of the "facial" genre and Florence Turner's repertoire of facial expressions, Christine Gledhill argues that although "the capacity for quick-change moods drew equally on the swings of melodramatic performance and on the impersonator's art," the emotion was ultimately grounded in "the expressive power of the human body." It would have been easy to "translate" such discourses of early cinema acting drawn from British and American film culture into the colloquially familiar terms of *rasa* theory. As early as 1915, we find a hybrid of *rasa*-based performance aesthetics and Delsartian facial types in Dhiren Ganguly's *Bhaver Abhivyakthi* (An Expression of Emotions), "a book of photographs showing himself in various impressions and disguises." The title comes from *rasa* aesthetics, but the "various impressions and disguises" may have borrowed equally from the "facial" genre that Gledhill discusses. In the Indian star profiles of the 1930s, the emotion read on the face of the star seems to have nothing to do with any particular facial expression "put on" by the actress. There is a distinction here between "doing" and "being," and a focus on the latter allows reviewers to see Indian actresses in terms of emotional types divorced from particular films or roles. The tendency to isolate a characteristic emotion as a classifying device also permitted Indian writers to read Hollywood films through a similar lens. One article explains "what makes a star" by resorting to a typology of the kind that is a favorite analytic device of Indian traditions of aesthetics. The various kinds of stars, assumed always to be female, are "the woman in love type" (Norma Shearer), the woman of mystery and gloom (Garbo and Dietrich), the "namby-pamby class" (Janet Gaynor), "the submissive homely type" (Ann Harding), and "the queen type" (Jeanette MacDonald).[69] Although the classification here is based on character type, it is still detached from specific roles and enables the writer to see Hollywood stars in terms of aesthetic categories rather than embodied performances.

A profile of the star Manorama shows some of the constraints under which writers of (female) star profiles were working.[70] It has a section describing her as in a still photograph, but without the emphasis on a specific emotion that we see in other examples of star profiles. Rather, the description leads up to the statement: "It will not be exaggeration to say that she resembles Mary Philbin very much, and those who have personally seen her, I dare say will agree with me." Underlying the claim about "those who have personally seen her" is the unspoken assumption of a radical difference between photographs and the physical presence of the actress. Yet such a difference is immediately undercut because those who have seen Manorama in the flesh and will notice that she looks like Mary Philbin can only make that judgment based on photographs, since they have not seen Philbin "in the flesh." The quotation suggests that seeing Manorama on the screen or even in the photograph that accompanies this article cannot give the viewer an accurate impression of what she really looks like, which would also explain the need for a detailed passage describing her. In other words, the "reality function" of photography is implicitly denied in order to engage in a typical rhetoric of star discourse: the promise of revealing the "reality" behind the screen image. Here, that revealed reality is tied to the journalist's role as mediatory figure facilitating audience-star relations and representing the first point of contact. Rather than operating within the revelatory rhetoric of the paradigm of private life/professional life, the writer reconceives this rhetoric in terms of giving the viewer a privileged look at the "real" *ap-*

pearance of the star. Conceptions of star "aura" by contact and the"truth" of interiority are transferred to facial and photographic surface.

Star profiles such as these indicate almost the exact point up to which Hollywood could function as a model of stardom. While the Hollywood machinery of stardom was regarded as the ideal economic system whose lessons were to be learned, the micro-details of how this machine functioned became impossible to emulate in the Indian context. What was the writer of an Indian star profile to do after providing the scanty biographical information and the frequently padded filmographies? If Ramamurthy, for example, were to follow the model of the Hollywood star profiles available on other pages of *Varieties Weekly*, he would then have had to turn to personal details about the star, ranging from information about her tastes and opinions to even more private details having to do directly or indirectly with her sexuality. Thus, what remained was to conceive of the star profile (and by extension, the rhetoric of stardom itself) as a sort of panegyric, and to accomplish that, the writer emulated models with which he was familiar, such as the tradition of praise of the heroine drawn from poetry.

The "Unofficial" Discourse on Indian Stars: Theorizing Gossip

Put simply, no knowledge about the personal lives of actors and actresses, coded as "private," was circulated in the official print discourse until the early 1940s, so that in terms of deCordova's definition of the star, as opposed to the picture personality, it is true to say (as does the *filmindia* editorial) that in the 1930s "India has no stars." In addition to the circulation of Hollywood stars and an "official" discourse of Indian stars, a third, unofficial site of stardom can be gleaned only indirectly. Even though the unofficial, oral version of fame in the 1930s actually bore a closer resemblance to the articulation of stardom in Hollywood at the time, its scandalous and gossipy content was regarded as unspeakable in its details and was kept out of "respectable" film magazines. In the unofficial mode of stardom, gossip had primarily to do with issues of female sexuality, the boundaries of private and public, and notions of the respectability of the new medium, all of which were integrally tied to conceptions of gender and class. That there was also a clear link between gender and the prohibition of private information is evident in *filmindia*'s response to a 1939 reader's request for the address of story writer Agha Jani Kashmiri: "As he is not a film-she, I shall give you his home address."[71] Clearly, a female star calls for greater reticence.

Gossip itself has been gendered feminine, with women as both the subject and the object of the forms of unofficial knowledge associated with it. With stardom as an institution fundamentally constituted by gossip, the link between gender and stardom was thus framed by the feminized status of cinema in India and its performing women as the generalized object of gossip. In the case of Hollywood cinema, stardom became a technology of publicity with the express intent of controlling and channeling such extra-cinematic knowledge. Gossip, rumor, and scandal belong in a shared network of rhetorical forms of public discourse, but can be usefully distinguished from one another. While gossip usually pertains to knowledge about private or other aspects of personal lives that are not meant to be publicly available and are coded as privileged information, scandal is, by definition, knowledge of a public nature. Tanika Sarkar notes the role of public forums such as trials in constituting gossip as a "shared field of discussion" and "an interpretive community." But while "gossip flourishes within an intimate group . . . scandal performs the same function within an anonymous abstract public: it draws an unseen community of concerned people together." But what are the rhetorical qualities of gossip itself, and how does it lend itself to historical analysis? Sarkar's distinction between scandal and gossip points to "official" sites such as court cases, where the historian might look for traces of gossip. In cinema, for example, some of the court cases that I discuss in the next chapter became a site of specificity where gossip could be anchored to individual names and events. Unlike scandal, however, gossip and rumor function rhetorically in a field of uncertainty, lacking accuracy and with no source capable of verification. Unverifiability and anonymity are also the source of their power in shaping the reputations of institutions such as the cinema and figures such as Gandhi.[72] Generalized gossip about the institution of cinema took a hybrid form that combined gossip, rumor, and scandal, with rumor appearing in the form of stories and films about the goings-on in film studios, scandal taking the form of court cases, and gossip more closely tied to individuals' star identities.

In the Indian cinema of the 1930s, gossip, in its absence or its presence as innuendo, was constantly framed within a discussion about the reputation of the institution of cinema as a whole. The dominant antigossip stance was explicit: "One of the things we have learnt is to observe complete indifference to the 'yellow talk' of our contemporaries. A few of them deserve some respect but the others are just dealing in cheap pander to get the support of some of our depraved producers."[73] Such statements, which regularly appeared in *filmindia* and other mainstream magazines, indicate that, structurally or ideologically, gossipy revelations were frowned upon and relegated to the margins of respectability. Yet antigossip statements in respectable publications also lent credence to the overall bad reputation of cinema as a profession because of references to such elements as the "depraved producers."

The status of gossip in the construction of Indian stardom in mainstream journalism of the 1930s was a paradoxical one. On the one hand, there was no explicit gossip attached to individual names or narrating specific events. On the other hand, gossip was the primary lens through which the cinema and its stars were viewed. It was the very substance out of which the cinema was constituted in the public imagination. Yet these two aspects of the status of gossip, its simultaneous presence and absence, were really two sides of the same coin: because the very "being" of film stars was one of ill repute, the public did not need to *read,* though they may have *heard,* unsavory details about a specific star. At the same time, part of the overall agenda of anyone associated with the cinema—and this would certainly include film journalists—was to rescue it from its bad reputation, and this dictated an unspoken taboo on gossip pertaining to individual stars.[74]

Since there were never any concrete stories of scandal pertaining to specific people, the numerous innuendos force the assumption that concrete stories were circulating elsewhere in public—that is, outside the pages of these magazines. One example that bears out this assumption pertains to the figure of Devika Rani, considered at the time and in recent histories to be the "first lady of the Indian screen."[75] If one looks at film journalism both then and now, even the most acerbic writings on her, such as *filmindia* on her role as producer, remain silent on any aspect of her private life other than the most public and respectable events, such as the death of her husband and her marriage to the Russian painter Svetoslav Roerich.[76] She was mostly celebrated as the preeminent female Indian star, the one who represented the best of Indian cinema in pre-Independence times. Not until 1950, in a work on Indian stars by Saadat Hasan Manto, written after he had left Bombay and in a self-consciously provocative style, do we get a glimpse into what oral gossip around her might have been like. Manto begins his first "story" in this collection with the shocking statement: "When Najmul Hasan ran off with Devika Rani, the entire Bombay Talkies was in turmoil. . . . The worst affected man at Bombay Talkies was Himansu Rai, Devika Rani's husband and the heart and soul of the company. . . . Without saying anything to Rai, [director S. Mukerjee] somehow managed to persuade her to come back, which meant that he talked her into abandoning the warm bed of her lover." Not only does this account reveal scandalous information, but its tone is as intimately narrational as oral gossip. It provides a glimpse into the rhetorical style and emphases of oral gossip with its use of vivid detail, such as "the warm bed of her lover." But Manto's "gossip" here is "old news" in terms of the more than ten-year time lag between event and narration, and points to the regulation of such information in print discourse.[77]

The rhetoric of improvement, examined more fully in chapter 2, not only decried the absence of real stars in India, but also repeatedly protested against the low social status of (female) stars and censured those who indulged in gossip regarding them. Framed as a defense of cinema, these articles participated in a regulatory discourse that managed the public face of cinema, identified with its women. Yet even while explicitly refusing to participate in gossip, these magazines themselves implicitly contributed to the generalized framework of gossip through which stars were viewed, by their innuendos and oblique references to *other* sites where such information might be had. The fear of the unsavory in "respectable" magazines led to a wholesale avoidance of any, even the more "innocent," details of private life that were to be found in any American film magazine of the time.

Because gossip and scandal existed at the fringes of mainstream publications, such as *Rangbhoomi, Filmland, Cinema Sansar,* and *filmindia,* the historian has to look for indirect sources of evidence that there was an unofficial circulation of gossip in the oral sphere, which is no longer empirically available. In an indirect reference to a flourishing gossip press, a *filmindia* editorial asked why film stars "allow themselves to be slandered by the public, the gutter press, and by their own films."[78] It referred to a Hindi magazine from Calcutta, "an insignificant little paper," which, under the headline, "Film actors are all pimps and film actresses are all prostitutes," published an article whose "content and . . . tone . . . can very well be imagined." It is clear from this that gossip was widely in circulation. But while any *details* given in such gossip pertained to the industry as a whole, only the generalizations could be taken to refer to individual players, so that the general and the specific were inseparable in the rhetoric of this type of gossip. Moreover, the same paradoxical relation between general and specific gossip extended even to references to gossip papers. Mainstream publications made generalized remarks about them but always shied away from actually naming any specific gossip magazine. In the example just given, *filmindia* censured the Hindi gossip magazine, which remained the unnamed "insignificant little paper." When gossip magazines were mentioned by name, as in the case of Manto's *Mussawar,* the mention was usually accompanied by the assurance that its gossip was "in good taste." Richard deCordova notes a similar vagueness about gossip in the early years of Hollywood star discourse. He writes that in the 1910s one could find "fairly strong generalizations about the moral atmosphere of film production [from which] one might infer all kinds of atrocities. What is striking . . . is that the concern expressed for these women never departs from the most general level. One does not see stories about specific scandals. . . . The charges about Hollywood may have been titillating, but they were also extremely vague." Such an avoidance of direct gossip was short-lived in Hollywood. The shift in the mode of gossip took place in a very short span of time. Around 1913, "the [Hollywood] publicity apparatus became geared toward the presentation of the love lives of stars," but in 1912 *Photoplay's* question-and-answer section had announced that "this department is for answering questions of general interest. Information as to matrimonial alliances and other purely personal matters will not be answered. Questions concerning the marriages of players will be completely ignored." In the Indian discourse on stardom, similar disclaimers were still being made in the "respectable" film magazines as late as 1937. But apart from the time lag, what was different from Hollywood, as I will argue, was the very nature of the prohibition on gossip and its connection to ideas about the representation of private and public.[79]

Even when personal accounts regarding stars were present, the only "revelations" were about the profession and its people, as opposed to private relationships. The editorial in the 13 July 1932 issue of *Rangbhoomi* announced a new format for future issues. Besides articles on cinema, occasional stories from or related to films, serialized novels, and lighter features, the magazine would also feature a new section "The Devil Has Brought News" ("Shaitan Samachar Laya Hai"), whose tantalizing title seems to promise gossip. However, the description of this section reveals it to be nothing more than studio news on films to be released.[80] The alignment of gossip with studio news is indicated in the *Times of India* news item "Studio Gossip: Sagar News," which is entirely about a forthcoming Sagar Studios production.[81] If there was any gossip or rumor published in this and other magazines in the early 1930s, it was exactly this type of studio news, which included rumors about contracted stars being lured away to other studios or the professional doings of various directors, some of whom were more likely than others to be in the news.[82] Thus, what went for gossip then was privileged information regarding the institution of cinema, and this was also the focus of star profiles. An example of professional gossip is the negative publicity around the actress Shanta Apte's hunger strike "for non-payment of her dues" for the days she was away on leave. The editorial comment on this news was that it did her no good other than giving her some newspaper publicity.[83] No comment was made on the labor issues implicit in this news item, particularly the weak position of stars with regard to the studios. This explicitly antilabor position, which actively discouraged actors and actresses from protesting their contracts, again confirms the close connection between the interests of film producers and film journalists, and suggests that journalistic discourse functioned in a disciplinary mode in matters of labor, in addition to matters of gender and morality.

A 1934 article recommending improved publicity for stars modeled on Hollywood, suggested the kinds of information about stars that should be made public, but the author's recommended scenarios tellingly featured only the "behind the scenes" professional, rather than the private, aspects of star identity, at the same time that they drew upon a melodramatic notion of stardom: "What actor refused a part and for what reason? Why should a particular actress alone was [*sic*] selected for a part among thousands of competitors?; what made an artiste walk out of the set?; the playing of which role resulted in the swooning of an actor for hours?; what stars are seen doing between scenes?; how one of the cameramen escaped an accident? :—are some interesting items that are bound to create unusual attention upon their being announced by the publicity department of a studio."[84] Similarly, the August 1931 issue of *The Cinema* mentioned studio gossip about the silent star Sulochana leaving Imperial Studio so that "the famous team of Sulochana and Billimoria was split up. . . . For a time everybody was anxious to know if Sulochana will play lead against any other actor . . ." Here too, the implied gossip was professional in nature.[85] Six years later, the same subject elicited a potentially scandalous piece of private information:

> Question: "There are rumours at Meerut about Sulochana. They say she has left Imperial Co., and has eloped with someone."
>
> Answer: "Don't believe any rumours. Sulochana has been married to Dr. Weingarten and if he had 'eloped' for effecting a marriage, there was no wrong done. Her future with the Imperial Co. is still in the balance, and for that matter no one can at present tell whether she is ever going to work in any pictures."[86]

Despite the apparent interest in the private here, we find that gossip and questions about private lives ("Has Sulochana eloped with someone?") at this time were still legitimated through their connection with a star's professional career ("Has Sulochana left Imperial?"). The editor's response is typical of the late 1930s, with its simultaneous denial and indulgence of gossip. Thus, although gossip and scandal were significant ways in which the star image was circulated, the events described were not usually coded in terms of access to the inner being or personality of the star. For example, a news item about Sulochana allegedly assaulting a vendor appears in the *Times of India* as a report on a court case.[87] This news was a factual report, with no further examination of Sulochana's personal opinions or "feelings" regarding this allegation.

Reticence, Innuendo, and the Production of the Private

Much has been written on the emergent notions of private and public in nineteenth-century Bengal and, by extension, in other parts of Western-educated India. The distinction between the personal/domestic and the communal/public constituted by modern civil society centered on debates about domesticity, which took place in "public narratives"—documents that are "both the products and the constituents of a print-culture or the public sphere." But key to the construction of the private were the new genres of biography and autobiography in nineteenth-century Bengal that emerged with "a new concept of the 'individual' among the English-educated elite," and that presented the private in a public forum. The modern individual constituted by these new literary genres is "supposed to have an interiorized 'private' self that pours out incessantly in diaries, letters, autobiographies." That is, "the bourgeois individual is not born until one discovers the pleasures of privacy." But what was the precise nature of "private" self-presentation here? Contrary to expectations of outpoured feelings in such genres, we find that indirections and reticence are endemic to the practice of biographical discourse in India. Rather, private discourse is marked by "conventions of self-effacement" or "a selective silence" or "embarrassment" at "the kind of confessional self-revelation that has been seen as a characteristic of Western biography and autobiography since Rousseau."[88]

The avoidance of interiority and the relative absence of direct gossip, linked to a general prohibition of the private in discourses of cinema stardom, is consistent with a wider sphere of cultural practice in the 1920s and 1930s concerned with redefining norms of respectability pertaining to women's participation in the public sphere. Francesca Orsini points to the attenuated articulation of interiority even in the case of "an ostensibly 'private' genre like the novel." Novels, confessional literature, and other low-brow forms of reading material were closely tied to cinema in their capacity to address the desire for expressions of interiority.[89] Although many novels rated familial and communal well-being higher than individual desire, the conflict between the two was rarely represented through a discourse of private feeling: even "realistic novels [of the 1920s and 1930s] show literally *no place* for a private language of feelings and for private aspirations in the family or elsewhere. Indeed the fictional worlds of the novels themselves, the extraordinarily popular 'social' romances that originated in these decades, seem to have been the only place (perhaps with films?) where private feelings could be securely indulged." In her reading of the 1920s autobiographical writings of Mahadevi Varma, with their keenness to "deflect attention away from herself" even in "sketches which revealed aspects of her private life," Francesca Orsini shows that such reticence is also gendered by the constraints of appropriate female behavior in public life. Orsini interprets Mahadevi's reticence in aesthetic and personal terms, but also includes a cultural explanation of silence as "a much-approved attitude particularly in women." Like Mahadevi's work, the scores of Indian personal writings that began pouring out from the mid-nineteenth century onward "seldom, if ever, reproduced in writing the other side of the modern citizen, the interiorized private self unceasingly reaching out for an audience."[90] Given the broader context of a half-century of personal writings marked by reticence, it is no surprise that the official star discourse in India remained in the mode of the picture personality even as it relished the private disclosures of Hollywood stars. It was precisely because film narratives did explore private emotions that the extra-textual information about the stars who played such roles downplayed discourses of interiority. Thus, the tension between private expression and concealment worked to deflect interiority onto other signs of private identity, moving away from a discourse of feeling to one of doing. In the case of cinema, a curriculum vitae style of public information could stand in for private details.

In cinema discourse, when private information *was* circulated, reticence was transformed into innuendo as the dominant rhetorical mode through which it was expressed in public. Unlike reticence, whose urge is to conceal, the stronger urge in innuendo is to reveal through indirections. Even magazines that explicitly saw themselves as gossip papers resorted to innuendo rather than direct reporting. For example, Saadat Hasan Manto, screenplay writer and editor of the weekly Urdu film magazine *Mussawar,* makes it clear that his paper sold gossip, but that it was always indirect. "My columns *Nit Nai* (the latest) and *Baal ki Khal* (splitting hair) were popular and always in good taste, but Sitara did not like what I had written. . . . When my spies gave me details of her affair with Asif and I made *indirect references* to it in my columns, she asked him to beat me up, adding that if he didn't, she would hire someone to do it."[91] This account of Manto's experiences as a gossip columnist, written many years later, is itself a piece of gossip, revealing the violent reactions of the subject of his column and suggesting what the consequences of explicit gossip might have been.

In the same spirit as other articles proclaiming the absence of stars in India, the May 1936 issue of *filmindia* says that "star-value" has no meaning in India because "the 'Face Value' that pleases the 'tastes' of the producers immediately builds a 'Star Value.'"[92] Here we see more innuendo of the kind that fed the generalized gossip about illicit liaisons in the cinema: it is the star's physical attributes, the beauty of her face, rather than her talent that gets her the personal rather than professional attention of producers. The focus on the face, rather than the body, is a further form of innuendo, but it also participates in a more general tendency to substitute the face for the body, as in star profiles. *filmindia,* in particular, specialized in innuendo mixed with evasive answers. The responses to the following, fairly innocuous, requests by readers are examples of this:

> Question: I am an admirer of Raja Sandow. Can you give me some particulars about him?
> Answer: No! I want you to go on admiring him.[93]
>
> Question: I learn that Barua is in love with Jamuna. How far is this rumour true?
> Answer: It is not a rumour, it is a fact. He is in love with her work and so am I.[94]

The answer to the first question suggests that any "particulars" about Raja Sandow would have to be negative and would therefore put an end to the reader's admiration. The answer to the second question successfully deflects the focus away from the private meaning of "in love with" to a generalized, professional context of work in the film world. Even questions of a more professional nature, such as inquiries about the salaries of leading stars, elicit evasive answers: "I know, but I won't tell you. It is bad manners to ask people about their earnings. Someday you might ask me how many children they have got."[95] Of course, there is an element of "witty" showmanship to such answers, and readers would have come to expect such refusals to give any straight answers.[96] Yet other journalists read even what I am designating as innuendo in the responses quoted here as "indecent" scandalmongering, creating further layers of innuendo in their own work.[97]

In the December 1937 issue a reader asks why *filmindia* doesn't feature a star biography every month. The editor's reply is another example of the type of innuendo that served to fuel an atmosphere of gossip, without providing any concrete information. He starts by saying, "I don't believe in telling lies and misleading my readers," which implies that most star biographies are filled with gossipy lies. But his next sentence reverses this by suggesting just the opposite: "If half the truth in the life of these people was told, the paper would be banned as obscene. I have therefore left this job to the 'liars' of this trade." The "liars" are therefore not the ones who gossip but those who present a "clean" image of stars. This answer slyly acknowledges food for gossip while tantalizingly remaining silent about its details.[98]

Privacy is the commodity that sells magazines, through its promise of revelation of secrets. Even though the official Indian star discourse tended to emphasize the professional history of stars, it did not hesitate to use the lure of private information to attract readers who were used, perhaps, to similar fare on Hollywood stars. An example of this is the essay entitled "Love," written by Sulochana, which appeared in the Puja issue of *Filmland* in 1934.[99] The title, which seems to promise insight into Sulochana's personal ideas about romance and thereby into her private self, is merely a decoy to lure readers, and turns out to be an essay on the profession of acting and the role of good personal relations in this profession. She is using "love" in the widest possible sense to mean "not . . . the elemental, self-conscious love between man and woman," but "the love of close kinship. . . . the idyllic, unselfish love of friendship and understanding." Rhetorically, this essay is thus similar to the evasive replies to fan mail in *filmindia.*

The persistence of innuendo can be explained in terms of reticence, but more specifically by norms of respectability and notions of what is appropriate for public discussion. Discussions on the place of private information in public discourses inevitably centered on the etiquette of what is or is not appropriate for public display. The nineteenth-century theater director and playwright Girish Ghosh, in whose theater company the actress Binodini worked, critiqued her autobiography for its inappropriate revelations: "The concealing of the personal which is the essence of the technique of writing an autobiography has been compromised." Girish recognized that Binodini had her reasons to feel bitter, "but such bitter words are best left out of one's own life-story."[100] The taboo against such private revelations continues even in more recent writings about Binodini. Sudipto Chatterjee explains that Binodini never mentioned the names of the "young gentlemen" she was involved with and that Soumitra Chattopadhyay and Nirmalya Acharya, "the editors of Binodini's memoirs and collected works (first published in 1969) decided to be quiet about it on the basis of the following determination: 'The general reader may be curious about the men who were Binodini's paramours. We believe that Binodini has exposed quite enough. She revealed only what she felt was relevant in the context of [the history of the Bengali] public theatre and her life as an actress. It may be possible to find out more, but the history of our theatre has no need for that information.'" Even a recent biography of early twentieth-century Marathi female impersonator Bal Gandharva takes a similar position on aspects of his life that might arouse unseemly curiosity. Written as part of the state-run National Book Trust's official biography series, the book states that "while close associates of the thespian vouch for . . . his personal life, the last few years of his association and reported eventual marriage to Goharbai are apt to remain shrouded in mystery." Therefore, even though an earlier chapter mentions intense controversy over his relationship with Goharbai, the author's impulse is to maintain reticence over its details.[101]

Reticence marks not only the production of gossip, but also its reception, and we get a vivid sense of the perceived effects of explicitly published gossip in the following letter of protest written by a woman after Saadat Hasan Manto's serialized accounts of Bombay stars began to appear in the newspaper *Afaq* in Lahore, Pakistan, in the early 1950s:

> I do not consider going to the movies to be a cardinal sin, neither do I wrap a bandage over my eyes when I look at a picture. . . . I am no child, but there are certain pictures which I do not dare to look at because if I do so, it will lower me in my own eyes, as if I had violated someone's privacy which would be against good manners. You can turn around and say that such things, such magazines, newspapers and books should be kept out of the reach of children. But that is easier said than done. . . . Now please read [Manto's article on the film star Shyam] once again and tell me what you think of it. Regardless of how far a person has strayed from the path of virtue or how morally depraved he is, can you imagine him sitting at home, surrounded by his wife and children and regaling them with the experiences . . . that you have described? . . . He would never talk such filth. . . . What service to mankind or to public morals is being performed by printing such things in newspapers? People have their homes and families, something which should be kept in mind. . . . What newspapers, magazines, and literature are now propagating is perhaps designed to induce parents to raise their children according to such values.[102]

In this critique of public gossip, the writer invokes the presence of family and domestic space, both when talking of the subject of the gossip and when describing the effect of such gossip on the reader. In speaking of how she feels when confronted with such material, the writer mentions the sense of embarrassment that comes from a violation of social etiquette and the sense that the gossip "will lower me in my own eyes." Here, too, we see gossip framed in terms of appropriate social behavior ("good manners") and a domestic ideology. Moreover, the sense of identification, rather than distance, with the subject of the gossip ("regardless . . . of how morally depraved he is") is so keen that it prevents the kind of pleasure in the moral transgressions of stars that fueled the interest in scandals in Hollywood film magazines.

Although norms of public behavior might account for such reticence, gossip also served ultimately to transform the individual into the representative. Partha Chatterjee argues that most autobiographies were more interested in "the facts of social history and the development of new cultural norms for the collective life of the nation" than in exploring the individual.[103] If we view gossip as a form of biography, we find a similar emphasis, in the official discourse of stardom, on the representative rather than the individual in the figure of the star, which also explains the interest in fictional accounts of starlike people in these magazines. Instead of targeting specific individuals, gossip in the official discourse was generalized and tended to fall into certain recurrent categories. Two variants of the same category, for example, were (1) the (upper-class) innocent female star endangered by the sexual advances of male studio bosses; and (2) the (lower-class) female star of "loose" morals presenting a threat to the reputation of others associated with the studio. Another category of gossip had to do with the amorous relationships, always coded as disreputable, between female stars and other studio figures, usually the director or producer. All these categories of gossip articulated recurrent tropes in the social construction of female performance and hence functioned more as representative comments on the institution of cinema ("the facts of social history") than on the private being of a particular star ("the exploration of individuality"), since no individuals were ever named.

The hesitation in representing the private and the consequent differences between Indian and Hollywood star profiles in Indian film magazines can best be understood in the context of a complex discourse of Indian nationalism in which the cinema, too, was a participant. In the case of cinema, the question of the codes of etiquette governing the representation of the private in public was framed in terms of the moral improvement of cinema. In the next chapter, I argue that discussions of the status of cinema in the public sphere were closely tied to Indian nationalist ideologies and the role of the modern cultured woman in improving both cinema and nation.

2. *The Morality and Machinery of Stardom*

> We cannot expect to produce a heavenly picture like "Song of Songs" with artistes recruited from the slums of North West Calcutta. It is a happy sign that the pick of the society have come into the producing branch of the industry.
>
> —Amar Das Mullick, "1934 Heralds a Brighter Dawn: Renaissance of Bengal's Motion Picture Industry," *Varieties Annual*, 1 January 1934, 7

> Wanted Cultured Ladies Only!!
> For a Leading Role in "BHAI-BAHEN"
> If you dream of shining in
> the film firmament as a star
> and wish to see your dream
> come true
> Apply (With Photographs)
>
> —Full page advertisement in *filmindia*, July 1943

The film "star" in India was constituted out of the competing demands of a Western model of celebrity derived from Hollywood, which defined identity in terms of interiorized private lives, and an Indian model of public identity, with its deep-rooted avoidance of a written discourse of gossip. In the 1930s, a decade of intensified struggle for Indian independence, the divided Indian star discourse was shaped by a wider nationalist project, even though cinema's direct engagement with the actual events of the day was minimal. The earliest Indian filmmakers, such as D. G. Phalke and Baburao Painter, who were producing mainly mythologicals in the late 1910s and 1920s, were often operating on an overtly nationalist agenda. One expression of nationalist sentiment was through the presentation of explicitly "Indian" subject matter drawn from India's "glorious heritage," as constructed by Orientalists and nationalists in the nineteenth and early twentieth centuries and expressed in visual practices such as the nationalist iconology of the painter Raja Ravi Varma.[1] Phalke and Painter, and other filmmakers in the 1920s and 1930s, were also avoiding colonial censorship by means of oblique and allegorical references either to national culture or to other historically or mythologically displaced sites of struggle.[2] Mythological characters could also double as references to contemporary nationalist figures, sometimes in ways transparent enough to attract censorship.[3] Entire genres, such as the costume drama and the stunt film, could be read as nationalist allegories through their anti-establishment narratives set safely in a legendary or fantasy space. Films were also circulating recurrent tropes of nationalist pride in historical scenarios particularly associated with nationalist and Hindu masculinity, such as Shivaji's wars against the Mughal empire or tales of the heroic Rajputs. A random example of nationalist readings of historical films can be found in a review of the Hindi film *Meerabai* whose Bengali title was *Rajrani Meera* (Debaki Bose, 1933), which praised the film for its "happy blend of Bengal's culture and

"Wanted Cultured Ladies Only!" Advertisement in *filmindia*, July 1943.

Rajasthan's heroism."[4] If the films themselves engaged national issues indirectly, there was only a distant echo of major current events in the pages of mainstream film magazines until the mid-1940s. Such echoes could take the form of advertisements, such as one for a *swadeshi* directory, which listed *swadeshi* products and companies producing them. Such a directory, the ad promised, would eliminate the practical problem of knowing where to find decent *swadeshi* products to replace foreign ones.[5] Appropriately enough, given its context, this advertisement represents the commercialization of nationalism.

The overall distance from current events in film magazines was partially the product of censorship, as in the case of the films themselves, but can also be seen as a sign of the marginalization of cinema from the nationalist mainstream. Perhaps because of its inability to engage directly with the nationalist agenda, the cinema was never recognized as a legitimate site of nationalist expression. This attitude to the cinema was true not only of the national leadership, but also of those who were writing about cinema, mainly in English-language film magazines. While these magazines frequently deplored the contemptuous attitude toward cinema of leaders such as Gandhi and of Westernized elites who preferred to watch foreign rather than Indian films, they nevertheless expressed a similar attitude in their own critique of the absence of social commentary and nationalist sentiment in Indian cinema.[6] Nationalist concerns in journalistic discussions regarding the role of cinema often took the form of an entire category of film journalism, which I would call the "What's Wrong with Indian Cinema?" genre.[7] This is where Indian cinema seemed never able to measure up to Hollywood and norms of international cinema in terms of social relevance and national representation.[8] Such articles were almost always couched in prescriptive terms, the implied consensus being that Indian cinema had not yet acted on its potential status as a participant in the nationalist struggle. Until films adequately represented national culture and concerns, cinema as an institution would remain marginalized.

The call for the improvement of Indian cinema may be situated in the wider context of the discourse of "improvement" that characterized British colonial and Indian nationalist thought. In a pivotal discussion of the "British idiom of Improvement," Ranajit Guha includes within this discourse "the introduction of Western-style education (*siksha*) and English as the language of administration and instruction; official and quasi-official patronage for Indian literary, theatrical, and other artistic productions." The British idiom quickly became internalized and, beginning in the nineteenth century, "generations of nationalists" were captivated by "the promise of 'improvement,' of being allowed into the tiny coterie of the 'leading' nations of the world." The British rhetoric of improvement was a civilizing one with the notion of "improvement" implicitly and sometimes explicitly linked to that of "civilization." For Indians, improvement also entailed a counter-civilizational rhetoric against Western civilizational norms, pitting the glories of ancient India against contemporary claims about its fallen status, particularly over questions of gender and the status of women in Indian society.[9]

In the sensory-visual regime of cinema, questions of nationalist legitimacy centered on the female figure, both film character and actress, who bore the burden of representing the moral core of national identity. The desire for improvement produced a split discourse on film stardom, divided between Hollywood efficiency and Indian moral superiority, and participating in a version of Partha Chatterjee's well-known model of the dual domains of anticolonial nationalism. While Hollywood set the agenda for a rationally functioning machinery of stardom, the actual enunciation of a discourse on female stardom was dictated by the needs of a nationalist conception of the moral space occupied by performing women. Chatterjee's discussion of the gendered separation of two spheres of anticolonial nationalism in the nineteenth century locates an inner or "spiritual" domain of nationalism in the domestic sphere of language, family, and women, and an outer domain of nationalism in the institutions of the modern state. While the inner domain "insisted on its own marks of cultural difference from the West," the outer domain demanded that "there be no rule of difference" from Western models. Chatterjee's reading places areas constituted by literary and aesthetic forms such as drama, the novel, and art within the inner domain. However, I would argue that, rather than such a complete separation of the two domains of national culture, there was often a fractious coexistence of both inner and outer domains in the same site of cultural practice. In the area of cinema, for instance, it is obvious that "Western" technology is used in the service of "Indian" stories, drawn usually from sources similar to those that fed the theater. Similarly, as I will demonstrate, the cultural sphere of film stardom in the 1930s shows both domains in uneasy coexistence. While Hollywood stardom functioned in the Indian discourse as a superior Western technology worthy of emulation and constituting the outer domain of nationalism, Indian star profiles, especially in their articulation of the private discourses of female stardom, were constructed in terms of a language of difference from Hollywood. As one commentator put it, "The Indian mind is very conservative and will not—quite rightly too—allow their women-folk to be exposed to moral danger and contamination. The stories one hears of the life at Los Angeles are not such as to reassure the public mind."[10] Thus, while Hollywood's star *system* served as a model, there was nothing paradigmatic about its scandalous articulation of the private lives of stars. Cinema's discourse of improvement, shaped by both domains of nationalism, fell into two categories. The first was textual and technological, having to do with audiovisual quality, narrative style, formal choices (such as the prevalence of songs), and film length. The second category was a moral one having to do with the bad reputation of cinema as an institution and the need for its improvement through the involvement of educated, upper-class women in the role of actresses.

One of the recurrent rhetorical practices in this discourse of improvement was the claim that the state of the nation was reflected in the state of its cinema, a strategy that similarly marked such widely divergent spheres as sanitation, domesticity, citizenship, and the management of civic society. For example, Nagendrabala Saraswati's book on improved domesticity, published in the 1880s, uses the same rhetorical strategy, asserting that "there cannot be any improvement in the state of the nation without improvement first in the domestic and political spheres."[11] One can immediately see a parallel between these kinds of sentiments and statements in film magazines such as "just as the improvement of a nation depends on its literature, similarly it is upon theater and cinema that a nation's customs, culture, and civilization depend. In other words, it is crucial to pay attention to these areas."[12] The relation between the state of cinema and that of the nation also became a defense of cinema when that relation was posited as a causal one. The argument was that the low esteem in which cinema and the arts in general had been held in India had caused the nation's fallen state, since "the development of a nation's art is an indication of the development of that nation."[13] Such ideas linking culture, literature, civilization, and national health were themselves drawn from British colonial education in India.[14]

The Hollywood Machine

The most basic mechanism for an improved cinema was emulation of Hollywood in technical matters. But how could Hollywood *stardom* serve as a technological model? Already in the late 1920s, the strongest emblem of the exemplary nature of Hollywood stardom for Indian cinema was the obligatory use of Hollywood epithets for Indian stars.[15] The most frequently mentioned example is the silent star Master Vithal, who was dubbed "the Indian Douglas Fairbanks." Suresh Chabria refers to other examples, such as "the Indian Mary Pickford" (Ermeline) and "the Indian Eddie Polo" (Nandram). Where such epithets were not used, we see an effusive abundance of comparisons with Hollywood stars. For example, as late as 1942, the captions accompanying photographs of the actor Mazhar Khan compare him to Bela Lugosi, Paul Muni, and Boris Karloff, among others.[16] The point of comparison in all these cases centered on screen roles and physical appearance, rather than on the star's "inner" identity, and the comparison served to cement a relationship of equality with Hollywood.

But this naming practice was also derided, as in the following exchange in the letters section of a 1939 issue of *filmindia*:

> Question: Why is Master Vithal called "the Indian Douglas" [*sic*]?
> Answer: . . . I know half a dozen girls who are occasionally called the "Greta Garbos" of India—and one particular girl who was called Greta Garbo, Norma Shearer and Lupe Velez, all at the same time. . . . Don't you think that Americans should retaliate by calling Douglas Fairbanks the "Master Vithal of Hollywood"?[17]

It is also noteworthy that among scores of unselfconscious usages of Hollywood epithets, only explicitly nationalist film magazines, such as the Hindi *Rangbhoomi,* critique this type of overt referencing of Hollywood. For example, Master Vithal stated outright in *Rangbhoomi* that he hated the popular epithet of "Indian Douglas Fairbanks" and pointed out that "such names go against our national pride."[18]

The Hollywood model was invoked in a variety of other ways, but there were two dominant forms that Hollywood stardom took in the Indian imagination. The first was in the context of articles on the improvement of Indian stars, in which Hollywood was viewed as the model of a perfectly oiled machine that knew how to *produce* stars. The second was simply a form of *participation* in that machinery by disseminating knowledge about Hollywood stars in ways that were similar to American film magazines. On the one hand, there was a focus on publicity, which was identified as the institutional framework that contributes to stardom. On the other hand, at the individual level, the road to stardom was equated with good acting, where Hollywood again served as the model for the professionalism and work ethic that produces good acting. Talent and luck played no role in such visions of Hollywood as an efficient modern institution that used scientific methods to train and promote stars.

One could argue that we have here another version of the Americanism that was so popular in Europe in the 1920s. For Indian cinema, too, Hollywood represented "a new model of industrialism" that was both rational and economically profitable.[19] In Germany, even as debates over Americanism were far more central to questions of national culture, Hollywood served a similar role as a technological model: "The American star system . . . elicited enormous attention and imitation in Germany," and there were "study trips to New York and Hollywood to be schooled in everything from business organization to camera types and lighting." Yet, even though German cinema culture in the interwar period "was first and foremost American," as in India, Germans saw Hollywood as having no "serious contribution to make to culture."[20] Thus in Germany, too, there was something of a split discourse separating technology and culture. But as a point of contrast, Hollywood's position in Indian cinema was inflected by the context of British colonialism, with America functioning as a positive example of democracy and freedom, at least in part as a provocative contrast to the British. Some magazines took delight in unfavorably comparing British cinema to Hollywood cinema. The British authorities, for their part, were anxious about the influence of Hollywood cinema. B. D. Garga, Brian Shoesmith, and others have discussed the colonial anxiety about representations of Western moral codes in Hollywood cinema, which were regarded as detrimental to colonial authority.[21] The *Report of the Indian Cinematograph Committee* of 1927–28 mentions a witness who says that "the exhibition of films depicting European social life were very harmful as they produced very mistaken notions of European social life."[22] Such anxieties, in Garga's argument, were actually not so much about the harm done to the image of English culture in Indian eyes, as about the growing economic hegemony of Hollywood.[23] The anxiety regarding American films was shared by other European countries and resulted in various policies designed to curb Hollywood's growing economic power. This context might explain why, in Indian film magazines, Hollywood could serve, fairly unambiguously, as a rational model for the economic management of the cinematic institution, even if not as a model for female stardom or for the types of stories to be told; such areas were clearly seen as impinging upon areas of cultural identity constituting the inner domain of nationalism.

A "how-to" manual written in 1931 by K. T. Dalvi is representative of the attitude to Hollywood as a well-oiled machine.[24] In *A New Profession or Manual of Indian Talkies,* Hollywood served as a model at both individual and institutional levels. For the individual star aspirant, Dalvi recommended that "intending artistes would do well to read the careers of Douglas Fairbanks, Charlie Chaplin, Harold Lloyd, Mary Pickford, Lillian Gish, Colleen Moore, Talmadge Sisters, and others and how hard and conscientiously they do their work." At the institutional level, Dalvi notes that "in America there are academies for actors and actresses and persons passing from these academies are given preference by the studios over the untrained persons," and suggests that Indian studios follow the same practice. In his view, it is the combination of individual work ethic and institutional training in acting that produces the Hollywood star. There is a frequent slippage in his writing between "actor" and "star," so that the qualifications for attaining star status are the same as standard training for an actor. In his attempt to provide rational guidelines for star aspirants in India, Dalvi suggests that "a person seeking to qualify as a star, should first try to get admission into the studio as an 'extra' . . . if the person is able to make some impression as an 'extra,' he will surely be preferred for a better part in the next film." His recommendation that star aspirants begin at the bottom and work their way up relies on a model of success through hard work, an ideology central to the American dream and entirely unsuited to established practice in India, where actors and actresses, more often than not, received good roles by virtue of their elite social status and their family connections with the directors or producers.[25]

The view of Hollywood as a scientifically run star factory derived from the notion that in every detail of its various operations, Hollywood functioned on the basis of carefully researched formulas. K. M. Multani's "Public Taste" in the May 1936 issue of *filmindia* elaborated on Hollywood's scientific formula for assessing and manipulating public taste: "As a result of investigation and inquiry into the subconscious and palpable needs of filmgoers, producers in America had arrived at a formula according to which they have been turning out hundreds of successful feature pictures." The successful formula includes "25% romance and sex, 15% strong melodrama, 15% music and dancing, 10% sentimentalism, 10% kid stuff, 10% strong meat, e.g., fights and brawls." He ends with a lament that repeats the absence of a healthy work ethic in India: "But how many would undertake this painfully arduous and onerous research work in our own lethargic country of dreamers?" It is probably no coincidence that the same issue of *filmindia* has an article on the hard work involved in retaining star status in America.[26] In the implicit rhetoric of improvement here, we hear echoes of colonial perceptions of the laziness of tropical natives. One thing to note in Multani's description of the Hollywood recipe for successful films is that this formula very soon came to resemble more closely the *Indian* conception of a good film, with its balancing of a variety of attractions.[27]

By 1939 the discourse of Hollywood as a model of scientific efficiency was so much in place in India that no further reference to Hollywood was necessary in, for example, the recommendations that Y. A. Fazalbhoy makes in his book *The Indian Film: A Review.* Beginning with the observation that "picture publicity, like all advertising, is a scientific business," he counters the "haphazard methods" of publicity in current Indian practice with recommendations of a more rational system of film publicity emulating the manner of "foreign distributing companies." In his view, "it should be the duty of the publicity department to develop the star value of the actors and actresses so that when a picture is released, the mere mention that so-and-so has an important part in it will bring people to the theatre." Fazalbhoy also emphasizes star merchandising, suggesting that "the illiterate millions" should be targeted by "coloured pictures of stars [which] if manufactured on a large scale would be extremely cheap and are never thrown away." His choice of words, especially his emphasis on the "duty" of film publicity to produce stars, makes it almost a moral imperative rather than a form of practical economic manipulation. Underlying these various recommendations was not only the model of the Hollywood star machine, but also a consensus on the chaotic methods of Indian film production.[28]

When the rhetoric of improvement turned to the state of Indian stars, the focus was on the irrational economic basis of the star system and of star popularity. Thus, a sub-genre of the "What's Wrong with Indian Cinema?" genre of film journalism devoted itself to the vexed question of why India had no stars, with the goal of analyzing why the actors and actresses who were referred to as "stars" did not deserve that appellation. The relation between star salaries and box office returns was usually the crux of these arguments, which explains the obsession in film journalism with listing, analyzing, and critiquing star salaries.[29] The sign of a rationally organized star system, for many of these writers, was not the stars' salaries, but an efficient "nursery" for stars, a "scientific" publicity machinery to launch them, and the work ethic of the individual star. The goal of such a system and, consequently, the ultimate measure of star status for Dalvi and others was a film's financial returns. In a functioning star system, operating on sound capitalist principles, the star's salary should reflect the box office returns resulting from his or her presence in a film. Instead, the complaint was that salaries, in and of themselves, had become the main criterion of star status: "The supposed 'star-value' in India has no box-office or art rating, but it is merely measured by the monthly earnings of these supposed 'stars.'"[30] Yet, because these film commentators assumed such a correlation with box office returns for Hollywood stars, they felt free to discuss star popularity there in terms other than salaries. One article measured the popularity of John Stewart by the number of letters he received—about a hundred a week—and by the fact that members of the professional classes ("doctors and critics") wrote to him. The article concentrated on one letter, in particular, which was a letter of complaint from the lover of a female fan who had asked for Stewart's photograph and had fallen in love with it.[31] In this contrast between stardom as training in India and stardom as mass appeal in Hollywood, we see again the professional orientation of the Indian "picture personality" placed alongside the private orientation of the Hollywood star. There was no such discussion of fan mail or obsessive viewers as a measure of stardom for Indian stars.

The emulation of Hollywood produced its own constraints. One author recognizes the constructed nature of Hollywood stars: "Publicity is the life of a star's career, without it he is a failure."[32] Marveling that Hollywood stars even pay for publicity out of their own pockets in order to send photographs in response to fan requests, he also notes that publicity prevents Hollywood stars from being happy in normal lives. Thus, as soon as the subject turns to the private lives of Hollywood stars, a marked ambivalence enters his discussion. Even as publicity is crucial to their economic role in Hollywood, stars would gladly give up their fame "if they could only wear cotton dresses, sweep porches and sew buttons on shirts." The shift to the inner desires of Hollywood stars immediately produces the feminizing domestic discourse of "cotton dresses" and sewing buttons, with even Hollywood stardom being gendered as female. The goal of a rationally ordered publicity machine, then, sits uneasily with the full implications of publicity as a system of communicating private lives. Yet, despite its vivid picture of the deprived lives of (female) Hollywood stars, unable to fulfill their domestic desires, the article is able to conclude by returning to its critique of the absence of a comparable publicity machinery in India.

If these writers were correct in stating that there was no correlation between star salaries and box office returns in India, then the continued maintenance of stars in Indian cinema, despite their unprofitability, suggests that the rhetoric of Hollywood stardom was in place, but without its economic motivation. In other words, the star was functioning in India as a rhetorical practice rather than as an economic practice. This rhetoric is evidenced in the extravagant and indiscriminate epithets used to describe "stars" in film advertisements and magazine photographs. The discrepancy between the rhetoric and practice of stardom is also borne out by the fact that there actually was more interest in news about producers, studios, and directors than about stars until the late 1930s. In his article in *Filmland* bemoaning the absence of true stars in Indian cinema, Charu

Roy tacitly denied his main argument by concluding with an alphabetized list and description of contemporary directors and "stars."[33] Here was an example of the coexistence of an unqualified rhetoric of Indian stardom alongside a critique of its economic viability.

But stars existed as an economic commodity not only as conceived by these writers, as an investment toward box office returns. Ironically enough, all film magazines, including the ones that carried articles critiquing the true financial worth of stars, made commercial use of the star image, both figuratively and literally. Even if they did not sell films, stars did sell magazines, if one is to judge by the number of full-page photographs of stars in most film magazines of the time. Not only the presence of photographs of players sold magazines, but also the *promise* of special photographs in forthcoming issues.[34] There was, in general, a telling contrast between the printed matter in magazines such as *filmindia* and their visual material, such as advertisements and pictures with effusive captions. Sometimes an article might severely critique the entire institution of Indian cinema and its stars, while the photograph on the same page, which was unconnected with the article, had enthusiastic captions celebrating the talents of the star. In this gap between the rhetoric and practice of stardom, it was as if there were two separate magazines in one: one for the elite literate reader, and the other for the uneducated reader who might buy the magazine for the photos and ads. Such a division between the educated elite and the uneducated masses dominates much of the writing on cinema audiences at this time and matches the suggestions for improved publicity made by Fazalbhoy, who recommends an increased supply of visual material to target the "the illiterate millions."

Perhaps the most obvious way in which the star functioned commercially in Hollywood cinema was as a mode of product identification, to sell not just films and film magazines, as in India, but also other products. There is minimal evidence for stardom as a broader economic practice in India in the 1920s and 1930s, with no consumer culture surrounding stars or advertisements of products using star images. However, we do know that matchboxes featured the faces of both cinema and theater stars, while at least one company put out a numbered series of postcards featuring Indian stars that ran into the hundreds.[35] A more extensive use of stars to sell cosmetics and other products emerged only much later, in the 1950s.[36]

The "Cultured Lady" and Cinema's Moral Status

Alongside discussions of the efficiency of Hollywood compared to the Indian film industry, if there was a single unifying concern in the rhetoric of improvement, it was the issue of the moral health and respectability of cinema. Generalized gossip about cinema as a disreputable institution was tied to its class status and to anxieties about female public performance. Early cinema in colonial India did not have the low-class associations it initially had in the United States. While in the West early film shows were mostly low-brow entertainment, exhibited alongside other low-brow forms like vaudeville, in India they represented "a relatively higher class orientation inflected by the colonial formation of British India," since "initially travelling film shows were accommodated within a well-established European variety entertainment circuit." Thus, often Hollywood's low-brow offerings, such as serials and Westerns, became highbrow entertainment in India because their audiences were mostly the colonial and Indian elite. However, once Indian film production took off, concerns over its moral impact changed cinema's class affiliation, in part because of the association of prostitution with any form of public female performance. In Indian cinema, class discourse focused on all aspects of the cinematic experience. Manishita Dass's reading of the interviews conducted by the Indian Cinematograph Committee in 1927 shows the assumed equivalences between "educated," "sophisticated," "high class," and "cosmopolitan," and similar equivalences at the low-brow end of the spectrum.[37] Not only audience types, but also film genres, movie theaters, and actresses were mapped onto a hierarchical axis of "culture," with low-brow genres like the stunt film assumed to be popular with low-class audiences. By the late 1920s, such evaluations based on "cultured" status had become focused almost exclusively on the quality of the players in films. Now the class composition of actresses associated with the cinema became the single most important issue for redefining the moral status of cinema, with the greatest emphasis on education and well known families.[38] One sign by which the social respectability of female stars was prominently announced was to attach degrees (B.A., M.A.) after the names of educated stars.

Certain basic assumptions about class permeated all levels of film analysis in the magazines and newspapers of the 1930s and 1940s. Class hierarchy was directly linked to education, with the explicit desire to convert the much derided medium to one produced for and by the educated elite. This was a question of national identity, not only because of the perceived neglect of the medium by national leaders, but also because it was felt that Indian cinema suffered from a lack of respect internationally as well as nationally from the Western-educated Indian elite. A series of equivalences emerged: the moral status of cinema became feminized as it was conflated with the moral status of its stars, and their moral status, in turn, was determined by their class origins.[39] This gendered construction of cinema itself, paradoxically perhaps, enabled cinema to participate in the nationalist discourse in terms of the long-standing argument linking the status of women with that of the nation.[40] A 1931 article cements the chain of equivalences between cinema, woman, nation, and international status via the ubiquitous discourse of improvement, complaining that Indian cinema is so flawed because "our characters are misrepresented, our ladies demoralized, our nation mispriced [*sic*], our country degraded in the eyes of others."[41]

Despite the constant references to Hollywood in the context of recommendations for the technical and economic improvement of cinema, there was a striking absence of Hollywood as a standard of reference in discussions of the *moral* improvement of cinema. Hollywood in the 1920s was having its own problems with a public image of scandal and licentiousness. In *Picture Personalities,* Richard deCordova's chapter on Hollywood scandals describes the ways in which attempts were made to recuperate this licentious image within the discourse of family romance. In the Indian discourse on Hollywood stars, the scandalous aspects of private information on stars were downplayed, with the emphasis placed more on love, romance, hobbies, and personal tastes of the stars. The image of Hollywood circulating in the pages of Indian magazines was a relatively "safe" and "clean" one, and yet, in the context of the moral improvement of cinema, it could not serve even as a horizon of possibilities in which the modern Indian woman negotiated new limits of public identity.

In other national cinema contexts in the 1920s and 1930s, such as in Shanghai or Berlin, the "new woman" is a recurrent figure, emblematic of the anxieties of new gender relations under modernity. In the Indian context, the "new woman" is quite different in meaning and appears half a century earlier as a figure of domestic anxiety over the intrusion of British administrative and legal control into the space of the home. By the early twentieth century, the "woman's question" was "resolved" to the extent that a new model of "modern Indian womanhood" aligned with nationalist goals had emerged.[42] Reconciling the modern woman with the nationalist project entailed redefining the modern in terms of a reconstituted Indian "tradition." The ideological power of "tradition" came from its identification with the gendered inner domain of nationalism, outside the control of colonial authority, and centered on the figure of the woman.[43]

The Indian modern woman was identified not only with the domestic sphere, but also with education, which was not contrary to female propriety but rather was entirely appropriate to the newly reconstituted domestic sphere. Appropriate education and social engagement, together with class origins, constituted the "cultured lady," the specific form in which a positive image of the modern Indian woman was invoked. Education and literacy, of course, centered on topics like "home science," the development of virtues like modesty, and public efforts in the cause of other women. A nineteenth-century book on female education, for example, "waxed eloquent on 'true modesty,' which it distinguished from the 'uncivilized' modesty in uneducated women." Such "nineteenth century tracts on new domesticity" took pains to establish the link between education, domesticity, and the nation by presenting "women without any formal education" as "bringing the nation into disrepute." Partha Chatterjee elaborates on exactly how the seemingly contradictory options of education and domesticity for women could be reconciled: "Once the essential femininity of women was fixed in terms of certain culturally visible spiritual qualities, they could go to schools, travel in public conveyances, watch public entertainment programmes, and in time even take up employment outside the home." In cinema's discourse of improvement, such "culturally visible spiritual qualities" were repeatedly identified with education and class, which alone could provide actresses with the protective armor of "true modesty" in the face of the licentious world of cinema. Discussions about the 1930s studios emphasize their familylike atmosphere, which helped manage the potential contradiction between home, education, modesty, and public performance.[44] Yet it is important to remember that the redefined modern woman was not a homogeneous category. The essays of Mahadevi Varma, writing in the 1930s, are representative. She "distinguished between three kinds of modern Indian women: (a) Those who were taking part along with men in the political movement, defying age-long constraints; they gave proof of great strength and sacrifice, earned well-deserved respect and benefited all women by dispelling false notions of women as being weak and emotional beings. (b) Then there were 'some educated women who, despite their favourable conditions, could find no solution to social ills and turned their education and awakening into a source of livelihood and into public service' . . . . (c) Finally, there were those fashionable and wealthy women with a little education who had refashioned their home life under the influence of Western modernity."[45] In cinema discourse, the desire was for women in the first category, with educated women's work in the movies discussed in similar terms of courageous defiance of taboos, even if not directly in the cause of political action. These were the terms in which stars such as Durga Khote and Devika Rani were discussed.

Such a nationalist framework of thinking continued to be dominant in the discourse surrounding cinema even in the 1940s. The female author of an article in *PicturPost* in 1943 again reiterated the link among nationalism, ideal womanhood, and female performance in cinema, a link cemented by class and educational status. According to her, it is the duty of educated women to take up film acting as a career because "they will be utilising not only their talents and education, but *will also enable the films to portray Indian womanhood in all its phases and reveal to the world at large its glorious achievements and ideals.* It is not by hiding in their homes, and by their hearths, that women will help in the advancement of their country, but by urging forward every cause which can benefit, and be benefitted by their individual gifts—and in this the film industry is a very great factor."[46] The author strategically couches this argument in favor of women in public performance in terms of class affiliation and national service. The rhetoric of improvement, through its valorization of cultured women, completely rejected the democratic aspiration underlying Hollywood star ideology. Where the Hollywood stories offered the star's success as proof that anyone—with talent or luck—could make it in America, in India, cinema itself aspired to class mobility. But by relying on upper-class women as its means to social respectability, the discourse of improvement was caught in a paradox: cinema's low reputation made it impossible to attract educated women, and yet educated women alone could redeem cinema's low reputation.

The recurrent clarification of distinctions between cultured and vulgar actress can be tied to a general bourgeoisification of culture that was reshaping other areas of cultural practice as well: "Respectability was the key to the making of a middle class in colonial India" and a way to "draw distinctions between themselves and other social groups." These distinctions became urgent in the case of cinema because of its aspiration to the status of middle-class respectability. The defining characteristic of the middle class was not merely economic status, but also a shared background of education: "A certain group of people became producers and products of a new cultural politics in a transformed [and changing] historical context."[47] But cinema had no legitimate access to this new cultural politics in which classical music, dance, literature, and religious practice were being reshaped. The two axes of the moral rhetoric of cinema were thus the explicit one of gender, having to do with anxieties about women performing in public, and the implicit one of class, having to do with what type of woman might legitimately perform in the cinema in order to improve its reputation. By the 1930s, since there could no longer be a prohibition against women's public performance, the rhetoric of improvement turned to the implicit axis of class. The prohibition of gossip and the constraints regarding the circulation of private knowledge about stars can be explained in terms of these two axes of gender and class.

Discussions of representations of the private in Indian cinema have tended to center on the unofficial prohibition of the kiss, although such a ban was not yet in effect in the silent and early sound period. Madhava Prasad argues that the prohibition of the kiss in post-1930s Indian cinema was not the result of some essentialized characteristic of Indian culture, but the product of an alliance between premodern feudal power blocs and the modern state. Writing mainly about post-1950s cinema, he defines the prohibition on the kiss in terms of a taboo on filmic representations of the private, defined specifically as conjugal space. He explains this prohibition as a type of contract between "new and traditional elites," specifically, as a way of preventing "the dissolution of pre-capitalist patriarchal enclaves" such as the family. In Prasad's usage, however, "the erotic display of the female body as spectacle" is not coded as a representation of the private but, in the context of song-and-dance sequences, is regarded as "contracted voyeurism," producing a representation of public, rather than private, space. Prasad also makes the important point that the emergence of private discourse can be tied to the development of middle-class respectability for cinema as an institution: "The problem of the couple is the problem of the formation of a middle class."[48]

In the scholarship on cinema's early history, discussions of public and private usually center on the production of new public spheres both through filmic representation and through the communitarian space of film viewing. Annette Kuhn sees the public space of cinema in terms of where films were consumed and also in terms of a public sphere of regulation, which emerged as a response to the perceived threat of such a space as constituted by mass consumers of films. Miriam Hansen approaches the gendered connotations of public and private spaces from the point of view of women's increased participation in the public sphere via cinema. Her more recent work focuses on the difference between the public sphere of cinema and earlier public spheres produced through print culture and, more crucially, on mass media's transformation of the "raw material of human experience into an object of capitalist production."[49]

In the context of star discourses, my interest in constructions of stardom extends from the film text and the space of exhibition to questions of the public circulation of private star identities. Miriam Hansen's discussion of the capitalist and technological appropriation of human experience provides a useful starting point in considering two key aspects of cinema that might explain anxieties in India regarding the interpenetration, rather than the separation, of the private and public. First, as a visual-sensory medium, cinema not only *represents* private feelings and actions (such as the kiss), but also *produces* private feelings through mechanisms of identification and also through the conditions of spectatorship in movie theaters. There is an inscription of intimacy in the very medium of cinema, not only by virtue of the darkened cinema theater and the individualized viewer's experience of the large screen, but also, more importantly, by the increased flexibility in the viewer's perspective, which is permitted by the potentialities of camera movement and varied camera distance. Second, through its commodification and transmission (through mechanical reproduction) of feelings, cinema produces a seeming proliferation of spaces of intimacy in the public sphere, not only through film screenings, but also through star photographs, interviews, and profiles, even when the focus is carefully on the professional. The possibility of such images and feelings becoming saleable, reproducible, and mobile property puts a new meaning on the public availability of women. Both of these aspects of cinema's role in producing an interpenetration of public and private center on the figure of the star, who quite literally becomes the point of intersection between fiction and biography, the film text and outside realities, and the public space of screenings and private space of spectatorial response.

Before the cinema, female performance in the urban theater was coded as public in a new way because such women were available for viewing by anyone capable of paying the price of a ticket, while performances by women (dancers and singers) in the homes of the rich were coded as private since they were by invitation only. Concerns during the 1920s, by colonial authorities as well as by Indian writers on cinema, about the availability of Western women for Indian male viewing can be presumed to have extended to similar concerns about the availability of any (that is, Indian/Hindu) women for public viewing.[50] Not only the cinema, but also other media had contributed to the increased circulation of female bodies. For example, in speaking of appropriate subjects for representation in paintings, Sister Nivedita, writing in 1907, voices concerns about proper etiquette regarding public space. She says, in a critique of the paintings of Ravi Varma, that "not every scene is fit for a picture. . . . In a country in which that posture is held to be ill-bred, every home contains a picture of a fat woman lying full length on the floor and writing a letter on a lotus leaf! As if a sight that would outrage decorum in actuality could be beautiful in imagination! In a country in which romantic emotion is never allowed to show itself in public, pictures of the wooing of Arjuna and Subhadra abound."[51] Given that such representations were often transposed from the medium of painting to that of cinema, Sister Nivedita's reaction serves to explain why the sight of actresses playing such scenarios might arouse even greater concern.

Films increased the public circulation of women's images and made women's bodies available in the public sphere in a wholly new way, not only through their circulation in film magazines, but also through techniques specific to the medium, such as the close-up. Kamalabai Gokhale, a stage and silent film actress, points to the unavoidable intimacy specific to the medium of cinema and uses this to explain why film actresses were particularly looked at askance: "Theatre acting is done within the norms of restraint. It is symbolic, particularly in love scenes. On the stage you can keep your distance, decide your limit and say that I would go no further than holding hands. . . . But, in a love scene in a film, you have to embrace—really embrace—the other fellow in front of the camera. Otherwise, it would make no sense."[52] Since the cinematic medium itself encourages the impertinence of an intimate gaze, this explains, in part, the impulse in printed discourse on female stars to maintain a distance from the "private" identity of the star. The hesitation with regard to gossip stems from a discomfort with actresses as public figures who expose to the public gaze the *fictional* private beings of the characters they play, an exposure that already feeds the generalized gossip about the institution of cinema. The presentation of private emotion and feelings in fictional settings creates an illusion of intimacy that threatens to spill over into and contaminate the real identities of stars. This is similar to the "autobiographism" that plagued women writers like Mahadevi Varma, whose narrative scenarios featuring women *like* her were invariably read as autobiographical. In terms of its ability to explore intimate and private concerns, the novel was arguably the closest medium to the cinema in India, closer even than theater. Yet here, too, what I have called "innuendo" in the context of cinema discourse became "strategies of obliqueness and the reluctance to speak directly about oneself." In both novel and cinema, the indirections of private expression were shaped by the gendered anxieties caused by the interpenetration of private and public, as fictional identities tended to be conflated with those of the actress/author.[53]

We can look to the Parsi theater, a precursor of cinema, for some of the mechanisms of managing anxieties about the women who were performing such scenes of intimacy. Kathryn Hansen's observations on the presence of Anglo-Indian and Jewish actresses on the Parsi stage may be extended to the cinema. She argues that there is a simultaneous distancing (women "other" than our own are on display) and identification (with the fictional Hindu women they played) through Hindu names and roles: "The Parsi theater demanded that its actresses be Other, and that its own women stay strictly beside their male chaperones in the audience." This is why there was no attempt to conceal the actresses' real names or Anglo-Indian background. But at the same time, we also get no further details of their biographies, details that might render them too "other" for the possibility of their identification with Hindu roles. We can easily surmise a similar split dynamic of at once Othering and Hinduizing in the case of Anglo-Indian silent stars such as Sulochana (Ruby Myers) and Sita Devi (Renee Smith).[54]

Anxieties regarding female public performance on stage and screen included not only the public display of female bodies and of private feelings, but also—especially in the case of the new professions of stage and screen actress—issues of impersonation. Female impersonation by male actors was acceptable in urban Parsi theater in the early twentieth century, especially because it produced a space of control for defining and modeling the ideal woman.[55] But when it came to female actresses impersonating not only respectable women but also absolute ideals of womanhood derived from mythology, the persistence of autobiographism caused intense discomfort. That is, the precise relation between the actor and the role was at stake, and the tendency to conflate the two was in tension with the knowledge of the social origins of most actresses. In both theater and cinema, there was much discussion of the direction in which the relation between the two identities, actor and role, went: would the vulgar actress lower the role of mythological character, or would the sanctity of the role purify the actress? For example, the stage director Girish Ghosh converted the "theatre into a moral-pedagogical space . . . redeeming prostitutes by the aura of the characters they enacted." In many cases, no such redemption was claimed for lower-class screen actresses playing similar roles. On the contrary, the screen itself was defiled by their presence.[56]

Discussions of female stars implicitly extended the argument of a link between class and moral status of women to criteria for evaluating acting ability. For Dhiren Ganguly, cinema's problem was not the moral danger to "respectable ladies" in the studios, but rather the harmful effects on film texts of the presence of lower-class women as actresses: "their unfitness lies neither in their birth nor in their downfall; it lies in their mode of base living, in their vicious environment, in their want of culture and their indifference to education." In his view, the penetrating eye of the camera would see through the masks of histrionic impersonation to perceive the true class status of the performer, because "lack of culture and education . . . can never deceive the screen" or escape "the eye of the camera [which] is as penetrative as that of a thought reader."[57] Here is a version of Dziga Vertov's kino-eye at the service of moral perception. If the camera eye can see through the artifice of impersonation to the true class origins of the actress, then by implication the camera's penetrative eye ultimately would interfere with the full articulation of fictions on screen. Furthermore, it also implies that the "truth" about the identity of the role/actor is framed in terms of social origins rather than private feelings. The question, however, remains as to who precisely these actresses of low character are: since such women are never explicitly named, they remain the invisible hordes who ruin the reputation of cinema. Yet, there were several well-known stars, such as Ermeline or Gohar, who might fit the description, but would never find themselves explicitly discussed in such terms in print.

With the widespread and long-standing cultural bias against female public performance, the low social status of film actresses was a given, but the reformist voice in the discourse of improvement advocated greater respect for female stars, promoted the image of their hard work, recommended that educated women become actresses, and critiqued old prejudices against the profession. Yet it shared the ingrained assumption that women of "loose morals" make poor actresses, unquestioningly linking the absence of education to moral laxity. By reiterating the need for the educated classes to send their daughters to this profession, many articles reinforced the assumption that all other female performers who were uneducated or from low-class families were *justifiably* identified by the public as little other than prostitutes. Articles advocating a change in attitude toward upper-class actresses wanted to bridge the binary between the woman at home and the woman in public, but they maintained the ideological value of the distinction by ascribing the superior moral characteristics of women in the home to cultured women in public performance.

In cinema discourse, the moral domain of women's space is a private space that is publicly understood through a tacit insider knowledge that recognizes the boundaries between the speakable and the unspeakable. Woman's domain, in public discourse about it, is an idealized and therefore publicly exhibited space of tradition and feminine virtue. It is constructed as insider knowledge, and, like purdah, it is outside the view of foreigners and the lower classes. But that other private domain of the prostitute's existence is also equally, but negatively, idealized as the antithesis of the domain of home. Public knowledge of specific details of private lives of actresses is therefore, in a sense, redundant. Certain iconic and recurrent tropes, such as references to the actress's education and "cultured" origins, function to evoke the entire realm of idealized female space, while silence on her everyday private self functions just as iconically, by suggestive innuendo, to open up the opposite type of female space. The early film actress therefore occupies, in the public imagination, both spaces.

3. *Real and Imagined Stars*

In writings about the bad reputation of cinema, there was usually a slippage between the loose morals of individual actresses (never named, but referred to in generalized insinuations) and of the cinema as an institution (in the form of lewd producers and directors). Several types of texts that appeared in the pages of mainstream journalism give a sense of the contradictions marking this type of discourse. All these texts concerned the work environment to which actresses in the cinema were exposed. Although they may have taken opposing stands on the question of whether the cinema was an appropriate work place for respectable women, they all shared certain deep-rooted premises about the nature of this environment.

In this chapter I read a variety of texts about female stars that display a recurrence of many of the tropes I have discussed in chapters 1 and 2. First, I discuss different journalistic sites in which real and fictional female stars appear. The texts I analyze include short stories about fictional stars, a debate between two stars, and a legal case as reported in a newspaper. Then I look at the discourse about stardom as it appears in some of the films themselves, focusing on the three major studios, New Theatres in Calcutta, Prabhat in Poona, and Bombay Talkies in Bombay. My discussion centers on two "respectable" female stars, Devika Rani and Durga Khote, who were both exceptions to the generally negative image of female stars and who serve as a contrast to my argument thus far. In my discussion of two Prabhat films, *Amar Jyoti* (V. Shantaram, 1936) and *Aadmi* (V. Shantaram, 1939), I shall suggest that one of the ways to piece together a star text from the 1930s might be to resort to the very same indirections that marked the rhetoric of innuendo in star discourse.

The 1933 Hindi short story "Chitrapat" by Bhudev Sharma summarizes some of the concerns that recur in discussions on actresses.[1] It is about an actress who helps a beggar boy and is painted in that role by a European painter. In the painting, she is depicted wearing a sari, which the story suggests is unusual for her. The painting represents her as a model of virtuous Hindu womanhood: "that blotless character is an inspiration not only to me but to all," says the painter in an interview. Seeing herself represented thus, the actress refuses to continue filming and remains very thoughtful as she closets herself in her room. The rest of the story details her moral transformation from actress to respectable Indian woman, the two categories being mutually incompatible. Painting, a more respectable form of female public display, succeeds in morally transforming her. This story encapsulates several clichés, such as the hierarchy between painting and film, and the location of national pride in Hindu womanhood, with its potential for teaching the superior moral values of India to the West. Typical of this and other texts in film magazines voicing similar values is the implicit condemnation of female stardom, as well as the overall institution of cinema, even while actively participating in the very institution it is condemning. The story goes further in its simultaneous condemnation and participation by incorporating several references to the magazine *Rangbhoomi*: the actress reads it, receives a letter from it, and is featured in it. While clearly inviting a comparison between the fictional actress and the real actresses who are featured in the pages of *Rangbhoomi,* the magazine blatantly promotes itself by association with a fictional star who is rendered safe through her moral transformation.

A news item, "Film Star's Story; Incidents at Hill Station," which appeared in the *Times of India* on 15 September 1927, reported that the silent star Ermeline went to court, charging the director and chairman of the Shri Krishna Cinema Company with indecent assault.[2] Often, as in this case, such "personal" court cases turned out also to be about professional issues, such as contract violations.[3] The first magistrate who tried the case "found that . . . the complaints were false and ordered her to pay Rs. 100." A second judge reversed this judgment because he found the first magistrate to have been biased by the fact that Ermeline "and her ayah were untutored women of loose morals and bad association. His honour held that in neither case the evidence on record justified the inference that the accusation was false and frivolous. . . . The orders were therefore set aside and the compensations deposited were ordered to be refunded."[4] Such news items were reported in a carefully neutral, matter-of-fact voice, relegating their more sensational aspects to the pages of "yellow journalism."[5] It is noteworthy that while the second judge found the first magistrate to be biased because of his knowledge of the "true" identity of the complainant, he did not overturn the basic premise that the actress was a woman of "loose morals" by virtue of her profession. This judgment is emblematic of the contradictions found in even the most reformist voice in the debate on the social status of female stars. Against this news item, we might place an interview with Ermeline herself in which she voices very similar opinions. Women of low character in cinema lose their virtue, not because of some danger presented by the studios, but because of a flaw in their own characters. No matter what line of work a woman is in, she needs strength of character to protect her virtue. Ermeline, herself regarded as a woman of loose morals, concludes the interview by reiterating the call for women "of good families" to join the profession in order to improve its reputation.[6]

The two sides of the debate over whether the screen was a suitable profession for "respectable" women can be found in two articles, "Should Respectable Ladies Join the Films?" and its rejoinder, "Why Shouldn't Respectable Women Join the Films?" which appeared in *Filmland* in 1931. The anonymous "Lady Artiste" who wrote the first article had thought that the cinema "would be an honest means of livelihood" but soon realized that "it would require a high moral courage and character to withstand the scandal that accompanied the actress in and out of the studio." By this she does not mean that the scandals are unfounded, but that the work atmosphere in studios makes scandalous behavior inevitable. It is difficult for ladies such as herself to have to work with actresses who come "from houses of ill-fame" and are "naturally very free in their behaviour and are easily accessible for corruption." Because of the behavior of such women, a "society girl" cannot "expect any better treatment from the hands of those persons who are accustomed and habituated to low morals." She concluded by urging the film industry to "first learn to give the respectable ladies their due honour" before expecting them to take up this profession.[7]

This article serves to confirm, from an insider's point of view, all the gossip about cinema. The author's anonymity further authorizes her views, even as it works as a substitute for the rhetorical mode of innuendo. As an anonymous writer, she cannot be identified, but at the same time, she is also free to tell the truth. The rejoinder to this article, "Why Shouldn't Respectable Ladies Join the Films?" was by Sabita Devi (Irene Gasper). She insists that Indian studio bosses are "thorough gentlemen, who in trying to embody the aspirations of the West with those of the East, still hold to the traditions of the East in respect of their attitude towards women." This statement places the burden of nationalist representation on women, who constitute the pure site of the superior traditions of the East. She charges those who regard actresses as morally fallen with a "mid-Victorian conception of ladies on the stage" and reminds readers that "as artistes we are not concerned with the private life of an individual . . . rather we are concerned with the attitude and behaviour of that person during working hours." Yet, having vigorously defended the honor of the profession and of other actresses such as herself, she nevertheless shares the opinion that "some of the lesser lights in Filmland have been recruited from the lowest strata of society," while cautioning that "it is far nobler to sympathize than to criticize" these "unfortunate women." Certain bedrock assumptions linking class status with improper sexuality are therefore ingrained on both sides of the debate over cinema as a morally appropriate profession for women. Sabita Devi insinuates that "A Lady Artiste" is perhaps herself to blame for any unwanted advances she may have experienced and suggests to her that, instead of talking of "'weak and helpless girls' being at the mercy of unscrupulous libertines," she should remember "the old story of Eve tempting Adam" and recognize that "Eve still wields her subtle influence over men more often for evil than for good." By the end of Sabita Devi's essay, we find that the old binary of the home and the world is still in place. Placed against the "Eves" of the film industry, who no doubt belong to the lower classes, are "society girls" of "true womanhood" who command respect through their "womanly and modest" behavior so that "no man can approach her in any other spirit than that of the deepest reverence."[8] Sabita Devi, as identified author of this rebuttal to the "Lady Artiste," speaks in the voice of the dominant discourse, but also reveals its own contradictory pressures toward sanitizing, on the one hand, and moralizing, on the other, with class remaining the dividing point.

An exchange similar to the one between Sabita Devi and the Lady Artiste also took place in the pages of *filmindia* ten years later, in 1941. This time, Snehaprabha Pradhan, an educated actress, complained about the low social status of film stars and accused society of hypocrisy and snobbery. Now the focus was turned on society, rather than on the film industry. In her view, "whether a film artiste comes from a good high-class family [as she herself does] or she has the misfortune of belonging to a class of people which this very society of moral people maintains (secretly of course) and to which class the society owes the safety of many of its daughters from the beastly passions of its own members she becomes a mere actress to the very men and women who spend many an evening with her in the cinema theatre."[9] In her argument, the bad reputation of female stars is not the product of actual misconduct on their part, but a result of the gossip network of a hypocritical society and self-serving press. Pradhan's strong indictment of class politics and the double standards of norms of respectability rests on the key phrase "mere actress" by which, she says, society identifies women like her. A crucial disjuncture enters into conceptions of stardom here. In this stark representation, stardom is not the equivalent of fame, glamor, popularity, or enviable lifestyle—all those qualities representing the American dream—but is, in the end, nothing more than "mere actress."[10]

"A Snob's Reply" by Sindhu Gadgil, a lesser-known actress, reiterated the right of society to scrutinize the activities of stars, since "society has certain expectations from you—you who boast of your education, culture and high parentage." The "old uneducated film star" could be excused for her behavior since she "came from a low class." But the new upper-class actress, who "should be the pioneer . . . [and] guiding star for the new spirit," has "severely disappointed" her viewers. Gadgil's generalized innuendo specifies the exact meaning of "mere actress" when she justifies that epithet with almost cinematic images, such as "a girl . . . who straightaway walks on the set and gets a four figure cheque by coquettishly playing with the tie of a director" or "spectacles of broken homes, sorrowing husbands and neglected children."[11] She transforms "stardom" into the melodramatic scenarios associated with "mere actress." The rest of her essay, like Sabita Devi's, counters the norms of "mere actress" with those of Indian womanhood aligned with domestic virtue. Gadgil spells out such norms as specifically domestic virtues and suggests that domesticity and stardom are at odds.

The argument in "A Snob's Reply" used generalized gossip against actresses to validate society's condemnation of them, and insisted that only domestic virtues could win them back their reputation. This is almost identical to the argument in Baburao Patel's "Housewife Becomes a Glamor Girl; Sulekha Patankar's Pathetic Story; A Bridge of Sighs between the Home and the Screen," a short story replete with purple prose and clichés about the star who neglects her duties as wife and mother, until her child dies. It ends on a cautionary note: "On the burning pyre of little Arun, let others stop and think." It is ironic that this cautionary tale appears in the midst of several articles and replies to letters to the editor, which constantly argue *against* the prevailing prejudice that stardom ruins a woman's character. As editor of *filmindia,* Baburao Patel used his columns to lash out against "the so-called well-born classes" for having "unreasonably condemned [film stars] on grounds of personal morality."[12] Snehaprabha Pradhan's protest against the hypocrisy of society was a very common argument in the early 1940s. The March 1940 issue of *filmindia* carried an essay by socialist writer and filmmaker K. A. Abbas, who critiqued the suggestion that film stars are no better than dancing girls.[13] Yet despite a spate of articles in *filmindia* (and other magazines), all presenting the same defense of stars, we find the "snob's" argument also represented, perhaps more insidiously, in other short stories in the magazine as well. For example, the December 1940 issue of *filmindia* had another lurid story by Baburao Patel entitled "Sandhya—The Prostitute-Actress! Is a Star Born in the Producer's Bed?"

The story slyly takes the trouble to insert a caption that claims that "the characters and names mentioned in this short story are fictitious. Any similarity to actual persons, living or dead, is purely coincidental." Rhetorically, this statement serves the same function as the references to the magazine *Rangbhoomi* in its short story about the painting of the star. Such rhetorical devices solicit comparisons between fictional and real stars. The story of Sandhya was, on the surface, a sympathetic rendering of the sexual exploitation faced by actresses.[14] But as a moral fable about the dangers of cinema as a profession for women, it was fully participating in, and even pandering to, the overall gossip about the goings-on in film studios, even while protesting the undeserved ill reputation of actresses. An indication of the double-talk of film journalism at this time is the fact that this short story is accompanied by several photographs that have nothing to do with the story but, in their captions, celebrate stardom.[15]

A reader was quick to notice the contradictory messages put out by this magazine. His question and the editor's answer to it were as follows:

> Question: So often you write articles urging educated girls from good society to join the film industry. While on the other hand you write short stories vividly describing the bad practices of the film industry. How do you reconcile these two things?
>
> Answer: . . . when a woman leaves her home and family to become a film star, her one aim in life should be to bring back to her home greater comfort, greater happiness and greater glory. . . . The stories of Sudha, Surekha and Sandhya which appeared in 'filmindia' are intended to serve as lighthouses in the stormy seas of glamour and greed. They show the mariner danger spots. . . . Light-houses have never scared away good mariners. Similarly, these stories should not scare off really good girls.[16]

Once again, "decent" female stardom is linked to the domestic virtues of Indian womanhood where "really good girls" belong.

The close economic and personal connection between the interests of film journalism and the cinema industry in India is evident from innumerable references in the memoirs of film critics like Saadat Hasan Manto, who write about their intimate social interactions with film personalities.[17] In many ways, the two institutions of film journalism and film production were so inseparable in their public construction that it was not unusual to see a film journalist like the editor of *filmindia*, Baburao Patel, referred to as a star.[18] Similarly, there were many, like Manto and K. A. Abbas, who worked as both film journalists and as film personnel and moved easily between the two professions.

Given the impossibility of any serious separation between the views of journalists and those of film professionals, it is not surprising that cinema engaged in a negative self-representation at this time, whether through films about stars or through statements by professionals, and actively distanced itself from Indian cinema as an institution, but not from Hollywood cinema. One sign of such a disavowal of cinema was the tendency of stars to emphatically deny any exposure to Indian films in their upbringing. In the 1950s a new generation of stars, who might conceivably have been brought up on Indian films, often claimed that they were raised exclusively on Hollywood films and only watched their first Indian film under duress, after they had acted in the films themselves.[19]

Studio-era films of the 1930s that were about stardom critiqued Indian cinema while distancing themselves from it, by displacing their narratives onto the world of theater. Such a displacement occurred routinely in the films produced at the Calcutta-based New Theatres studio. But considering this studio's own name, its representation of theater stardom was also transparently self-reflexive. Although their construction of stardom was rarely as extreme as the dire warnings in Baburao Patel's short stories, New Theatres productions such as *Street Singer* (Phani Majumdar, 1938), *Dhoop Chhaon* (*Sun and Shade*, Nitin Bose, 1935),[20] and *My Sister* (Hemchandra Chunder, 1944) participated in a similar negative discourse on stardom.

Stardom at New Theatres

Dhoop Chhaon features the blind singer K. C. Dey playing a blind street singer, Surdas.[21] He is wooed by a (stage) producer who represents the cutthroat commercialization of his profession. Surdas is opposed to the producer's view that only those who pay for tickets should be allowed to hear his music. Here, music is transformed from a free gift to a saleable commodity, and stands for the commodification that corrupts the enterprise of cinema and stardom. *Dhoop Chhaon* represents the process of stardom in a montage sequence comprising a series of metonymic shots from a poster, to fighting crowds at a ticket counter, to a scene at the theater, where shots of the audience are intercut with the anxious glances of the producers who cannot yet be certain that they have a star. The climax of this sequence is enthusiastic and rowdy applause, which cuts to a shot of Surdas (Dey) being garlanded as he emerges victorious from the theater. The montage sequence ends by bringing us to the present, which is twenty tears later, when Dey's character is a famous and wealthy star.

Dhoop Chhaon represents male stardom in terms of a conflict between family values and the pressures of popularity and commitment to the theater. At the end of the film, Surdas's son, who had lost his memory in an accident, regains his memory and his family when he recognizes his father at one of his performances. The film recuperates the moral image of its fictional theater company when the producer addresses the internal audience and, by extension, the film's audience to say that, even though theater companies usually ruin upright people and destroy families, "this theater company [and New Theatres Studio] brings families together." In this concluding statement, *Dhoop Chhaon* asserts its own distance from the ill-repute of cinema, while also perpetuating that reputation. Thus, in its equivocation regarding the moral status of the cinema as a profession, its rhetorical strategies are similar to those of the short stories I have discussed.

New Theatres' other productions, *Street Singer* and *My Sister,* both starring K. L. Saigal, make an interesting contrast between representations of male and female stardom. *Street Singer* relentlessly details the breakdown in a female star's home life as she rises to stardom. While the immediate cause of this breakdown is the lecherous behavior of the theater director, the star herself is also willing to be led astray into the corrupt values of this world. Only through the agency of the man in her life, played by K. L. Saigal, does she recover her moral values at the end of the film. *My Sister* is very similar to *Street Singer,* but with the significant difference that the rising star here is male (played by K. L. Saigal). Although the theatrical profession is shown to be just as corrupt in this film, the star himself is untarnished by it. Instead, the film focuses its moral opprobrium on the female star at the theater, even though she is actually a minor character in the film's narrative. Rekha, the female star, sexually pursues the male star (Saigal) and causes his estrangement from his family and fiancée, but at the end of the film she is literally eliminated when she courts death in a Japanese bombing raid, in one of Hindi cinema's rare references to World War II.[22] Together, *Street Singer* and *My Sister* make the argument that a male star's profession is just that, a means of supporting his family, while the female star's profession is unequivocally a downward path of moral and sexual degradation. In the gendered difference between stardom as profession and stardom as sexuality in this fictional scenario, we see the recurrent trope of the "mere actress." Yet, despite a repeated discursive clarification of the equivalence of "stardom" and "mere actress," numerous fictional scenarios such as this, of female stardom outpacing male fame, play out the anxieties of the actual distinction between the two.

I turn now to the methodological question of how best to discuss specific film stars of the 1930s when the only available extra-filmic material about them merely reproduces their professional identities and adds little or no new information about them. If extra-filmic material is hard to come by, it is even harder to gain access to the films made in the 1930s because of the indifference to preservation that marked cinema production in India until 1964, when the National Film Archive was established and began the task of collecting and preserving films.

Stardom at Prabhat Studios

My discussion focuses on two female stars: Durga Khote and Devika Rani. Durga Khote of Prabhat Studios was repeatedly hailed as an exemplar of the educated actress of "good family" whose participation in films would improve the moral reputation of the cinema. Devika Rani, who was mainly associated with Bombay Talkies studio, was a foreign-trained architect of illustrious family. Her background and achievements aroused so much admiration that it rendered her fans and critics virtually speechless.[23] The March 1940 issue of *filmindia* is representative; it carried a full-page photograph of her with the caption: "Devika Rani: And need we say more?"[24] My discussion of Durga Khote centers on the Prabhat Studios film *Amar Jyoti* (*Immortal Flame,* 1936), which is representative of her star vehicles at this time. I approach Devika Rani via the more circuitous route of *Aadmi* (*Man*; also titled *Life's for Living,* 1939), a film that does not feature her. *Aadmi* lends itself easily to such a use because it is actively engaged in defining itself and its own studio against rival film studios. Made by Prabhat, rather than by Devika Rani's own studio, this film has no explicit connection to her except through a recognizable parody in a comic sequence involving a film shoot. As I will argue, this is not the only self-referential moment in *Aadmi,* as the film also contains a subtext about female stardom in general, through the figure of its central character, a prostitute, and more importantly, through the new actress, Shanta Hublikar, who plays her. Both *Amar Jyoti* and *Aadmi* were made by the same director, V. Shantaram, who was himself something of a star in the 1930s, with a strong reputation for making socially progressive and stylistically innovative films. A significant number of his films, including *Amar Jyoti* and *Aadmi,* centered specifically on women's issues.

Amar Jyoti is a costume/action film in which Durga Khote plays Saudamini, a pirate queen who has chosen to be an outlaw in order to pursue her principled rebellion against a corrupt monarchy's oppression of women. This was a fairly typical role for Durga Khote.[25] In *Maya Machhindra* (V. Shantaram, Prabhat, 1932), she played the queen of "a kingdom of man-hating women." *Jeevan Natak* (Debaki Bose, New Theatres, 1935) combined the two principal aspects of her public identity by having her play a stage actress playing a warrior queen, who turns out to have been one of her previous incarnations.[26] Her public image was constituted by two frequently repeated details about her: that she played rebellious warrior women, and that she was the first middle-class, educated, upper-caste (though caste was rarely referred to explicitly) woman of good family to dare to become an actress. As the *Encylopaedia of Indian Cinema* notes, she was also the only star of the 1930s to have worked in two of the major studios, Prabhat and New Theatres.

"Devika Rani—And need we say more?" Full-page photograph of Devika Rani in *filmindia,* March 1940.

Durga Khote as Saudamini in *Amar Jyoti* (V. Shantaram, 1936).

It may have been fitting that this social rebel should play action-oriented roles that displaced her rebellion onto fantasy or historical settings. But the fact that she was only rarely placed in social films also had the effect of distancing her from contemporary domestic constructions of female identity, which were focused mainly on romantic and sexual norms. Action-oriented female roles can be read as a performative space for trying out alternative femininities. Displaced onto a legendary site, these anti-authoritarian narratives could play out "progressive" models of femininity that were specifically associated with political rebellion. Sexual and domestic rebellion became framed by a protonationalist context. In a sense, action roles were safer than domestic roles because they did not directly raise the question of the extent to which the actress playing the role did or did not share the womanly virtues or sins of the character she was playing.[27] So it is appropriate that, in *Amar Jyoti,* Durga Khote played a woman who has renounced love, motherhood, and domesticity. Interviews and articles featuring Durga Khote invariably contained an implicit contrast with other actresses when they emphasized her professional acting ability, relating her class and educational background to the moral and aesthetic improvement of the cinema. One interviewer, stressing Khote's dedication to her art, noted that she had little interest in physical beauty and bodily adornment, and recommended that "other Indian actresses . . . similarly concentrate all their energies on acting and thereby improve the quality of films."[28] Khote, more than anyone else, embodied the freedoms and constraints of the "cultured lady." While her social class was routinely touted so as to anchor her public image more firmly in her origins than in her present occupation, she also strained the limits to which class and education would serve as protection from the shadow of the "mere actress." Her autobiography describes her traumatic loss of social and familial face after her first few screen appearances. The realignment of her image with normative models of femininity resulted, quite literally, from the concerted efforts of journalists, producers, and princely patrons who supported her studio, Prabhat.[29] Khote became emblematic of the type of cultured lady the cinema desired.

In her action roles, she played regal figures, and this also served to parallel and confirm her class origins. In keeping with her screen roles and her class origins, Durga Khote's photographs in magazines typically featured her in a full-length, commanding, low-angle shot. In *Amar Jyoti,* her first scene initially withholds a clear glimpse of her and then introduces her in a low-angle shot emphasizing her regal look. The film opens with the spectacle of her pirate crew capturing the royal ship that carries the Princess Nandini, the daughter of the royal family that Saudamini (Durga Khote) is fighting. Her speech to the captured princess to persuade her to join her cause is the centerpiece of her philosophy and is worth quoting in full:

> After my marriage I came to understand that woman is slave to man. The law says it, religion supports it, and the state puts its stamp of authority on it. My heart broke when I realized this truth and in that instant, I vowed to eradicate our slavery. Even if you become queen someday, you still won't escape this slavery. You will have to become the lesser half of your husband. This means that you will have to act according to his wishes. . . . If you go against his wishes you will be punished. As queen you might overcome your status as woman, but as wife, your status will remain even worse than a slave's. . . . I have begun the task of tearing up this system and replacing it with equality between men and women in order to create a new image of freedom. (my translation)

Framed by the context of political rebellion, norms of marriage and domesticity become open to question. On the lips of Durga Khote there was also an extra-filmic resonance to her statements here. Her own status as the emblematic upper-class film actress placed her in a reformist role of eradicating old prejudices against women in performance and of persuading other women of her class and background to join the film profession.

Those privy to oral gossip at that time and current viewers who have read her autobiography would also recognize the parallels with Khote's own unhappy first marriage. Her speech suggests that domestic life, society's preferred alternative for women, is itself another form of slavery. The feminist subtext in this speech could, of course, be read as a thinly disguised nationalist allegory of a master-slave relation transferred from the political to the domestic sphere. Such a reading is further sanctioned by the debate between Saudamini (Durga Khote) and her assistant, an old man, on the relative merits of violence and nonviolence as a means of effecting political change, an issue at the forefront of public debate in India at the time. In keeping with the national current, the film sides against Saudamini in this debate by negatively representing her acts of violence and revenge, and by having her views persistently challenged by the wise old man.

The film's narrative ultimately contains the transgressions of linking femininity and violence, while delinking femininity and domesticity. At the same time, it provides a visual space for their representation, a space that spills out of the diegesis to accommodate Khote's off-screen persona and contemporary nationalist politics. The end of the film shows Saudamini's renunciation of "womanly" qualities such as romantic love, motherhood, and domesticity to be an unnatural distortion of her true feelings, which the viewer sees in "unacted" moments—for instance, when she takes out and looks at the baby clothes of her long-lost son. The film thus uses an essentialized norm of femininity aligned with motherhood to defend and identify Saudamini's "true" self: she is "actually" a good wife and mother forced by circumstances to take on unconventional positions.[30]

As an outlaw and an outsider to social norms, the pirate queen occupies a position that is hardly different from that of an actress. The film emphasizes the similarity of the two positions when its point of view subtly shifts from Saudamini to her son. Not realizing that the pirate queen is his mother, the son treats her as a fallen woman unfit for respectable society. The film establishes the son's attitude as normative by having Saudamini herself act according to this view. That is, she prefers not to let her son know who she is for fear that the knowledge will shatter his childhood memories of his noble and upright mother. Clearly, there is no question of transforming the son's notions of what defines good motherhood, notions rooted in a clear divide between the virtuous womanhood that resides in motherhood and domesticity, and the distorted womanhood of the pirate queen. The film makes no attempt to transform the values of its fictional characters, even as the narrative destabilizes the fixed binaries of good and bad womanhood. Saudamini's "true" nobility of character can only find expression and fulfillment in supporting the son's views, through her renunciation of all claims to a respectable social position. As is frequently the case with commercial films, despite its progressive vision, in the end *Amar Jyoti* is compelled to participate in dominant constructions of ideal womanhood. At the end of the film, Saudamini's moral status can only be rescued by an act of sacrifice that reasserts and acknowledges her maternal feelings.

In the words of a contemporary review in *Bombay Chronicle, Aadmi* is "the story of a common prostitute, Kesar, and her heroic struggle to escape from the evil shadow in which she had been condemned to live."[31] Through the figure of the policeman, Moti, who falls in love with Kesar, the film explores the question of whether the individual or society as a whole is culpable in the perpetuation of prostitution. *Aadmi*'s overt project is to critique the social hypocrisy behind the stigmatization of prostitutes. However, since the prostitute is specifically a performing woman, living in a brothel where the women sing to entertain their clients, the entire discourse on her position in society also works as a representation of the position of an actress in society. The film's sympathetic delineation of the actual moral worth of its fictional prostitute parallels reformist journalistic arguments, which condemned the social ostracism of film actresses.

Early in the film, Moti reacts angrily to a song sequence in which Kesar performs before a male audience. In the scene immediately following the song sequence, Moti accuses Kesar of refusing any help in changing her lifestyle because she enjoys being a prostitute. His perception of a correlation between performance and loose morals parallels the debates surrounding female performance on stage and in the movies. In response to Moti's accusation, Kesar immediately challenges him to be the one who will help her out of prostitution. His weak and vacillating reaction, and his constant fears of being seen with Kesar, expose the casual and abstract nature of Moti's condemnation. From this point on, the film occupies itself with a relentless examination of the impossibility of moving out of prostitution, by detailing the obstacles placed before Kesar by a "superstitious, taboo-ridden social order."[32]

Early in the film, seemingly unaccountably, the smooth-flowing narrative of the attempt of a prostitute to change her life is interrupted by a digression. On their way to his village, Moti and Kesar stumble upon a film crew in the process of shooting a song sequence. This scene is a rare example in Hindi cinema of the 1930s of an explicitly self-referential look at cinema *as* cinema. The scene taking place is a romantic declaration, shot in multiple takes. The heroine is sitting on a tree branch, while the hero declaims a few lines about love, after which they break into song. The actress says, "A storm is raging in my heart. Tell me, is this what they call love?" The first line of the song is "I will live in the city of love." Their conversation is accompanied by a birdcall, which very quickly turns out to be a sound produced by a musician in the orchestra.

The actress is immediately recognizable as an Anglo-Indian stereotype by her atrocious Hindi accent. Between takes, she petulantly smokes a cigarette, and afterward we see her swiftly remove her sari and false braid to reveal a Western dress and close-cropped hair. In the British colonial context in which this film was made in pre-Independence India, the term *Anglo-Indian* referred to any person of mixed Indian and Western parentage. On the face of it, the choice of an Anglo-Indian stereotype here makes obvious sense because so many female stars in the silent era of Indian cinema were Anglo-Indians.

Our reaction to the scene being filmed is guided by the response of Kesar and Moti, who break into disruptive and uncontrolled laughter. Without their response, this scene might have appeared to be another run-of-the-mill filmed romantic encounter. Not only at the level of this song and its inane lyrics, but at other levels as well, the film draws attention to the constructed nature of this romance. For instance, the frantic editing, combined with the canted and upside-down framing during the sequence of shots showing the orchestra, is noticeably inconsistent with the style of the film as a whole. Like the fake birdcall, they are there to foreground the filmmaking process itself and are meant to be the stylistic equivalent of the stilted language of the romance scene. The film's goal, of course, is to establish its own unacted status in contrast to the film within the film.

After the film director throws Moti and Kesar off the set, they stop by a pond and begin parodying the filming, in what amounts to a parody of a parody. They expand upon the absurdities of the original conversation about love and then break into their own parody song. The lyrics mimic the original parody song: "I am a priest in the temple of love." This second song, though meant to be a parody, is thoroughly consistent with the style of music in the rest of *Aadmi* and clearly functions as a proper song sequence with all of its entertainment value.[33] It is clear that their parody song is superior to the song being filmed because the entire film crew follows the sound of their song as if in a trance. When the director enthusiastically offers Moti and Kesar the starring roles in his film, promising them instant wealth and renown, they leave in haste.

Their fear of such an association with the movies is fully in keeping with the deep-rooted disavowal of cinema that marked even this film. At this point, the Anglo-Indian actress responds to the director's offer of stardom to Kesar by stomping off in anger. She removes her "Indian" costume, revealing her true identity and confirming her representation of Indian womanhood as entirely fake.[34]

Aadmi has its hero, Moti, recall the "bad" song in this sequence at two other points in the film. These reminders point to the filming sequence's thematic relevance to *Aadmi,* even if it is unnecessary to the film's narrative continuity. Its overt function is to add to the film's discussion of various models of love, by contrasting the artifice of film love with that of the main characters. But Moti and Kesar are not the film's ultimate exemplars of love; rather, an older couple, Moti's neighbors Meghram and Bijli, are the unlikely model for an ideal male-female relationship. Moti's mother repeatedly describes Meghram and Bijli's relationship as a perfect example of the Indian notion of romance, which, linking innuendo and sexuality, needs only indirect expressions of love and is "so deep rooted that it thrives on domestic quarrels."[35]

In the filming sequence, although the stereotype of the Anglo-Indian actress may have had a generic resonance, the reference was arguably much more specific. The tune of the song being filmed, the mise-en-scène, the Anglo-Indian actress's weak voice, and her amateur style of singing all strongly recall a famous song sequence in the Bombay Talkies film *Achhut Kanya* (*Untouchable Girl,* Franz Osten, 1936). Made in 1936, three years before *Aadmi, Achhut Kanya* featured the major star-pair of Bombay Talkies, Devika Rani and Ashok Kumar. Because of this recognizable reference, the parody in *Aadmi* functions as a submerged review of the film *Achhut Kanya,* and by extension, as a commentary on the practices of Bombay Talkies studio.

The scene in *Acchut Kanya* that *Aadmi* parodies was a popular song sequence in which the Ashok Kumar and Devika Rani characters expressed their love through poetic allusions to nature ("I am a bird in a forest . . ." and so on).[36] The film was highly acclaimed for its "serious" theme of the problems of the caste system and untouchability, especially as it was responding to contemporary discussions initiated by Gandhi and other reformists.[37] Devika Rani played the untouchable daughter of a low-caste railway signalman, while Ashok Kumar played the Brahmin son of the village grocer. The idealistic core of the film centered on the friendship between the grocer and the signalman, but the impossibility of their children's love was made clear by the reactions of the other villagers and even of the grocer's wife. *Acchut Kanya*'s critique of the

Devika Rani and Ashok Kumar singing "Main ban ki chidiya" (I am a bird in a forest) in *Achhut Kanya* (Franz Osten, 1936).

caste system was coupled with a similar critique of traditional forms of medicine, village justice, and moral codes, against which were placed modern medicine (practiced by the grocer) and the impersonal law of the state, enforced by the police who intervened at the end.

Both because of its critical look at "traditional" Indian social practices and because of its polished film style, *Achhut Kanya* was (and still is) considered to be one of the high points of Indian cinematic achievement. Yet, embedded in Shantaram's parody of the romantic song sequence in *Acchut Kanya* is a negative commentary on the film as a whole. The appearance of humorous parody, however, allowed one review to see the film as merely a "brilliant example of comedy of nonsense used for dramatic effect" and this sequence, in particular, as containing "no malice . . . because no particular 'victim' is aimed at."[38] But another review in the same newspaper explicitly asserted the "refreshing contrast" between *Aadmi* and "the fatalism of Devdases and Achhut Kanyas."[39]

The overall inauthentic quality of the sentiment of love displayed by the Anglo-Indian actress, in comparison to the more authentic relationship between *Aadmi*'s real hero and heroine, is cast in terms of the ability or inability to sing complex songs. In turn, the ability to sing such songs is shorthand for an entire edifice of oppositions, underlying which is the implicit contrast between Prabhat Studios and its rival Bombay Talkies. According to the film's values, all these oppositions can be subsumed under the categories of authenticity and artifice, with Indian identity on the one side and a derivative Western identity on the other. However, the film avoids essentializing some of these categories by presenting them through multiple lenses. For instance, "Indian" love can also be read, instead, as "old-fashioned" love, or the relationship protocols of another generation, since the neighbors are an older and physically unattractive couple. At the heart of these oppositions in *Aadmi* is a play on performance and borrowed identities and a discourse on acting and metaperformance, as the characters play actors in their parody of the filming sequence. In the film's diegesis, the obvious contrast to the Anglo-Indian actress is Kesar, the poor but spirited singer-prostitute, while behind them is the unstated opposition between Devika Rani, top star of Bombay Talkies, and Shanta Hublikar, new star at Prabhat Studios.[40] Their unequal singing abilities function as an external sign of a deeper difference between the two studios' handling of serious social issues. Prabhat Studios' treatment of such issues often involved taking the risk of using no-name talent and concentrating on the quality of the singing voice of its actors rather than on their appearance.

Aadmi's parody of overly poetic romantic conventions and poor singing also works as a front for a more devastating critique, which is contained in the casting of the Devika Rani parody character as an Anglo-Indian actress who unsuccessfully borrows an Indian identity. The implication is that Devika Rani's Westernized, upper-class upbringing and her education and long years of residence in England and Germany make her an unconvincing choice for the role of a poor, untouchable village girl. According to this argument in the film, *Achhut Kanya,* unlike *Aadmi,* ends up treating social issues inauthentically because of an absurd mismatch between star and role, and voice and appearance. Like the Anglo-Indian star in *Aadmi,* who cannot shed her foreign accent, Devika Rani cannot discard her upper-class appearance and manner.[41] This critique was rarely made explicitly at the time, given the high status that Devika Rani enjoyed. But a recent biography of the 1950s star Nargis contrasts Nargis with Devika Rani because they were both, at different times, referred to as the "first lady" of Indian cinema. The contrast, made many decades later, relies on a view of Devika Rani as out of touch with Indian realities, which echoes the terms of Shantaram's indirect critique in *Aadmi.*[42] Also relevant to this reading of the filming sequence in *Aadmi* as a submerged review of *Achhut Kanya* is V. Shantaram's open expression of his desire to be a film critic in another life.[43]

Aadmi's critique of *Achhut Kanya*'s inauthentic construction of Indian realities also takes on an added layer when one considers that contemporary reviews often mildly castigated Bombay Talkies productions for their lack of Indian feeling. The studio, founded by Devika Rani's husband, Himansu Rai, was unusual in that it employed two Germans, Franz Osten and Josef Wirsching, as its director and cinematographer, the idea being that they would train Indians to eventually take their place. The following critique of Bombay Talkies is illustrative: "While no one doubted or questioned the technical excellence of Herr Franz Osten's work (and those who knew him testified to his painstaking efforts and personal amiability) it was clear that he was unable to infuse into the picture that characteristically *Indian* spirit which one finds in the pictures of a Barua, Devaki Bose, Nitin Bose, or Shantaram. . . . The psychological import and social significance of everyday incidents dramatized in his films naturally escaped him. Which, of course, was not his fault. Shantaram, directing German pictures, would be confronted with the same difficulty." This account of Franz Osten's work fits my earlier discussion of Indian stardom in the 1930s as a site of uneasy coexistence of two separate but related domains of nationalism. In critiquing Franz Osten's work in Bombay Talkies, the author makes a similar division between the outer domain of technical competence, which is the province of the West, and the inner domain of spiritual understanding, which the West can never master. Bombay Talkies was also the only Indian studio that commentators praised for its Hollywood-like efficiency and the "factory-like regularity" with which it "turned out four or five pictures a year." When Osten and Wirsching were interned by the British at the start of World War II, their unfinished film *Kangan* was completed by the Indians working under them. The same *Bombay Chronicle* review claimed to notice "a refreshingly original quality about the handling of certain scenes which were free from the all-too-familiar Osten touch."[44]

In making its critique of Devika Rani, *Aadmi* successfully inverts all the values regarding class and female performance that pervaded cinematic discourse in the 1930s. Here the problem is *not* about "low class" women unable to do justice to lofty roles. Rather, it is about the most acclaimed upper-class actress of the decade inadequately playing a low-caste woman. But *Aadmi* does not stop there. It presents, without innuendo, a low-class prostitute (and by extension, the unknown actress Shanta Hublikar) as someone who, unlike the Devika Rani parody character, is superbly adept at performing various Indian identities.[45] The film's most celebrated song sequence showcases Kesar's (and by extension Shanta Hublikar's) performative abilities as she moves easily between different Indian identities. In this scene, Kesar entertains a group of men from different parts of India, singing "Why sing of tomorrow?" ("Kisliye Kal ki Baat?") Their regional identities are signified in various ways, but mainly through their different headgear. Shanta Hublikar performs the same song in five regional languages, borrowing the hats and other headgear of the men in the audience. The setting is not a stage, but Kesar's room, in which the men are seated on the floor while she performs, casually leaning against a dresser and moving among everyday furniture. Between shots, there are changes in the style of wearing the sari, which reinforces the effect of distinctive regional identities signified by the hats. But the editing smooths over such clothing changes, focusing instead on Kesar's apparently casual use of objects in her environment, such as the hats, walking sticks, and glasses of the men in the audience, masking the actual technology of such an effect.[46] This song sequence also works against a single essentialized notion of Indianness as, both musically and sartorially, Hublikar slips easily in and out of a multiplicity of Indian "nationalities" (this was the preferred term of the period for regional affiliations).[47] *Aadmi*'s overall self-definition relies on the contrast between the Anglo-Indian actress's (Devika Rani's) false borrowing of an Indian identity and the demonstration, in this sequence, of Kesar's (Shanta Hublikar's) authentic Indian identity, through her playful borrowing of regional singing styles. The difference is encapsulated in the Anglo-Indian star's false braid and Kesar's borrowed hats.

The multilingual sequence is not only a linguistic and musical performance, but it also incorporates, in the case of some of the regional songs, a parody of song styles from different regional film studios. The Bengali-language segment of the song, which parodies the style of New Theatres films, starts with a close-up of Kesar's face, wearing borrowed glasses, as she sings while gazing out a window at a nature scene. Between the "natural" setting and the "intellectual" look conveyed by the glasses, she fits the image of the literary sensibility of New Theatres films and also the Bengali poetic stereotype, both of which the "real" audience of the film would recognize. But as the camera pulls back, we see that she is still in the same room and that the "window" is a painting on the wall. This sequence ends by underscoring the economic and sexual basis of

Shanta Hublikar, with different regional headgear, performing the song "Kisliye Kal ki Baat" in *Aadmi* (V. Shantaram, 1939).

this performance with a dissolve to a close-up on the coins that Kesar's male audience has tossed on the floor.

As in Shantaram's *Amar Jyoti, Aadmi*'s ending sadly undermines its progressive message. In a negative deus ex machina, Kesar inadvertently murders a persistent admirer and ends up imprisoned for life. The film is caught between a desire to expose the social hypocrisy that perpetuates prostitution and its need to assign blame to no particular character in the diegesis, such as the mother or Moti himself. Moti brings Kesar home to his mother with the intention of marrying her, but the film cannot go through with that narrative trajectory, and one wonders if *Aadmi* would have received the rave reviews it got had it ended with Kesar happily married to Moti. Who is to blame for Kesar not marrying Moti? To preserve the moral uprightness of all the characters, the renunciation of marriage has to come from Kesar herself. In a sudden reversal of her critique of social norms throughout the film, Kesar appears to internalize all those norms that render her outcast and refuses to "ruin" Moti by marrying him. At this point the film has left the register of parody.

The film's representation of Moti's mother is central to its problem of what to do with Kesar at the end. Although K. A. Abbas's review of the film identified the "superstitious, taboo-ridden social order" as the culprit in the film, it did not associate any character with these values. As Abbas says, the mother is "kind, gentle, religious . . . [she] may be the mother of any of us," and the film goes to great lengths to construct her in terms of religious and social tolerance, as she accepts Kesar with no questions about her background.[48] Yet it is precisely her religious values which lay out the norms of what a "good wife" for Moti would be, and her innocent acceptance of Kesar as Moti's ideal domestic partner is what prompts Kesar to give up her desires for social acceptance. Not only does the film stop short of identifying the mother's values as the actual basis of the incompatibility of "fallen woman" and "wife," but it also makes the mother an unequivocal and compelling image of virtuous womanhood. Thus, as in *Amar Jyoti,* the "fallen" woman in *Aadmi* can only be redeemed by her acceptance of dominant social norms and by an act of renunciation that serves to maintain the status quo without identifying any villains. To make Kesar's renunciation unequivocally permanent, the film uses the gratuitous narrative device of having her commit a murder. It is also significant that, like *Amar Jyoti, Aadmi* ends by shifting its narrative point of view from the "fallen" woman to the man in her life. After the murder, *Aadmi* focuses exclusively on Moti's perspective.

Both *Amar Jyoti* and *Aadmi* represent a type of fallen woman, and therefore may be read as indirect representations of actresses, while their stars and star references invoke the opposite kind of woman, the upper-class, educated actress who was viewed as holding the key to the moral improvement of cinema. But both films end up indirectly reasserting dominant social values regarding such women and thereby undermine their progressive statements. K. A. Abbas, a respected film journalist of the 1930s, had enthusiastic praise for *Aadmi*'s progressive vision.[49] He was himself to make the 1952 film *Anhonee,* which, as I will argue, had a similarly equivocal representation of a "bad" woman.

4. *Spectatorial Desires and the Hierarchies of Stardom*

In the preceding chapters I argued that the dominant cinematic and extra-cinematic discourse on female stardom in 1930s film worked from an implicit structure of oppositions. On one side, there was low-class status aligned with public performance, and implications of sexuality and immorality, while on the other side there was upper-class status linked to a type of modern female identity that combined education, social responsibility, and female propriety. Such a model of normative femininity could propose only a certain type of acceptable female star, emerging from the educated upper classes, and playing roles matching the social norm of domestic virtue in genres such as the social, which allowed and showcased such roles. Yet even as such norms were being debated and refined on-screen and in the pages of magazines and newspapers, the full spectrum of female stars in the 1930s presents a far more unruly picture. In this chapter I consider two competing models of fame and public self-presentation that challenge any notion of a fully homogenized and contained discourse of female stardom. Both models are figured on white or semi-white bodies that either were superseded, as in the case of the cosmopolitan modern woman played by Sulochana in her silent films, or remained on the margins of high-brow star discourse, as in the case of the stunt star Fearless Nadia. Together, Sulochana and Fearless Nadia occupied two extremes in the hierarchy of 1930s Indian star discourse. While Sulochana, by the early 1930s, was reified as the queen of Indian stars, self-evidently and unquestioningly understood as the most popular Indian star of the silent era, Nadia, by the late 1930s, was equally self-evidently understood as a popular but ultimately marginal actress whose identification with the low-brow stunt genre did not qualify her for the designation of "star." Moreover, as both actresses were associated with mass audiences, they offer insights into the relation between spectatorship and star culture at this time. Audience responses and the passions of spectators figured only marginally in discussions of stardom in the 1930s, though the cinematic tastes of different classes of audiences were scrutinized in the context of recommendations for the improvement of cinema. As stars who did elicit enthusiastic responses, however, Sulochana and Fearless Nadia offer an opportunity to uncover traces of spectatorial desires that might fall into the category of fandom, even if it was not always named as such.

In any history of stardom in Indian cinema, Sulochana is the embodiment of the idea of the star in the earliest years of Indian cinema. While there is no disputing the centrality of Sulochana to the emergent discourse of stardom, I suggest that as early as the 1930s, her silent-era dominance became a discursive idea that rewrote the realities of cinema culture in the late 1920s, and that her popularity was, paradoxically, in inverse relation to the degree to which her star persona engaged central discourses of gender formation in early cinema in India. In the context of cinema's participation in the wider social discourse of "improvement" and its obsession with "cultured" women, Sulochana's star persona between 1925 and 1933 occupied an ambiguous space. In her silent films, her star persona initially circulated an image of the "cultured" woman in terms of specifically cosmopolitan rather than national discourses, placing gender identity at the intersection of modernity and fantasies of capitalism, centering on sexuality, fashion, and imaging technologies. Thus, before the concern with respectability redefined female participation in cinema specifically in terms of education and class origins, actresses like Sulochana invited the audience's fascination through their ease in negotiating the experience and spectacle of cosmopolitan modernity even as they moved among the social, historical, and mythological genres.[1] But by the early 1930s, just as she made the transition to sound, Sulochana's star image was brought into alignment with the dominant discourse of female stardom, with her films literally playing out the trajectory of reform from the cosmopolitan to the national. Where in the 1920s her screen roles placed ideas of stardom at the intersection of modernity, technology, and fantasies of upward social mobility, the talkie remakes of her silent films literally engaged in the discourse of improvement, by placing her in roles that staged her regulation into norms of Hindu womanhood.

Publicity still of Sulochana/
Ruby Myers.

Sulochana as modern
Indian woman.

Sulochana's first film was *Veer Bala/Warrior Girl* (Mohan Bhavnani, 1925) made for Kohinoor Film Co., followed by *Cinema ni Rani/Cinema Queen* (dir. Mohan Bhavnani) in the same year.[2] Following their success, she made five to six films a year between 1925 and 1929. After a gap of a year, during the transition to sound, she returned to the screen in 1932 with her first talkie, which was a remake of her 1928 silent film *Madhuri* (dir. R. S. Choudhury). Many of her talkie hits were remakes of her silent films. It was during her hiatus from the screen, in 1930–31, that the idea of Sulochana as India's "star of stars" moved from the routinely hyperbolic realm of film advertisements to critical discourse on stars.[3] Ads for her films used such epithets, but other actresses were also similarly advertised. At this time, too, we find the repetition, which continues in popular discourse to this day, of some key details about her: that she was born Ruby Myers, variously described as Anglo-Indian, Eurasian, or Jewish; that she took the screen name Sulochana (the beautiful-eyed one); that she was working as a telephone girl when she was discovered; that at the peak of her career she earned more than the governor of Bombay; and that she played eight roles in *Wildcat of Bombay* (Mohan Bhavnani, 1927), many of them criminal male underworld impersonations. Her earnings became a repeated subject of discussion in film magazines, where the relation between income and star status was examined.[4] It was often in terms of earnings that Sulochana became reified as the "star of stars," and even her rival star, Gohar, placed lower than Sulochana in the hierarchies of stardom based on salary.[5] Sulochana herself measured her rise in terms of salary in her 1927 interview with the Indian Cinematograph Committee: "To tell you the truth, I don't know how others have begun, but as for me, I began on Rs. 150 a month and when the producer saw that I could work for my first picture he gave me a rise [*sic*] of another Rs. 100 on his own account and in two years I have risen to Rs. 750." Using the measure of salary, however, she is not yet the "star of stars" in 1927: "I know one actress who gets Rs. 1,200 a month. Some get a thousand."[6] Even a 1932 estimate put it that Sulochana and Sita Devi, another Anglo-Indian star, *both* earned Rs. 2,000 a month.[7] Thus, based on the early 1930s criterion of a correlation between salary and stardom, Sulochana's status as the top star at the time is questionable. My argument is that Sulochana's star status, like the term *star* itself, had become an independent idea, decoupled from the realities of specific measures such as popularity, acting talent, or earnings, even though such criteria were routinely mentioned. In terms of acting and popularity, for example, we find that it was Gohar, and not Sulochana, who won "Movie Show gold medal" in 1929 for best acting, and that she beat Sulochana by 9,007 votes.[8] In the early 1930s, then, the verdict regarding Sulochana's preeminent star status was already becoming fixed in the discourse, a verdict that has been repeated uncritically in subsequent histories of Indian stars. Such a view would also come to color later readings of her earliest films, such as *Cinema Queen* (1925).

In *Cinema Queen*, Sulochana's second film, she played a film star who inspires and rejuvenates a suicidal painter. The film presented the glamorous lifestyle of studio bosses and stars, and was one of several films in the mid-1920s, not necessarily starring Sulochana, that focused on the lifestyles of the urban rich.[9] Sulochana's role in *Cinema Queen* has been read as exploiting "the autobiographical ambiguities generated by a star playing a star" and using "Sulochana's persona to project a new image for actresses and studios."[10] But having acted in only one film before this one, Sulochana was not a star yet. If *Cinema Queen* could safely associate Sulochana with a fictional star who matched some of the rumors about actresses (daughter of a prostitute attracting or being seduced by married men), it was only because she was *not* famous yet. She is credited in the film as Miss Ruby Myers, not as Sulochana, which was the name of the fictional character she played in a film the following year, *Bamto Bhoot/Wandering Phantom* (Mohan Bhavnani, 1926). This was the source of her screen name.[11] As one among many popular Anglo-

Indian actresses, Sulochana could be initially cast in roles that enabled her to play with fantasies of the transgressions associated with stardom. *Cinema Queen* narrates the fictional star's biography and has no trouble making her the daughter of a prostitute or representing her in an adulterous relationship with the painter for whom she models. Kaushik Bhaumik argues that in making the main character's *mother* a prostitute, the film presents "the prostitution-cinema nexus as a thing of the past," belonging to "the senior generation," so that the present generation's actress "was a respectable entity."[12] However, such screen depictions may have served both to fuel and to confirm rumors about the low moral milieu of cinema, whether in the past or the present. *Cinema Queen*'s appeal, like that of *Telephone ni Taruni/Telephone Girl* (Homi Master, 1927), another Sulochana film, may have been its titillating insider look at the cinema industry, one that enabled a critique of the industry even as it circulated a new star-in-the-making of ambiguous moral standing. Yet it is also likely that Sulochana's ability, as a relatively unknown actress, to play a transgressive role in *Cinema Queen* brought her stardom in the form of multiple film ventures in the following year.

Sulochana as cultured cosmopolitan star.

Sulochana's sartorial transformations in *Indira M.A.* (Nandlal Jaswantlal, 1934). Full-page spread in *Filmland,* Puja issue, 1934.

By the early 1930s, when Sulochana had become reified as the most popular Indian star, films such as *Cinema Queen* and *Telephone Girl* could be seen *retrospectively* as offering a privileged glimpse into her private life—for example, that she worked as a telephone operator before becoming an actress. But alongside their presentation of titillating rumors about Indian actresses, these films also circulated a well-known type drawn from Hollywood films with similar titles and stories, where ordinary working girls "made it" in Hollywood. Thus the biographical connection to Sulochana has to be understood as part of a highly constructed framework of references drawn from both Indian and Hollywood ideologies of stardom, which served to anchor her cosmopolitan image and align her with associations of class mobility and the American Dream. Yet despite the impression that Sulochana's star identity was constructed, like that of Hollywood stars, out of a complex negotiation of private and professional, cinematic and extra-cinematic knowledge about her, her biography, as referenced in *Telephone Girl,* recast privacy in the professional terms of her former job as telephone operator.

The price of Sulochana's embodiment of the idea of "the star" in the early 1930s was the increasing need to cast her in reformist narratives. In her talkie films, her star persona became realigned with the dominant nationalist discourse of Indian womanhood, marked by filial piety, sartorial modesty, and contained sexuality. We can look at the remnant of a film that no longer survives, in the form of a five-page publicity spread for *Indira M.A.* (Nandlal Jaswantlal, 1934), a remake of her 1929 silent film, *Indira.*[13] Sulochana plays Indira, whom the publicity material for the remake describes as follows: "The glitter of the Western Civilization blinded her to the culture in which she was born. Her life was in line with that of a 'flapper' in the West." Sulochana's screen identity in films like *Cinema Queen* and *Telephone Girl* had put her in alliance with Hollywood-derived models of femininity, and *Indira M.A.* works to reform that image through a narrative of transformation. The film takes Indira, the Oxford-educated Westernized "flapper" girl, in love with a "playboy," Pyarelal (played by D. Billimoria), through marriage and divorce to a return to Indian roots and recognition of her Indianized suitor, Kishorilal (played by Raja Sandow), as the true hero. The cause of her Westernization is her alcoholic father, "the old block from which the chip of a flapper had sprung," but it is also his illness that brings Indira back to his bedside, producing "the turn of the tide—the inborn Indian Culture breaks through the veneer of Western Culture." Visually, the five-page spread also shows Sulochana's transformation in sartorial terms, from sleeveless gown, to fashionable shirt, trousers, and hat, to

Sulochana's contrary impulses in *Indira M.A.* (*Filmland,* Puja issue, 1934).

Introducing Sulochana as "flapper" in *Indira M.A.* (*Filmland,* Puja issue, 1934).

Sulochana and the "veneer of Western culture" in *Indira M.A.* (*Filmland,* Puja issue, 1934).

D. Billimoria and Raja Sandow in *Indira M.A.* (*Filmland,* Puja issue, 1934).

several styles of sari. Yet there also seems to be a clear conflict in *Indira M.A.* between the interest center and the moral center of the film, with the trajectory of reform functioning as an excuse or framework for the continued interest in her cosmopolitan image. Given that this and other sound hits by Sulochana were remakes of her silent films, it is noteworthy that the moral trajectory provided a new legitimizing framework for the continued display of cosmopolitan lifestyle, fashion, emotion, and even language, such as "playboy" and "flapper." The caption accompanying the dapper Pyarelal says: "His definition of love crude—passion, in a manner of speaking," while for Kishorilal, the suitor her father has chosen, "his love was something sublime to him—it meant sacrifice." The film showcases the highly popular romantic couple, Sulochana and Billimoria, even while it reframes the Hollywood-style screen romances associated with their silent films in terms of a moral commentary on the distinction between "crude" and "sublime" forms of love. In the latter half of the 1930s, as the idea of the "modern" became recast in terms of nationalist models of female identity in stars such as Durga Khote and Devika Rani, Sulochana continued to embody a more ambiguous notion of the "modern." While one 1934 star profile, addressing Sulochana directly, declared, "You are remarkably modern and marvelous in your latest *Indira M.A.*," another stated that in *Madhuri*, she is "the embodiment of the Indian wife, who deserted by her husband, does not leave him, does not lose her chastity and remains faithful."[14]

If Sulochana embodied the idea of the star by the early 1930s, how did audiences respond to her? JBH Wadia remembers her in his memoirs: "She was easily the most beautiful woman to adorn the Indian screen. She was the cameraman's delight. Her chiseled features were such that they could be photographed in perfect proportion from any angle. And there was magnetism in her eyes—nay, seduction." Star profiles of Sulochana followed a formulaic structure as in other Indian star profiles, with her date of birth, educational qualifications, and lengthy physical description. However, another form of writing about Sulochana could also be found in these star profiles—erotically charged descriptions verging on the poetic. For example, Dushyant Chaubey begins his otherwise fairly typical profile of Sulochana: "And she is 'a thing of beauty,' blooming with youth and comeliness. Nay! not only that she is lovely, she is charming, she is delicate and active. Her every limb speaks—speaks of her unique attributes."[15]

It is in the tension between formulaic description and personal response that we can locate spectatorial traces, as in a 1933 star profile titled "Cinema Queen Miss Sulochana." Along with the repetition of key biographical details, V. S. Nigam includes a rhapsodic paragraph on a river bathing scene in *Madhuri* (the 1932 remake). He says nothing about Sulochana's face, but dwells instead on how she emerges glistening from behind a waterfall and describes her soft, delicate limbs and sculpted body "shaped as if by the hand of Brahma at a particularly auspicious moment."[16] In "Siren Sulochana," also written in 1933, F. Mohamed claims he is providing "the essentials lost sight of" by other film journalists, and proceeds to use similarly hyperbolic language to describe Sulochana's body, but constructed around Western classical themes: "have you seen an athlete so classically modeled like our heroine, with a rare blend of oriental features and a Greek-physique; We havent [*sic*]. A physique, perfect in its proportions, symmetrical in 'make-up,' mathematical in construction and geometrical in muscle-definition is the wonder of all humanity. She appears to have marched straight out of the classic world of the ancients even to have paced down from the olympian [*sic*] Goddesses themselves. Had she been living in those days . . . her fame would have been ornamented on the untrembling statues in the Athletic World. But fortunately for India, her birth was adjourned by the Great God Himself for the twentieth century."[17] Mohamed goes on to describe various aspects of Sulochana's musculature with physiological precision, and, like Wadia, emphasizes the sculpted qualities of "a human statue like Sulochana."

While such purple prose occasionally marked writings about other actresses as well, these accounts of Sulochana express an enamored gaze on implied nudity, and the arousal and desire that accompany it, barely contained in coded language of artistic and medical appreciation, or even cinematic technique, in the case of Wadia's account. "An Open Letter to Sulochana's Soul" by "Your Fan" expresses typical biographical details and fan sentiments ("Sulochana in your last role . . . you were really marvelous!") but couches the accompanying desire in the more "mystical" (and therefore nonsexual) address to her "soul." The pleasure of gazing at Sulochana is displaced onto praise of her fame: "I do enjoy the happiness of looking at you—you who sits on the top of glory—pinnacle of success."[18] In contrast, Mohamed is fairly obvious in his double entendres: "Physiologists will remember that her corporeal frame will afford them a rare opportunity to memorise their lessons." When Chaubey, commenting on Sulochana's skill as an actress, writes, "And her combination with D. Billimoria doubled the beauty. Of course, without each other they are not so successful," the fan reader might understand that beauty and success in terms of the erotic spectacle of Sulochana's celebrated screen kisses with D. Billimoria, her frequent costar.[19] Such screen moments as her kisses thus fueled the imagination of viewers and also sustained and satisfied their desire for private expressions of romantic emotion in the star.

The language used to describe the desire evoked by looking at Sulochana focuses on excessive emotion. Nigam says that if you have seen her in one picture, "your entire being craves another glimpse of her." "Your Fan" claims to be "not in the habit of writing letters to people's souls. However, I strive to restrain the urge." The prospect of not seeing Sulochana is equally excessive in its expression. "Your Fan" asks Sulochana's soul if it can "imagine what agonies the fans undergo" when film journalists circulate rumors of her retirement from films. Most significantly, Chaubey ascribes the viewer's uncontrollable emotional response to Sulochana's actual performances of emotion onscreen, using the language of a colloquial *rasa* theory that I discussed in chapter 1: "Sometimes she comes smiling, sometimes sobbing—and the effect is terrible. When she weeps it is impossible that you may not feel sorry; when she laughs, you also begin to smile; when she walks, you also feel to walk. (Mind! don't do so, else you will be out of the Cinema Hall.)" He makes the same claim again, more seriously, in the context of specific films: "Tragic scenes she handles so skillfully, that not a single eye can see them without tears. She weeps and makes others weep. Such is her sorrowful acting. She gains your sympathy. When she is driven out in the heavy rains in 'Saubhagya Sundari', you weep for her and resent at her husband's cruel temperament. It is the power of true artist that works [*sic*]." The *rasa*-based descriptions of Sulochana, like their more formulaic counterparts in other star profiles, are largely unrelated to any specific screen role. Couched in terms of the ideal aesthetic effect, where the emotional flavor (*rasa*) of a performance will produce a corresponding emotion (*bhava*) in the viewer, the panegyrics to Sulochana limit the fan-star relationship to the performance space. The spectator's passion for the star can only be explained in the language of the aesthetic impact of an ideal work of art. While the limits of spectatorial desire are here found in the framework of aestheticized response, in a different context these limits seem to be spelled out more clearly. A handwritten letter by another Anglo-Indian star, Sabita Devi (Irene Gasper), was published in *Bombay Chronicle* in 1934 as publicity for her film *Grihalaxmi/Educated Wife* (Sarvottam Badami, 1934). In beautiful cursive, she addresses her "patrons," rather than "fans" or "audiences": "I have always had a great respect and greater appreciation for the high ideals, characteristics, and culture of the Hindu Society. My heart has always bowed before the ideals of true Indian womanhood and in my sincere and simple way I have striven to portray the role of Malthi, the educated wife with these glorious ideals always before me. I would like to offer my heartfelt thanks to the cinegoers of Bombay who have appreciated my work in this film—your patronage has been a great source of inspiration to me."[20] This letter is significant in clarifying the desired relation between star and audience at this time. In keeping with norms of respectability in representing private lives, the relation is one of patronage rather than the passion or desire characterizing fans. Whether or not audiences felt those passions and engaged in fanlike behavior, the publicity machinery did not encourage this, even though, as here, it did acknowledge the audience's power as patrons. A decade later, *filmindia* characterizes "fan-dom" as "emotional escapism . . . the emotional meeting-ground of East and the West. They can let themselves go with wild abandon, forget all the taboos and restraints and touch-me-nots of the society in which their lot is cast and give the reins to their pent-up longings and suppressed lust, complexes, and inhibitions, without losing caste or their face either."[21] It is noteworthy that the implied fan here is male, since it would be unthinkable to discuss the "suppressed lust" of women.[22] The reference to the "East" and "West" seems to suggest that the fan is a hybrid product of Western and Indian forms of spectatorship. Not only does this description psychologize the fan, it also identifies sexual desire as the prime mode by which a fan relates to a star, and in doing so again feminizes stardom itself. In the panegyrics to Sulochana, the suppressions, "inhibitions," and fear of "losing caste" translate into a style of rhetoric borrowed from vaguely classical aesthetics. These classical references to Brahma, "Greek-physique," and the medico-scientific urge for physiological knowledge help to frame and contain the "suppressed lust" of these writers.

The image of Sulochana that emerges in this fan discourse presents her as unique among stars: "cinema queen," "screen's beloved," "the most beautiful woman to adorn the Indian screen." Mohamed writes, "Miss Meyers [*sic*] is no longer a star but the 'moon' among all the surrounding stars of movie skies." Using the silent era as a conceit, Chaubey goes so far as to present Sulochana as transcending cinema technology itself: "Though she did not speak, but sometimes it appeared as if she did. Perhaps then she was an orthodox believer in the old maxim 'Silence is golden,'—that is why she remained mute. But her Art did not escape brilliance. She, during her 'Vow of silence,' too, produced such rare films as 'Madhuri' and 'Anarkali.'" Through hyperbolic epithets and images that connote her transcendence of star status, the Sulochana star profiles produced the idea that she embodied the absolute ideals of stardom. The potency of this idea lay precisely in the limits of language, as only preexisting formulas of praise could be refitted to serve the new fan. This mode of fan discourse both demonstrated and was constitutive of Sulochana's status in the hierarchy of 1930s stardom as the "cinema queen." Through its turn to the language of *rasa* poetics, and the emotionally excessive expressions of sexualized desire for the body of the star, spectatorial passion was displaced onto and barely contained by more genteel modes of appreciation. In contrast, Fearless Nadia's popularity left few traces in contemporary film magazines and journals. She did not elicit articulations of desire from her equally enthusiastic fans, but, rather, embodied responses in keeping with the low-brow stunt genre with which she was associated.

Fearless Nadia and the Stunt Genre

In contemporary discourse, Fearless Nadia had no star persona outside her identification with the stunt genre, her studio Wadia Movietone, and its box office successes. Her films were directed by Homi Wadia, who later became her husband, and produced by his older brother JBH Wadia. Nadia's so-called Diamond Thriller film series at Wadia Movietone included titles such as *Hunterwali* (1935), *Miss Frontier Mail* (1936), *Hurricane Hansa* (1937), *Punjab Mail* (1939), *Diamond Queen* (1940), and *Jungle Princess* (1942).[23] JBH Wadia's description of his first view of Mary Ann Evans, who became Fearless Nadia, evokes her screen presence and her performance antecedents on the European stage circuit in India: "I saw a blonde young woman, milky white skin, pearly white teeth and a flaunting torso. She carried a sexy figure which was even then rather on the plump side. I learned that she had been in a circus as a young girl and was now a dancer-cum-acrobat on the stage in North India and a hot favorite with her audience."[24] Although the stunt genre became immensely popular starting in the 1920s, Wadia Movietone reinvented the genre by experimenting with formal and publicity mechanisms. A review of its *Toofan Mail* (1932) claimed that the Wadias "changed stunt technique and ideas," locating the change specifically in the type of stunts: in contrast to the "meaningless sword fighting and hand-fighting against impossible odds [that] have dominated the silent films," the Wadias "have introduced realistic original stunts."[25] This "realism" drew on the studio's technical competence, aligned, as I will show, with a specific form of cinematic spectatorship, and also on its participation in a wider social discourse of physical culture. Stunts and stardom become intertwined in the case of Fearless Nadia, whose public image became conflated with her first popular role as the eponymous *Hunterwali* (the woman with the whip).[26] In addition to "Hunterwali," Fearless Nadia was also variously known as "The Indian Pearl White" and "The Amazon." The audiences of these films were a heterogeneous, but mostly male, mix of classes and age groups, including teenagers, college students, and soldiers.[27]

My approach to Fearless Nadia is not an analysis of her star persona per se, but rather a consideration of the Nadia/stunt films/Wadia Movietone intertext, centered on the multiple spectatorial investments associated with this specific intersection of star, genre, and studio, which, I argue, brought two generations of film spectators into dialogue. The Indian stunt film, unlike the institution of cinema itself, was regarded not so much as a genre of ill repute as a genre of no consequence, one that had no place in the general discussion of cinema's status in the heated context of contemporary national and social politics. In the hierarchies of star discourses, the popularity of actors associated with low-brow genres was registered almost exclusively in the unofficial star discourse that was marked by silences. This means that, apart from the occasional review or news item about the studio or its latest productions, there were no articles, star profiles, or interviews devoted exclusively to Nadia, as there were for more "reputable" actresses.

Fearless Nadia in *Hunterwali* (Homi Wadia, 1935).

Box office success and stardom were delinked in Nadia's case because genre replaced stardom as the explanatory framework.[28] *filmindia's* review of *Hunterwali* (1935), for example, acknowledged that "Nadia's work as 'Madhuri' stands out, though she lacks expression," but moved on to say that "from the box office point of view it can go down as one of Wadia's successes and will play well in provinces where stunt stories are appreciated."[29] In its reference to the "provinces," *filmindia* marked its own sophisticated distance from such provincial tastes.[30] Its review of *Miss Frontier Mail* was more enthusiastic, but limited to a prediction that "the picture is expected to be a box office sensation, in as much as some absolutely novel stunts are performed by the amazon, Nadia."[31] Conflating Nadia with the stunt genre meant that she functioned as a constitutive contrast to the desirable star. One commentator condemned the poor imitations of *Hunterwali* and *Toofan Mail,* and reprimanded actresses for agreeing to make such films. He specified his condemnation with the example of Nadia: "The sad fate of 'Nadia' who, in spite of her hectic stunts and swift actions, has failed to secure recognition of her talents and achievements at the bar of public opinion owing to the bewitching but undignified temptations which she is constantly made to offer, should serve as a warning and reminder to other aspirants towards stardom." The quotes around her name suggest a refusal to grant subjectivity beyond the fictive construct of genre affiliation and also allow a momentary lapse from the rhetoric of innuendo, which would rather have identified her more coyly as "a certain popular stunt actress." Unlike Sulochana's, Nadia's sexuality, while "bewitching," is no better than "undignified temptations." The author then contrasts Nadia with reputable actresses such as Durga Khote, Uma Shashi, and Kamlesh, whose "solidarity [*sic*] of character and . . . dignity of conduct" make them fit for public acclaim.[32] The "bar of public opinion" in this case is the reformist discourse of improvement of the cinema rather than measures of popularity such as box office success. More tellingly, "public opinion" about actresses has little to do with talent, screen presence, or even genre affiliation.

It is no surprise, then, that Nadia's popularity left few contemporary written traces, but has been recovered almost exclusively in the form of oral and written memoirs, starting in the 1970s.[33] Thus, oral discourse, now no longer recoverable, and memoirs are crucially constitutive of Fearless Nadia's place in the history of Indian stardom. The low-brow connotations of the Wadia Movietone Diamond Thriller Series was not lost on the Wadia brothers. This exclusion from contemporary debates actually led Wadia Movietone to dissociate itself from the stunt genre, when the Wadia brothers broke up over JBH Wadia's decision to produce "artistic" films, such as the expensive dual-language flop, *The Court Dancer* (Modhu Bose, 1941).[34] Flop though it was, it certainly succeeded in gaining entry into the pages of film magazines, where it was widely discussed, in contrast to the dismissive single sentence that might announce a Wadia stunt release to "packed houses."[35] In Rosie Thomas's analysis, the brothers' partnership in Wadia Movietone was "invariably characterized as the clash of two visions," of low-brow entertainment in contrast to "despised intellectual pretensions" on the one hand, and "cultured," highbrow desires, seeking critical acclaim and international recognition, on the other; between the competing demands of "popularity" and "respectability." She reads these taste hierarchies in terms of "two different visions of the nationalist project . . . [that] tug between national self-definition and global modernity." Both visions acknowledged the transnational, but JBH's vision "was largely premised on an essentialized Indian cultural tradition, while [Homi's] better recognized the hybridity and fluidity within the porous borders of modern 'India.'"[36]

The heterogeneous affiliations of the Nadia/stunt film intertext complicate their low-brow status in the precise hierarchies of class, ethnicity, national culture, and performance expertise of the time. By their own account, the producers and stars of the Wadia films had been enthusiastic viewers of the Hollywood stunt serials of the 1910s featuring stars such as Tom Mix, Eddie Polo, Ruth Roland, Helen Holmes, and the popular Pearl White. Although these films had low-brow connotations in the United States, they had higher class associations in India simply by virtue of their equal appeal to European and Indian viewers. Hollywood serials circulating in India "consisted of fifteen episodes which in the early years were exhibited one at a time from week to week. They abounded in hair-raising stunts, breathtaking thrills, non-stop fisticuffs, acrobatics and spitfire gun-play, rounded off by nerve-breaking suspense at the end of each episode." The female action stars from that period "stood for a particular synthesis of femininity, athletic virility, and effortless mobility," and Helen Holmes's railway serials were especially popular in India. JBH Wadia's moviegoing memoirs refer to "'manly' heroines like Marie Walcamp and Pearl White. They were well equipped with requisite armament to assert their rightful place in society much before the Women's Lib became an organised movement. Marie Walcamp was a sharp-shooter and dare-devil rider who would not yield a place to Tom Mix." Wadia's nostalgic comments on the Hollywood serial draw attention to interpretive details such as "Women's Lib" and "dare-devil rider" that would become applicable to his own stunt films as well.[37]

Echoing the Wadia brothers' own conflict between the demands of art and popularity, recent accounts of the Nadia films have tended toward a reappraisal based on arguments of surface and depth, according to which, under their seemingly lightweight surface as "just honest-to-goodness stunt films," one can find socially and aesthetically serious motivations. The first of these arguments can be applied to other stunt and costume genre films as well: that the surface play and spectacle of the genre masks a serious articulation of nationalist aspirations toward independence in their narratives of struggle against usurping authority. Such a reading is validated because "reclaiming one's rightful patrimony remained a running motif throughout the stunt film genre's career." In this view, the stunt genre trappings also disguised the real intent of these films from the British censors. A second argument finds a similar value in the gender politics under the surface of these films' preposterous plots, pointing out the strong female roles showcasing Nadia. Wenner sees Nadia as a "radical feminist actress" who used "subversive methods" and "fought for freedom and also for women's rights in her films." Her reading produces a slippage between the motivations of actress, screenwriter, and textual form. Both nationalist and feminist readings are also present in Riyad Wadia's documentary, *Fearless: The Hunterwali Story.* A third reading of these films demonstrates their inherent Indianness despite their similarities to their Hollywood predecessors. Kathryn Hansen suggests that Nadia's *Hunterwali* role is in the lineage of Kavasji Manikji Contractor's female impersonation of a *jogin* (ascetic) in Harischandra who delivered "countless lashes to [a] tormented dancing figure." She says that Nadia takes on "the androgynous aspect of womanhood . . . associated with the virangana or warrior-queen in Indian myth and popular culture." Rosie Thomas develops this idea of Nadia's affiliation with the figure of the *virangana,* arguing that her role is a hybrid of Indian and Hollywood forms.[38] That Nadia's reception was shaped by the dominant discourse of respectability aligned with nationalism is clear in JBH Wadia's own defense of his stunt films, in which he himself uses similar surface-depth arguments to explain the success of his films against more high-brow productions:

> My friends, colleagues, and competitors, some of whom were really "big shots" in the industry in virtue of their respective achievements, could not understand why J. B. H. Wadia's "stunt" films should win universal acclaim from the masses of filmgoers when quite a number of their better class of social films went under.
>
> Of course, stunts, thrills, fast action, and slapstick comedy had a big way in the success of my films. But there was always something more,

> something different and something of vital importance in the life of the nation in them. I had made it a practice to weave my stories and screenplays around the burning problems of the day such as Hindu-Muslim Unity, and our Struggles for Freedom. . . . I also used to include themes of sociological value like Removal of Untouchability, Campaign for Literacy, Pleas for Democracy, Attack on Fascism, Emphasis on Physical Culture, Dignity of Labor, and last but not least Emancipation of Indian Womanhood. Sometimes the message was direct, sometimes indirect.

In this statement, Wadia bypasses the self-explanatory appeal of "stunts, thrills, fast action, and slapstick" to move on to the more socially responsible issues. The publicity programme for Nadia's first film, *Hunterwali*, pragmatically combined both nationalist aspirations and entertainment affiliations: "Hunterwali!: What visions does that film stir up! It is the story of a brave Indian girl who sacrificed royal luxury to the cause of her people and country," but it is also "a spectacular thriller, the first of its kind in India!"[39]

While all three readings are readily validated by the narrative details of these films, memories of the actual experience of watching these films tell another story. Responding to the dynamics of the genre itself, one of the rare contemporary accounts from 1940 has this tongue-in-cheek description:

> When you see a Wadia thriller, your habits have to be reorganized. You must sit on the extreme edge of the chair and keep your fists clenched in boxing on-guard pose. In between you must jump up and shout, "Come on Nadia, give them tight [*sic*]." If you have a friend sitting close by you must either shake him vigorously or slap his thighs tight or better still pinch him well. This must be done at least ten times during the two and a half hours to enjoy the entertainment effectively. The friend doesn't mind it. He is in the same mood and returns the compliment with equal sincerity and vigor. In these thriller theatres, I think the chairs are unnecessary seeing that so little of them are being used. Cross poles would be more suitable.[40]

Another, more recent, account describes it this way: "We were forced to keep ourselves under control everywhere: at work, in the family, faced with our superiors, on the street, there was nowhere we could give full rein to our emotions—apart from the cinema. There we could shout and laugh and cry without it being invasive or embarrassing. Everyone did it. And that is the reason too why the Nadia films were so popular because no other film managed to draw us in as much. Come the end of the film we were completely drained and exhausted. But at the same time there was a magnificent relief, a catharsis."[41] What if we were to stop at precisely the inconsequential surface pleasures of these films, at their impact on the viewers' bodies? How, then, would we account for their particular star effect, which clearly functioned outside the dominant moral discourse on female stars?

The first account of the experience of watching a Nadia film registers not so much the liberatory joys of nationalist and gender transgressions, as more simply a visceral and bodily engagement with the physicality of stunts, which it foregrounds to the exclusion of other plot details. The second account centers on pathologized emotional release in a wider, repressive social context. While discussions of Indian cinema, including the social genre at this time, routinely invoke the importance of emotion, this account's emphasis of being "completely drained and exhausted" aligns emotion with bodily experience.

The focus on the spectator's body and on the visceral delights of the thrills in the stunt genre allowed her fans to see Nadia as a figure in play, her stardom constituted through the serial iterative structure of the genre.[42] Genre and stardom intersected in the expectation of recurrent, even iconic, details, such as Nadia's "clarion call of 'Hey-y-y-y-y!'" After *Hunterwali* made Fearless Nadia a recognizable star, her presence in other films relied on a play between on- and off-screen space. In *Diamond Queen,* the villains are punched and thrown into disarray while Nadia remains off-screen, with only her arms and legs punching into the frame from its margins. Vision is decentered, as her presence is registered only as a form of corporeal impact. When we finally do see her, at the end of the sequence, it is in a low-angle shot as she stands in triumph over the cowering men.[43] Nadia's off-screen placement was also repeatedly linked to the trope of falling from heights. Nadia attacks villains by dropping on them from trees, walls, the tops of doors, and pillars. The iconic Nadia moment always featured her holding up a man on her shoulders and then whirling him around. Her physical prowess, as demonstrated in scenes such as these, was part of the Wadia films' participation in the wider sphere of popular physical culture at the time.

Physical Culture and Bodily Address

Entertainment and nationalist politics became intertwined in the discourse of physical culture in India. Nationalist discussions in the wake of the *swadeshi* movement in the early years of the twentieth century were shaped by the gendered discourses of colonialism that produced the idea of the effeminate Hindu (Bengali) male in relation to the "manly Englishman" and the martial Sikh.[44] Ideas about the effete Indian and the weak physique of other colonized races were further promoted by the worldwide celebrity of the bodybuilder Eugen Sandow, who, after his travels around the world, brought back a "weakling" from each country he visited in order to demonstrate how he could make them into strongmen. With gender mapped onto race and national identity in India, a secondary configuration of norms of masculinity and femininity replaced "traditional" gender roles, so that an upper-class woman like Sarala Devi Chaudhurani could organize gymnasia and physical culture clubs around 1902 to train young men and, later, young women. The discourse of improvement now included the human body, with "improvement of health and physique of young men . . . an essential step for the success of the national struggle." Joseph Alter shows how entertainment and nationalist sentiment came together in the figure of Gama the wrestler, who went to London in 1920 and returned to India a national hero after defeating British champions.[45] By the 1920s physical culture in India drew on a hybrid mix of wrestling, bodybuilding, circus acrobatics, popular medicine, sporting clubs, and gymnastics, in which distinctions between separate spheres of physical culture dissolved. In the "Amusements" section of the *Bombay Chronicle,* alongside film advertisements, readers saw ads like "Professor Eknath Murti's Bold Challenge. The Indian Hercules. Feat of Strength. Clowns, Jugglers, Acrobats." Other advertisements included the tonic Virol's promise to build up "weakly children" and Professor M.V. Krishna Rao's guarantee that with his "system of Physical Culture," "ten days from to-night, you'll see proof that I can make you a new man!"[46] Physical culture in the form of acrobatics and gymnastics was routinely featured in staged entertainments, too, as in the case of Fearless Nadia's own stage career.

Film culture in the 1920s and 1930s, and especially the stunt, costume, and historical genres, mediated many of these intertwined links among physical culture, entertainment, celebrity, and nationalist politics. In the *Bombay Chronicle* of 23 May 1929, for example, an advertisement for the stunt film *Masked Cavalier* (A. P. Kapur, 1929), featuring Master Vithal, was placed next to a Virol ad, and on the same page there was also an ad for a wrestling contest featuring Gama. Not only did films like *Masked Cavalier* feature a Ruritanian-style narrative of conflict between evil ruler and masked heroes, but its forms of resistance drew on a hybrid physical culture that included circus-style acrobatics, wrestling, warriorlike swordplay, and horse riding. Bodybuilders and wrestlers became film actors, perhaps the most celebrated being Raja Sandow, a former wrestler, whose screen name dissolved distinctions between his own wrestling career and the bodybuilding fame of Eugen Sandow, to whom the actor was not related.[47] Raja Sandow played mostly in the social genre, opposite stars like Sulochana and Gohar, and in *Indira M.A.* he played the Indian suitor to whom she returns, as a reformed Hindu woman, at the end of the film.

Physical culture is central to the Nadia films, their studio culture, and the forms of spectatorship associated with them. In addition to Nadia, a former acrobat herself, there was also John Cawas, "a physical culturist and weight lifter who had been adjudged the Body Beautiful Champion of India in an official contest." Auditions for new actors at Wadia Movietone consisted of gymnastic exercises, and the studio itself maintained a gymnasium culture: "To make our stunts and fights more realistic I had reserved a space at the north end of our estate for a gymnasium. . . . I had very efficient and bold extras on the staff. . . . Every morning they were ready for practice with Nadia, and later on John Cawas. There was a trapeze, a double bar, also a rope attached to a tree for practicing acrobatic swings and also weightlifting equipment."[48] Physical culture was closely linked to the execution of stunts in Nadia's films, not simply in preparing actors, but also as a form of cinematic spectacle. In *Diamond Queen,* the Nadia character attributes her physical prowess to the influence of the "Bombay Gymnasium." In many of her films, one recurrent item of spectacle was the gymnastics tableau of Nadia and her sidekicks. In *Hunterwali,* for example, a tableau shot presents Nadia in the center carrying a man over her head, while her sidekicks do gymnastics—this in the middle of a chase. Gymnastics as a form of entertainment can be seen in other stunt films as well. In *Diler Jigar/Gallant Hearts* (Agarwal Film Co., 1931), the acrobats who are the main characters put on a show that is merely a tableaulike display of bodybuilding and gymnastic exercises. One of the celebrated moments in *Miss Frontier Mail* united two kinds of body display in a scene in which Nadia, dressed in a skimpy bikinilike outfit, is exercising in a gymnasium in her home. Sexuality and physical culture come together as the extended sequence displays Nadia rowing, boxing, doing somersaults, and ultimately landing in the hero's arms. On the walls in the background are large photographs of men in classic bodybuilding poses made famous by Sandow and, more contemporaneously, Professor K. V. Iyer.

Supporting the new body culture in Nadia's films, there was also a whole array of technological marvels as instrumental devices for both villains and heroes. While premised on the perfectibility of the human body—though always with the risk of bodily dissolution through accidents—the core stunts relied on the interplay between the natural and the technological. Even in the titles of her films, the figure of Nadia was associated with the speed of transportation technologies like trains, airplanes, cars, and bicycles: "Is this a woman or a train?" asks one of the characters about Nadia in *Miss Frontier Mail.* Apart from the eponymous train around which most of the action revolved, *Miss Frontier Mail* featured car chases, dynamite rigged on a timer, high-tech intercom systems invented by the villain Signal X, and the most effective weapon of all, the motion picture camera, which the Nadia character's brother uses to trap the villain. The narrative of capturing evidence of the villain's crime on film integrates an explanation of cinematic process into the plot twists, as the villains steal what they think is the undeveloped film and expose it to the sun. With the camera, as with the human body, there is a play with accident and risk, where the act of filming alone does not guarantee the production of evidence. Again, as with the camera, technology and the human body are subject to control and perfectibility, but in a narrative scenario that always verges on absolute loss of control. In *Miss Frontier Mail,* for example, even though Nadia's instruments are technologies of speed, such as the motor car and the train, she is ultimately unable to prevent a train accident planned by Signal X, because the temptations of explosive spectacle override her narrative invincibility. Another stunt that plays with control and risk shows a man on the front ledge of a train engine snatching up a woman from the tracks seconds before the train would have run over her.

The discourse of control and risk extended beyond the human/technological body to the natural order, to include even Nadia's car, anthropomorphized into "Rolls Royce-ki-Beti" and given her own screen credit, and her famous horse, Punjab-Ka-Beta, with its "almost human performance."[49] Like Hollywood films featuring female stunt stars and their death-defying interactions with lions and tigers, the Nadia films referenced wilder animals as well, both in her various "jungle princess" costumes and in scenes of interaction with dangerous animals such as tigers.[50] In Jennifer Bean's reading, the wild animal in Hollywood stunt serials "upped the ante," using the unpredictability of wild animals to visibly put its stars at risk on screen, as a form of authentication that contested the norms of control and order that the well-oiled Hollywood mode of filmmaking projected. At issue were notions of the real, as the Hollywood stunt star system "brandishe[d] disorder and disaster as if to unhinge the progressive, utilitarian drive of the apparatus, and release it into the realm of the unpredictable real." The use of wild animals, risky stunts, and on- and off-screen accidents in the Nadia films, however, seemed to be more closely aligned with precisely "the progressive, utilitarian drive of the apparatus," especially in the context of the Wadia films' reputation for technical competence in an industry plagued by unfavorable comparisons with Hollywood. Even as accidents during filming were reported, their function was more to showcase and reinforce technical and physical competence than to reinsert the unpredictability of the real. In the Nadia films, the accidental fall was particularly effective when it left its indexical trace on the screen, as filmed accidents were retained in the final cut. Scenes in which accidents were known to have happened, such as Nadia's fall from a chandelier or her loss of control in a waterfall, signaled evidence of competency and physical prowess.[51] In her numerous athletic scenes, Nadia's body also inhabited a split discourse between control and loss of control over bodily perfectibility. The demands of generic verisimilitude demanded a belief in Nadia's physical prowess and the model of physical fitness she represented.[52] But those, like *filmindia*'s critics, who positioned themselves outside the taste affiliation of the stunt film, found much to deride in Nadia's weight. By the early 1940s, as ideas of star labor were being recast in terms of efforts to maintain norms of weight and beauty derived from Hollywood, Nadia became an easy target of satire.[53]

While the Nadia films have been discussed in terms of their liberatory gender and nationalist politics, there is also the persistent spectacle in these films, produced in the decade before Indian Independence, of a large white woman beating up a group of puny Indian men at her feet. The nationalist impetus toward physical culture may be attributed to the gendering of racial relations with masculinized English men, contrasted with feminized Indian men. In this way, a sado-masochistic reading of Nadia as dominatrix would have to be complicated to account for the pleasure Indian male audiences might take in watching themselves recast as a mob of "effete" native men being beaten up by a white woman. In her discussion of the complex ways in which Nadia's whiteness was negotiated as both Indian and white, "simultaneously recognised and disavowed," Rosie Thomas locates one explanation in "the classic colonial miscegenation fantasy." However, these spectacles could be read differently, and contradictorily, according to the shifting location of the Nadia/stunt film intertext in the different hierarchical axes of gender, genre (with its class associations), and nationalist categories. Thus, scenes where she singlehandedly takes on a mob of Indian men and reduces them to a cowering heap on the floor could be read variously as female empowerment, or the hyperbolic physical prowess associated with the stunt genre, or the strong white woman fighting for justice alongside other Indian men.[54] These readings certainly do not exhaust the possibilities, and I would argue that alongside these and other interpretations, we must also retain, rather than explain away, the potentially disturbing reading that sees a reinforcement of gendered racial hierarchies, where Indian men are so emasculated that even a white woman is physically superior to them. Retaining multiple and contradictory meanings enables the Nadia films to leave open old questions of pleasure and identification in the cinema in the specific context of genre. Clearly, based on the spectatorial responses we do have to the Nadia films, there was a prioritization of different types of reading strategies, with the readings elicited by genre expectations taking precedence over all else, including considerations of cultural taste, social responsibility, and national or racial identity.

The Nadia/stunt film intertext could accommodate contradictory affiliations not only because of her absolute identification with the iterative details of a recurrent character type, but also by a visible play of identities in a performative context that privileged ironic and comic distance. In one sequence in *Hunterwali,* she plays with domesticity as a disguise, putting on an ill-fitting sari that returns her briefly to her identity as Princess Madhuri, whose father has been imprisoned by his evil prime minister. In this sequence, the sari functions to hide her masked identity as the "Hunterwali" (woman with the whip) when the prime minister announces his plan of marrying her. Nadia's loud and derisive laughter at the mention of marriage frames both marriage and sari as ridiculous goals and creates an ironic distance from the normative goals of Indian womanhood. Although I describe the sari as ill-fitting, there is, of course, no such thing as an ill-fitting sari. Rather, it is Nadia's body that uneasily inhabits the sari. We can understand this better via Sulochana's testimony before the Indian Cinematograph Committee eight years before *Hunterwali.* When asked whether Anglo-Indian and European girls can find work in Indian cinema, she replied, "I do not think they would be able to do the Indian girl. It was a bit hard for me at first," and added that "it is not very difficult" if one has the knack "of walking and behaving like an Indian—just as I do."[55] Nadia neither has nor pretends to have this knack, so that both her masked and her domestic female roles look like disguises. This, I would argue, enables many of the "transgressions" that surprise audiences today. In some films, she smokes as part of the logic of her crime-fighting persona, even blowing smoke in the villain's face in *Hunterwali,* but smoking does not morally define her in the way that it does, for example, the gangster's moll in *Miss Frontier Mail.*

Nadia's visible whiteness remains an anomaly in the context of scores of Anglo-Indian stars like Sulochana, Ermeline, Patience Cooper, Sita Devi, and Sabita Devi because of her spirited refusal to make any kind of attempt at passing as Indian. Her response to the question of taking on a Hindu name was: "I am a white woman and I'll look foolish with long black hair. And my name is very well known all over India as Nadia. I refuse to change my name. It has been chosen by an Armenian fortune teller and it has brought me good luck. And besides I'm no devi!"[56] Anglo-Indians were already "passing" as Indians on the Parsi stage, but black-and-white cinematography further enabled these stars to "pass," while maintaining a look familiar to transnational star iconographies.[57] Given that film stock and lighting technologies were designed to naturalize whiteness, thereby constructing nonwhite skin tones as a "problem" for cinematography, Anglo-Indian actresses could "pass" for Indian even as they enabled easier manipulation of filmmaking technology.[58] Although Rosie Thomas argues that Wadia Movietone made efforts to Indianize Nadia, those efforts did not register on her screen presence and in stylistic choices such as backlighting, which drew attention to her blonde hair in ways that echo Hollywood lighting technologies. Her explanation for refusing a Hindu name ending in "devi" also seems to reinsert her into the fantasy world of stunt films, especially when she refers to the Armenian fortuneteller who gave her the name "Nadia."

If accidents, falls from heights, instruments of speed, and technological marvels shape the visceral response to the Nadia films, does this align the Nadia stunt films with the experience of modernity? Much of the recent work on early Hollywood serials is dominated by what Ben Singer calls the modernity thesis, which draws on Walter Benjamin's discussion of the analogies between the new experience of modernity and the new medium of cinema, both of which assault the senses with the shock of collision and proximity. As Singer puts it, "the modernity thesis stresses key formal and spectatorial similarities between cinema—a medium of strong impressions, spatiotemporal fragmentation, abruptness, mobility—and the nature of metropolitan experience." In this reading, the convergence of urban modernity and cinema is to be found specifically in very early Hollywood cinema and in the low-brow genres of the 1910s. Singer's own work points to the array of extra-cinematic entertainment forms, such as amusement park rides, that, like the stunt films, participated in novel ways of mobilizing the body. Thus, he says, "the *thrill* emerged as the keynote of modern diversion" where "concentrations of audiovisual and kinesthetic sensation epitomized a distinctly modern intensity of *manufactured* stimulus." Central to these ideas is the specific address of these cinematic forms to the body of the viewer. Miriam Hansen's work locates many of these sensory-perceptual convergences between cinema and urban modernity in "specific, and unequally developed, contexts and conditions of *reception*" of Hollywood film as they register on the senses. In their application to different national cinemas, these ideas have certain genre implications. Hansen's own reading of early Shanghai films sees the vernacular modern played out on the figure of the new woman, split between the competing demands of adulteress and self-sacrificing mother. Here, the preferred textual site of the vernacular modern returns us squarely to the dominant discourses of 1930s Indian stardom and its investment in the social genre.[59]

From these different positions on the relation of modernity and specific cinematic forms, most suggestive for the Nadia films is the emphasis on a kind of spectatorship that enables a theoretical investment in the surface pleasures of the text, at the level of bodily address and sensory stimulus, as opposed to their nationalist and feminist implications. In terms of the purely kinesthetic qualities of cinematic experience, where the viewer's body involuntarily registers some of the speed and movement on-screen, the modernity thesis provides a compelling account of the experience of watching Hollywood serials even in Bombay in the 1910s and 1920s. Yet if it also accounts for the popularity of the Indian stunt films of the 1930s, this very belatedness usefully complicates such a reading. It is belated not only in terms of the cinematic reference to Hollywood serials of the 1910s, but also in terms of the three-decade-old experience of urban modernity in India. That is, the belatedness of the reference is crucial in identifying the specific relation to Hollywood cinema and to mediations of modernity, and returns us again to questions of spectatorship. In 1934 the new *Perils of Pauline* was playing in Bombay, but by JBH Wadia's own account, the filmmakers and stars were acting on their fascination with the experience of going to see serials and movies in their youth, presumably in the 1910s and 1920s. Nadia remembers, "I used to go to the flickers at every opportunity I got. When I came home on weekends my mum used to give me a few annas and I'd rush to the cinema hall with my friends. There were not many girls who were allowed to see films in those days. Many considered it to be a little cheap. Of course I was only supposed to see pictures that were publicized as family fare. I once remember sneaking in to see Theda Bara's *Salome.*"[60] Here is JBH Wadia's own oft-quoted account of how he and his friends got tickets to the movies:

> My job was to run up to the main door of the third class and manage to push my way forward by hook or by crook. Sometimes, it was I who would be hooked up by others. The doors would be immediately thrown open after the entire audience of the previous show had gone out. . . .
>
> Then there would be a veritable stampede of cinegoers in the auditorium. The gold rush sequence which we sometimes saw in the Westerns was like a cake-walk dance compared to our adventure. So it seemed

> to us, at least. Then I would try to secure the best seats possible on the wooden benches by laying myself prostrate on one of them. This was the accepted technique for reservation of seats in those days.
>
> . . . for about the first half a minute or so one witnessed the strange spectacle of the first batch of cinegoers all lying supine and glued to their respective areas, motionless like so many corpses—a tempting sight for an undertaker wishfully imagining they never came to life. But as soon as their friends turned up, they would jump up and accommodate them.
>
> The next to turn up were the door-keepers. The speed with which they collected our tickets was certainly worth watching. It revealed a close parallel to the action of Keystone Cops on the screen cranked by the cameraman at slow speed of about six frames per second instead of the normal 16 frames.

The replay of film stunts in the experience of moviegoing, from buying tickets, to finding seats, to vocally responding to the screen, encompasses the entire spectrum of film culture in a form of embodied spectatorship.[61] Putting aside, for the moment, the question of belatedness, Wadia's description of moviegoing seems to be exactly paralleled in the experience of watching the Nadia films, as in the two accounts I discussed above, where we find an embodied spectatorship that decenters narrative and visual experience as the prime mode of experience.

But is there or does there have to be anything specifically Indian about such a response to stunts? Christopher Pinney's reading of Indian chromolithographs attempts just such an Indianization through his newly coined concept of "corpothetics" or "sensory, corporeal, or tactile aesthetics." Pinney argues that corpothetics constitutes a particular form of spectatorial address that, through the framing and organization of the image in early Indian cinema and in chromolithographs, "entails a desire to fuse image and beholder." Building his case on two points, mutuality and tactility of vision, Pinney tries to "sketch out a countertheory of Western visuality that can meet, halfway, a different tradition with which it shares much in common." Pinney argues that Indian chromolithography can be placed in the context of "strikingly similar oppositions between popular practices of corporeal visuality and elite 'decarnalized' practices." In his reading of the framing of action in early Phalke mythologicals, Pinney notes their tendency to stage the audience's gaze within the film, his examples of corporeal vision being the literal contact between gaze and object via a beam of light. While his reading is suggestive, this notion of corpothetics continues to privilege vision over other forms of sensory embodiment.[62]

When contemporary commentators in the 1930s made similar observations to Pinney's about embodied vision, it was less in terms of a specifically Indian mode of viewership than of a thoroughgoing articulation of class hierarchies, where it was the lower classes to whom such forms of embodied entertainment appealed. The 1938 book *Film in India* by Syed Assadullah provides a rare populist argument for film spectatorship when he recommends that films address not only the educated, but also the masses, through what he calls "brute incident" rather than "life at rest." The former does not arrest events for the sake of reflection and elaborate analysis; rather, it addresses the instincts, which are common to all classes. He says that the problem in film art is "of the human body and the concrete world around, not of abstract and intricate objects."[63] The mind/body split here matches the genre/class hierarchy of social film and stunt film, but it also provides a contemporary model of theorizing the relation of genre, class, subject matter, and bodily address: "brute incident," human "instincts," and "concrete world" form a universal substratum on which cinema culture can be built. At the same time, the claim that "brute incident"—presumably of the sort that attracted the viewers of the Nadia films—requires no analysis or reflection also goes to explain the easy dismissal of stunt films. In thinking of the specific spectatorial address of the Nadia films, it may be useful to consider the bodily impact of "brute incident" in the context of the global contours of film culture in India at the time. Equally, Pinney's notion of mutuality is relevant to the particular address of the stunt film and the type of spectatorial investment it elicits.

The Wadia stunt films were made by what was already a second generation of film viewers, just as the experience of modernity itself was an ongoing one that had begun in the nineteenth century. Given the belatedness of the reference, I would argue that it is "modernity" (expressed with quotation marks) that these films engage, in the form of an excessive mobilization of the tropes of technology, thrills, shock, and speed that its makers had encountered in the Hollywood originals. The star effect of the Nadia/stunt film intertext emerges from a playful engagement with an already mediated modernity experienced through the "original" (in Benjamin's sense) Hollywood stunt serials, rather than with everyday reality. This is not the same as the mediation of modernity that Hansen claims for Hollywood's role as the first global vernacular. That is, the "modernity" the Nadia films engage, and the source of their pleasure, is defined precisely by their separation from the tensions of modernity discourses played out in 1930s India in, for example, the nationalist conception of the modern woman. Rather, although the films engage contemporary concerns with the entire list of issues that JBH Wadia laid out in their defense, they also stage these engagements in a second-order modernity relayed from the Hollywood films. Signs of this second-order modernity range from film titles to the play with technology, to the spatial dynamics of the human body in action. For example, the credits of *Miss Frontier Mail* playfully announce Nadia as the Indian Pearl White; her costar, John Cawas, as the Indian Eddie Polo; and the villain as the Indian Frankie Dera. While this might seem similar to the wider practice in early Indian cinema of naming actors after Hollywood stars, it is different in its excess, with all the main characters as homegrown versions of Hollywood stars. Another difference is that these names appear in the film text itself rather than in extra-cinematic discourse, marking these productions as a form of fan appropriation, of "making one's own." Wadia's own wry reference to the surrealists places his investment in Hollywood serials in the context of a global culture of cinephilia: "Since our knowledge of European history was limited to singing 'God save the king' and 'Rule Britannia,' we were sublimely ignorant of the fact that the surrealists in France had already stolen a march over us and placed Hollywood film on a prestigious pedestal and squeezing subjective thrills out of cinema had found echoes of their heart's desire in it." In Wadia's memoirs and in other reminiscences, production history of the Nadia films is invariably framed in the context of a participatory engagement with Hollywood stunt films. For example, Wadia describes his silent film *Dilruba Daku* (1933) as "the reverse of Douglas Fairbanks's evergreen film *The Mark of Zorro*," and when Douglas Fairbanks visited Bombay in 1934, Wadia got him to agree to let him "show the silent movie *The Mark of Zorro* (1920) . . . in Indian cinemas with a synchronized Hindi version and soundtrack." When Fairbanks agreed, this was the Wadias' opportunity to collaborate with Fairbanks in a form of active remaking for Indian audiences. Wenner comments that the Wadias' Hindi version of *The Mark of Zorro* rekindled "their own, boyish enthusiasm for the daring, ironic action entertainment from America." Other signs of homage include a willful anachronism of cinematic style. In *Hunterwali* and *Miss Frontier Mail*, for example, vision is withheld through the use of off-screen space, but standard cinematic techniques denoting focused vision, such as close-ups, are rejected in favor of the iris, an earlier mode of focused vision. This form of engagement with older Hollywood films is not so much a matter of mimicry as of fans using and remaking their own Hollywood serials; that is, there is neither simple imitation nor the subversive edge that characterizes Homi Bhabha's notion of colonial mimicry.[64]

Even in their copyright violations, these films can be seen in terms of a kind of fan fiction modeled on, and ultimately increasing the prestige of, their originals. Wenner describes the techniques by which the Wadias would copy particularly exciting scenes from Hollywood films, such as "expensive shipwrecks, aeroplane crashes and raging fires." As she notes, however, it was not merely a matter of copying, or reusing cut-out footage from the originals, but also of skillfully integrating the "borrowed" scenes into their Nadia films. Although there was nothing amateur about the Wadia films, the negotiated boundaries between homage and creative self-assertion, between private ownership and mass circulation, which marks the current discourse of participatory fan culture, can also be seen in the Wadias' run-in with a representative of Edgar Rice Burroughs after "news of [*Toofani Tarzan*'s] phenomenal success had reached him." In the end, Burroughs's representative "sportingly agreed to give a go-by to this issue" once he was convinced "that [Wadia] had not hidden . . . the debt he owed to Mr. Burroughs nor the inspiration he had drawn from the American Jungle Films."[65]

In their exuberant remaking of Hollywood serials, the Nadia films remake not so much the plots and stunts, as the exhilarating *experience* of watching them. It may seem that in rewriting the Hollywood serials, these films are "mediating competing cultural discourses on modernity and modernization." I would argue, to the contrary, that the Nadia/stunt film intertext mediates the experience of cinema-going, of boyhood pleasures recast in adult memory and play, and provides a common platform for two generations of fans, the viewers of the Hollywood serials, such as JBH, and the viewers of the Nadia films, such as Girish Karnad. In Karnad's memories of watching the Nadia films, this mediation of cinematic experience occurs a second time and produces its own version of fan remaking: "The catharsis in a Nadia–John Cawas movie was not in the film itself. It came later. After watching the film at a matinee, our entire game had to re-enact the stunt scenes by throwing punches at each other to the accompaniment of sounds like 'dhum' and 'ttho.' Mother had strictly forbidden us to come anywhere near the living room after a stunt movie since an obligatory part of this re-enactment was to roll across a table or a chair and take that piece of furniture crashing to the floor." Here, too, spectatorial investment takes the form of a combination of cathartic release and bodily engagement that mirrors the action on the screen. While Sulochana's admirers found their emotions mirroring the star's performed emotions, fans of the stunt genre felt compelled to replay the performed actions.[66]

At the low-brow end of the hierarchy of stardom, the Nadia/stunt film intertext has important historiographic implications. For one thing, it serves as a reminder of other gaps in this narrative of Indian star history and foregrounds its necessarily provisional form, as other popular, but now overlooked stars might be brought back to our attention. The Nadia films also force a methodological shift to considerations of spectatorship. Arguably, the high end of the hierarchy registers itself in similar ways because Sulochana became so quickly reified as the star par excellence, needing no further elaboration. Popularity in both cases took on quantifiable explanatory frameworks—box office returns for Nadia, and salary for Sulochana—leaving questions of audience response at the margins of written discourse.

PART II

"This Stardom Racket"

5. *Monopoly, Frontality, and Doubling in Postwar Bombay Cinema*

> The logic is simple. The star must remain permanently in focus.
>
> —Jimi Hafizi, "The Double Role—Status Symbol for Footage-Hoggers?" *Filmfare,* 7–20 January 1977, 52

> Mainly, the star likes to play himself in every role because he knows he is an eminently saleable commodity.
>
> —Dilip Kumar, quoted in "The Big Three in the Dock; three top-notch stars of the Indian screen reply to common charges levelled against them," *Filmfare,* 25 October 1957, 55

In the 1930s cinematic stardom in India had been figured primarily as an absence, a recurrent complaint being the perceived lack of "genuine" stars, who were understood in the context of a general discourse of improvement of Indian cinema. Stardom in India was negatively conceptualized, both technologically and morally, against standards derived from Hollywood and from Indian nationalist concerns. From the rhetoric of absence, discussions about stardom from the mid-1940s began to shift to its polar opposite, a rhetoric of excess. Now there were too many stars crowding the film firmament, and anyone, it seemed, could become a star overnight. Star publicity, similarly, employed a hyperbolic vocabulary of excess to promote an increasing number of stars.

There were complaints about the indiscriminate overuse of adjectives, such as "Magnificent," "Thundering," "Bewildering," "Soul-Stirring," "Stupendous," "Spectacular," "Million-Rupee," "Sensational," "Never-to-be-Forgotten," "Thrilling," "Chilling," "Spilling," and so on. Going by film advertisements, "not one picture is less than any or all of these put together."[1]

During World War II, illegal money flowed into the Indian film industry, and economic control shifted from studios to independent producers, who were able to lure away stars and personnel with the promise of enormous fees. The breakdown of the studio system replaced a system of salaried actors on contract with a single studio with freelancing stars who signed multiple contracts with different film producers. Beginning in the early 1940s, discussions of stardom in the popular press centered on the abuses of this so-called star system. In its specifically Indian usage, the "star system" referred not merely to the hitherto unprecedented dominance of the star over the economics of film production. More specifically, it signified the practice of stars working in multiple films simultaneously, a practice that continues up to the present.[2] For the first time, the star system did not merely affect the hero and heroine roles, but extended to other specializations as well, such as the stock roles of dancing girl, villain, and comic actor.[3] Two shifts in the meaning of stardom here should be noted: first, "star system" continues to have local meanings at odds with Hollywood notions; second, the words *hero* and *heroine* gradually begin to replace and take on the meanings formerly associated with *star*.[4] This is almost certainly because of the strongly negative connotations of "star system," so that actors and actresses would rather be "heroes" and "heroines" than "stars." The shift in the meaning of "star" and the new economic value of stardom meant that new relational terms, such as "character actor" and "extra," also emerged.[5] Durga Khote, the 1930s star who became a "character" actress, critiqued the rigid fixing of female "star" roles in an article that clarified Bombay cinema's hierarchy between "star" and "character actor." She wryly observed that "the term 'film star' seems to have a different meaning in this country. It is generally applied only to the coy, young heroines who are the heart-throbs of the nation." The female star has to play "a girl of eighteen who loves a boy of twenty-two." Any other role is considered to be a "character" role and is just as fixed in its possibilities, being usually confined to mother roles. There is no question of a film being centered on an older female character because "the older or married woman in India has no individuality. She is part of family life and, as such, there can be no episode written around her alone."[6] Nargis adds a further nuance: "I would say no, a star was not a star at that time. A star is a star today. A star was an actress then." She distinguishes acting and stardom, noting that "people don't like to be called actors and actresses. They want to be known as a famous film star. I used to love it when people said she is a great actress."[7]

In the early 1940s fan magazines frequently carried editorials bemoaning the "too frequent appearances of . . . popular star[s]," because "people don't like to be overfed, however excellent the offering."[8] The blame for this state of affairs was placed equally on producers and stars. Stars were responding to the insecurity of short-lived careers by cashing in on their current popularity. Dilip Kumar, a top male star of the 1950s, described the double bind of the star system as follows: "No matter what Tom, Dick or Harry wants you to work for him, you realize, unless you are a fool, that these opportunities won't always be coming along. A star's life is highly ephemeral and popularity fades in a night. So, you take what comes and do what you are told. . . . If you are the exception, you don't stay one for long. . . . For an artist who takes acting seriously and wants to learn it, it is a disheartening set-up."[9] Producers, likewise, were unwilling to take the economic risk of launching new stars: "Unable to find a sure formula for success and wedded to the policy of pre-selling, most producers continue to bank on stars and songs, with the result that the prices of stars and the cost of music are mounting every day."[10] The Film Inquiry Commission of 1951 put an official stamp on these negative views by characterizing Indian cinema's new organizational principles as ruled by "leading stars, exacting financiers and calculating distributors" at the "cost of the industry and the taste of the public."[11]

Excess became central to the phenomenon of stardom in Hindi cinema of the mid-1940s onward, in the specific sense of creating multiple avenues of exposure for the star body within the films themselves and in the discourse about films. On the one hand, there was a sense of the outward proliferation of star presence in all aspects of cinema production. On the other hand, there was a stringent collapsing of all risk-producing variation and difference, as the inner logic of the star system led to monopoly of all specialized roles. The typecasting of stars was only one such form of monopoly. Behind the rhetoric of excess, however, certain staples of the discourse on stardom remained in place, such as the reliance on Hollywood as a standard of excellence, the social stigma against female performance, and the industry's own ambivalence about actresses.[12] For many during the war and postwar years, the discussion of stardom was a continuation of the 1930s argument that despite the economic significance of stars, there were still too few "real" stars since it was "the same damned faces" being recycled.[13] There was a sense of inflation overtaking the "stardom racket," not only because of the soaring prices of stars, but also because of the casual overuse of the term *star* itself: "Stardom is too cheaply won in India. What sort of film industry is this where every actress who isn't an 'extra' is a star and every actor who has the camera focused on him is a star?"[14]

While the term *star* was freely conferred even on extras, only a few stars appeared in film after film. Vinayak Purohit's comments become relevant from the late 1940s onward: "Indian film stars almost never die. They suddenly emerge as heroes, stay in the principal credit lists for a very very long time, continue to make flops year after year, and then at a very advanced age, begin to fade out very very slowly by way of character roles. . . . Once a producer-director-exhibitor gang has invested sufficient money in a star image . . . the investment is milked to the last drop."[15] In effect, this resulted in both excess (of the same star's presence across multiple, simultaneously released films) and absence (of variety among stars). Commentators no longer questioned whether India had stars, since the economic evidence of the star system was compelling, with producers willing to spend up to 30 percent of the budget of a film on its stars. Instead, the new subject of discussion was the effect on Indian cinema of its excessive reliance on stars and its recycling of the same faces. Indeed, already a note of nostalgia was sounded for the golden era of the studio system, with its domestic arrangement and in-house stars.[16]

Indian independence in 1947 did not bring about the hoped-for status of "industry" to the business of filmmaking. In practical terms, this meant that none of the subsidies, incentives, and safety measures guaranteed to other industries were available to filmmakers. On the contrary, in 1949, two years after Independence, "entertainment tax for film [was] raised to 50% in the central Provinces, going up to 75% in West Bengal." Rajadhyaksha reads the expansion of Indian film production at this time as the unusual case of a culture industry successfully taking on the function of producing a national culture, but entirely without state support.[17] According to one producer, the government was itself responsible for the poor quality of Indian films, its "undue taxation" resulting in "nearly 70 percent of its gross income going towards the central, provincial, and local taxes." With the odds against financial success, "film producers [are] . . . left with no choice but to trade in the most third rate subjects."[18]

By the end of the 1940s, the change in the structural position of stars in the institution of cinema, from employee to freelancer, coincided with other changes. The new system of production that fell into place with the demise of the studio system was to have a direct impact on the structure of the Bombay film text.[19] Given the economic volatility of the film business at this time, it is no accident that the shift to a system of star monopoly coincided with the codification of what came to be called the Bombay film formula. Because the tax structure significantly reduced the possible margin of profit from a film, there was an urgent imperative to reduce all economic risks. This translated to a heavy reliance on stars and the widespread adoption of the textual strategies of box office successes. Bombay Talkies' *Kismet* (Gyan Mukherjee, 1943), the first of these major commercial successes, initiated the use of elements of the action genre within the framework of the social film, to satisfy two types of audiences: "it was this fusion that made the Bombay-mode Hindi film gain its sway over a vast, country-wide audience."[20] In terms of overall narrative structure, the musical hit *Khazanchi* (Moti Gidwani, 1941) and the films produced by S. Mukherjee at Filmistan, the studio that broke away from Bombay Talkies, are often cited as major influences in the consolidation of the Bombay film formula, which relies mainly on music and star power to appeal to an all-India market. Another successful film that spawned imitators and influenced the Bombay formula was the South Indian Tamil film *Chandralekha* (S. S. Vasan, 1948), made by Gemini Studios, whose "signature was equated with multi-starrers and megabudget spectaculars, involving songs, sword fights, massive sets and huge battle scenes."[21]

Following Marx's distinction between organic and heterogeneous systems of manufacture, Madhava Prasad describes the production system of Bombay cinema, starting in the 1950s, as a "'heterogeneous form of manufacture' in which the whole is assembled from parts produced separately by specialists, rather than being centralized around the processing of a given material, as in serial or organic manufacture." This explains why, under the system of independent producers, the story in Bombay films "occupies a place on par with . . . the rest of the components, rather than the pre-eminent position it enjoys in the Hollywood mode." While fragmentation of space, time, body, and action is inherent in cinema as a medium, the overriding principle in Hollywood cinema is to mask this fragmentation by the mechanisms of continuity editing and a tightly causal narrative, which motivates and organizes all other aspects of a film. In Bombay cinema, by contrast, "the heteronomous conditions under which the production sector operates are paralleled by a textual heteronomy whose primary symptom is the absence of an integral narrative structure," which explains the discontinuities and incoherence of Bombay film texts that have so frustrated its critics. Apart from the story itself, other heteronomous elements have included dialogue, background music, and song sequences (with their own separate elements, such as "playback" recording and "song picturization"), dance sequences, and comic segments. It is well known, for example, that songs are recorded and song sequences filmed long before a conception has been thought out for the final film text. The same can be said about dialogue segments. Bharat Bhushan, a 1950s star, describes some of the pitfalls of this system of production: "During the filming of 'Hamari Shaan,' I was required to appear on the sets along with Durga Khote and the two of us participated in a good deal of dialogue. No one told us anything about the story which is supposed to be a top-secret till the picture's release. I addressed Durga Khote as my mother and the shots were 'okay.' Only when I saw the picture at its premiere did I become aware that she was my mother-in-law!"[22] Scenarios such as the one Bhushan describes would undoubtedly produce the impression of narrative inconsistency and uneven acting, which have been common complaints against Bombay cinema, as in a 1950 article in *Sound:* "The function of dialogue, songs and music, lighting and sound effects are not properly understood and correlated and mutually complementary factors with a definite and well-proportioned relationship in the narration of the story. They . . . often occur redundantly without any special purpose or significance."[23] Such critiques, usually relying upon the structure of Hollywood films as their model, consistently ignored the specific cultural imperatives that demanded such a film form. One critic only reluctantly acknowledged such imperatives when he could not explain the box office success of *Barsaat* (Raj Kapoor, 1949) despite its failure to subordinate other elements to the story. He conceded that what matters to the audience is "ample scope for lyrical dialogue and leisurely presentation of scenes . . . provided they are punctuated with beautiful songs and intimate love scenes."[24]

In Ravi Vasudevan's discussion of the seeming incoherence in the Bombay film text, he argues that "in a sense, instead of introducing discordance or incoherence into reception, the para-narrative [his term for the heteronomous elements in the Bombay film text] inserts the film and the spectator into a larger field of coherence, one that stretches beyond the immediate experience of viewing films." This larger field of coherence is constituted by culturally understood frames of reference. The example he gives elsewhere is of a song sequence in *Awara* (Raj Kapoor, 1951), which provides commentary on the traumatic event of the hero's pregnant mother being thrown out into the rain by his father. The song provides the key to its moral interpretation by explicitly referring to the well-known *Ramayana* story of the eviction of Sita by Rama, thereby opening up this event in the self-enclosed world of *Awara* to the extra-textual resonance of a familiar mythic event.[25]

The heterogeneous practices that went into the production of the Bombay film text also included the manufacture of the "star," who would then be assembled into the final film text. While the major film releases tended to utilize known and established stars, there were also producers who went to great pains to "manufacture" their own stars before placing them in a film. In such cases, this often meant that the "star" could be regarded as an autonomous text with little or no reference to actual film texts. An example is the case of Sushila Rani, the star promoted by *filmindia.*

The rise of the star system also led to a greater emphasis on the star as genre than on genre per se, especially since the vast majority of films were now socials, "the characteristic genre of the post-independence cinema."[26] Now genre and star became very nearly identical.[27] The story was subordinated to the star text, and the star text was not merely one among several heteronomous elements that went into the final film text, but rather, along with music, the overriding one that organized and structured everything else. The vast number of amorphous social films could be classified in advertising and in the public mind as, for instance, Raj-Nargis films or Dilip Kumar films. During the studio era, studios had performed this classificatory function, so that a Bombay Talkies film was understood to be different from a New Theatres film in ways that are analogous to the understanding of genre differences.

The combination of a heteronomous mode of production and the "star system" led to two major shifts in the public construction of stars in the 1940s and 1950s. First, the change in the industry and the new position occupied by stars demanded a more stringent application of Hollywood models of star publicity, which led to the demand for more details of private life and more gossip. Although this meant a new legitimation and desire for star gossip, the primary rhetorical strategy for conveying gossip in print was still innuendo. Second, various textual strategies emerged to maximize star presence in films.

The Production of Gossip

With a new emphasis on a publicly visible process of star promotion came a hitherto unprecedented interest in gossip. The star was now not merely constituted in terms of a professional history but also existed outside the context of the filmic text to a much greater extent than in the studio era. Professional history gave way to personal, though not necessarily overtly intimate, information about stars. For the first time, too, the machinery of stardom expanded to include fan clubs, advice columns by stars, beauty tips, advertisements for cosmetic products featuring stars, and explicitly gossip-based articles.

Despite the increase in the range of articles featuring stars and their doings, the standard of reference was still Hollywood. However, writers were no longer focusing on the economic aspects of the Hollywood star system, as they had done in the previous decade. Instead, with a conscious awareness of the difference in level of information about stars in India compared to stars in Hollywood, the focus now was precisely on those aspects of stardom in Hollywood that had not been regarded as worthy of emulation in the 1930s: sexuality and privacy. These issues were presented in the garb of old arguments about the efficiency of the Hollywood machinery of stardom, with its exemplary work ethic. For example, Hyacinth's article, "Show Us More of Their Legs. Cut Out Saris and Use Swimming Costumes" in the April 1942 issue of *filmindia,* compares Hollywood and Indian stars in terms of the amount of work they do. Hollywood stars, according to her argument, have to "work" for stardom by posing in swimming costumes, which means that, unlike Indian stars, they have to keep their bodies trim. The technological metaphor is still in place here: "Hollywood turns out perfect machines called film stars who in their films display large masses of bare flesh to the public. . . . This display of feminine 'charm' is having such an effect on the Indian public that they are beginning to look for the same display of 'charm' among our Indian actresses." This final statement is factually wrong, since Hollywood films displaying stars with "feminine charms" were equally available in the 1930s. Yet they did not have a similar effect then on the type of public desire that could be expressed in film magazines, even if their effect may have been similar in oral discourse.

The shift in star discourse in the 1940s is best exemplified by *filmindia*'s explicit call, unthinkable even in the mid-1930s, for more information on private lives.[28] In the 1942 article "Give Us Publicity with Pep—Tell Us about Private Lives," the anonymous writer says, "There is too much 'hush-hush' about the private lives of our stars in India," and contrasts this to Hollywood where "many stars make news by getting married and divorced in quick succession[,] and those conservatives who don't[,] have publicity managers who are clever enough to find ways to keep them in the public eye." Again, this call for more on private lives is still being framed in terms of the argument of the superiority of the Hollywood machinery of publicity. According to this argument, even when Indian producers do try to adapt Hollywood methods of publicity, they fail because an entire *system* of stardom is not in place:

> Hollywood's Garbo is a mystery woman but her "I want to be alone" complex is sensational only because the other stars' private lives are common knowledge and her silence is unusual by contrast.
>
> Here in India they are trying to publicize Neena as a mystery woman. This won't cause a sensation because as far as the public is concerned all the stars are mystery women.

The article ends with an attempt to practice what it preaches, but old habits die hard. In presenting a piece of private information, the author indulges in the usual innuendo: "Don't repeat this, but we have a sneaking feeling that before another year has passed Naseem will be Mrs. Something-or-other."[29]

In the 1940s and 1950s, there was a simultaneous call for more private information and less slander. A 1942 *filmindia* article complained about some "dirty posters in English, Gujarati & Urdu" that were "pasted all over Bombay attacking Film-star Naseem," and attributed such scandal-mongering to a loss of respect "not only for the womanhood of India but also for our own mothers and sisters."[30] In contrast, *filmindia*'s own profile of Naseem defined her precisely as one would imagine "our mothers and sisters." She is the "model" star who perfectly balances domesticity and glamor: "We just want you to realize that Naseem is a very human glamour queen." In this context, "human," means "cooking pulav and shamikabab."[31] "Private" information about her consists of details about her appearance and taste in clothes. At this time, the burgeoning private information is aligned with consumerism. While female stars such as Naseem were constructed as exemplary consumers in magazine articles emphasizing their domestic environment and taste in decor, clothing, and jewelry, the consumerism of male stars found expression in accounts of their hobbies, like fishing and tennis.

The Production of New Faces

Among the many critiques of the star system, the one that actors, producers, and critics cited nearly unanimously was its inevitable typecasting of stars. Stereotyped roles attached to specific stars are certainly not unique to Indian popular cinema, but the practice of stars working simultaneously on a bewilderingly large number of films inherently predisposes both actor and director to repeating the same roles. Raj Kapoor, for instance, himself said that the roles he played in *Awara* (Raj Kapoor, 1951), *Shri 420* (Raj Kapoor, 1955), and *Jagte Raho* (Sombhu Mitra, 1956) were all the same.[32] The 1950s actor Dilip Kumar frequently complained about the disheartening aspects of being an actor in Bombay: "The best way I can think of to illustrate the inherent limitations of stardom is this—ask a star to play an unpleasant role, say, that of a corrupt politician or a selfish, hypocritical coward. No matter how meaty the role, he will refuse it."[33] The great fear was that any deviation from a popularly established star persona would be punished at the box office or would transform a "star" into a "character" actor.

There were innumerable complaints, even from stars themselves, about the "bad" acting the star system encouraged. Actor and director Kishore Sahu, for instance, describes the difficulty a director has in drawing "the right expression and the right kind of performance from these stars, whose acting tends to become stereotyped from the very number and kind of roles they play each year." He contrasts such acting with his experience directing a new actress, Anuradha, who was "like clay in the potter's hands" when he directed her in *Bahurani* (1940). But in the same instant that he praises her acting (and his own direction), he suggests that the real source of Anuradha's success was not acting talent but publicity: "All that this young artiste required was a big build-up and publicity, and I spared neither the money, time nor labour to give her these. As a result, before 'Bahurani' was released, Anuradha had become a top star and after its release, I was established as a director."[34] There were many other cases where similar claims of instant "stardom" were made even before an actor was seen in a film. A reader of *filmindia* questioned the validity of conferring star status so easily. He asked, "How can you give the title 'India's famous film star' to Sushila Rani, before she comes on the screen? It is like predicting the beauty of a child before its birth." The magazine's response was that "the analogy is wrong. . . . The film star is born no sooner [*sic*] a producer finds a suitable role for her and is convinced of her abilities to acquit her duties efficiently. In the case of Sushila Rani, even the blind ones voted blindly where beauty, talent and music were concerned. Subsequently screen tests revealed a dynamic screen-star."[35] This answer implies a conception of stardom as a *potential* whose realization occurs after the release of the film text. Stardom was not the product of fame but precedes fame.

Sushila Rani was the secretary of Baburao Patel, the editor of *filmindia,* who after years of criticizing the products of Indian cinema, decided to launch his own star and produce a film, *Draupadi* (Baburao Patel, 1944). His venture provides an interesting case study in the details of

Advertisement for Sushila Rani in *Draupadi* (Baburao Patel, 1944)

star manufacture at this time, even if the final product failed at the box office. For over a year in 1943–44, readers of *filmindia* were inundated with photographs of Sushila Rani, articles by and about her, full-page spreads, lavishly eulogistic features stressing her educational qualifications, advertisements for her music performances on radio, and gossip about her marriage to Baburao Patel. The perceived importance of gossip for the construction of star identity at this time is indicated in Patel's response to an interviewer's question about slanders appearing in other newspapers. He explains that, instead of annoying him, the gossip about Sushila Rani "is going the way I wanted" because "counter-propaganda is most essential to create public interest," and he even implies that he himself paid for this "expensive experiment." The interviewer then suggests, with some astonishment, that it is "possible that Baburao Patel has himself hired people for counter-propaganda to create more curiosity for his picture 'Draupadi.'"[36] Despite the overwhelming presence of stars in the general discourse on cinema at this time, the idea that stars were a carefully manufactured product was still a novelty.

Yet whether manufactured in the manner of Sushila Rani or established through numerous simultaneously released films, the star was usually an already constituted package, ready to be assembled into each new film product. This mechanistic account of the use and presence of stars is, of course, a simplification of the enormous work that went into the suppression and containment of unpredictable and contradictory elements in a star's public persona, since stars "do not only exist in media texts" but "are carried in the person of people who go on living away from their experiences in the media."[37] These unpredictable elements were worked out in different screen roles involving the star.

Intensifying Star Presence: The Double Role

While publicity was one way to keep the spotlight on stars, various textual strategies emerged to intensify the presence of stars. One of these was multi-starrers, films featuring multiple stars.[38] Others were the promotion of unseen playback singers as stars, and the use of established star-pairs in film after film.[39] But the economic and ideological interests of the star system converged in films in which the same star appeared in double or even multiple roles. Although the star system naturally resulted in actors appearing in a concentrated burst of multiple film releases, the system's inherent tendency toward such multiplication found its logical end in films in which stars played double roles. It is no exaggeration to say that double and multiple roles have always been a staple of Indian cinema and even of precinematic performance modes.[40] Narratives involving twins separated at birth, multiple generations, and more rarely, reincarnation were some of the common narrative excuses for double roles. Dual roles were common enough in the early sound era for the Hindi magazine *Rangbhoomi* to complain that "people don't like to see the same actor in two roles in the same film because . . . the two roles don't mix together well and the whole thing looks bad."[41] Articles on the history of doubling in Indian cinema, written in the 1950s, could cite different cinematic progenitors for this type of film, suggesting that there were certainly enough precedents for critics to choose from.[42]

But only with the replacement of the studio system by the star system in the 1940s did the conditions fall into place that made double roles a matter of prestige for stars and producers alike. Since the 1960s every star worth the name, including minor players, has appeared in at least one dual role. A 1977 *Filmfare* article commented that "multiple roles have become a status-symbol for footage-hogging stars."[43] In the silent era, the source of dramatic interest in many of the dual roles had been based on class difference, as in Zebunissa's double role in *Beggar Meets Beggar* (Haribhai Desai, 1930) and Master Modak's double role as prince and beggar in *Vagabond King* (Master Vithal, 1933).[44] But by the 1960s it was moral difference that underlay the logic of the double role. Moreover, dual-role films began to be distinguished along gender lines. Male stars tended to have more doubling films than female stars, reflecting their increasing importance in Hindi cinema and the relative marginalization of female stars. Both male and female double roles worked to negotiate multiple and often contradictory ideological positions in the interests of clarifying the "authentic" persona of the star. But to this end, male double roles tended to make less use of moral binaries than female doubling roles, setting up oppositions based more on reconcilable differences and having the double roles complement each other. Female doubling roles only rarely broke out of a rigid polarization of good and evil. Since Bombay cinema has largely been unable to imagine "bad" womanhood in anything but the most formulaic ways, the bad double tended to be typecast in the same way that stars are typecast. For both male and female stars, the double role became an efficient way of managing and containing the fixed star image as constructed through film texts. In the case of female stars, it also took on the task of deflecting and containing the generalized gossip that continued to surround female stardom in Indian cinema.[45]

Few scholars have discussed the popularity of doubling in Indian cinema. Richard Schechner notes a propensity towards "multiplication of impersonations" in Indian performance traditions, which he explains, rather predictably, in terms of the philosophy of reincarnation. Ashis Nandy views double roles in Hindi films as "both ideal types and representatives of a fragmented self." The fragments of the divided self are "only separately manageable," and "one of the main functions of the Bombay film is to keep them separate." More recently, Lalitha Gopalan discusses a female double role played by the star Vijayashanti in the Telegu (South Indian) film *Police Lock Up* (1992), in which the fictional doubles are given the two halves of the star's name, thereby not only indicating that she is playing both roles, but also deliberately blurring actress/role boundaries. In contrast to most doubling films, *Police Lock Up* does not use the double roles "to recuperate the family" by explaining their resemblance in terms of a narrative of lost-and-found twins. Instead, the double role enables a further set of replications, with one twin masquerading as various male figures. By not recuperating the doubles under the sign of the family, the film also "allows and encourages a staging of lesbian fantasies."[46]

According to the very first issue of the film magazine *Filmfare* in 1952, "the success of *Afsana* and *Nishan* has started a new vogue in the industry—double roles."[47] The resurgence of films with dual roles in the early 1950s, and their increased prevalence thereafter, points to their close alignment with the logic of the star system. At one level, there is obvious commercial value in offering viewers a double dose of a popular actor's presence in the film, and economic sense in getting more of the actor for the same fee. But doubling also functioned to turn into an aesthetic advantage the constraints of the fixed star persona produced by the star system. The most visible function of the double role, in the public mind, was to exhibit the actor's versatility: "The stars treat their double roles as a practical test in measuring histrionic talent. Like our double graduates, they might soon start carrying impressive degrees after their names. How about Rajesh Khanna, D. R. (Hon.)—Double Role Honours?"[48] The spectacular and performative pleasures offered by the double exposure of the star body allowed a showcasing of the star's ability to incarnate different identities, while providing an arena for the clarification of the star's "authentic" persona.

Generally speaking, double roles solicit mechanisms of both identification and disavowal. Once the role that incarnates the "authentic" persona of the star is recognized, it becomes the primary point of narrative identification. The double role then serves to safeguard it from contamination by diverting disturbing subtexts in the star persona. Yet, even though multiple roles thus frequently function to authenticate the "true" persona of the actor, the actual operations of identification and disavowal are often more complicated than the binary logic of the double role might suggest.

Films with double roles exhibit a high degree of awareness of their potential for histrionic display and, hence, entertainment value. James Naremore notes that "any film becomes a good showcase for professional acting skills if it provides moments when the characters are clearly shown to be wearing masks—in other words, exhibiting high degrees of expressive incoherence." Beyond a straightforward display of two radically different characters played by the same actor, doubling films often also deliberately complicate the narrative by having the two characters switch identities. Such an exchange of identities is, of course, logically written into the very concept of the double role and is an opportunity for "metaperformance," or "acting persons who are acting." With the characters switched and only the viewer aware of the switch, doubling films offer many occasions for displaying expressive incoherence.[49]

Afsana (B. R. Chopra, 1951), one of the two films that supposedly started the vogue in doubling films in the 1950s, was the story of twin brothers, one evil, the other good, who are separated in childhood during a storm. The film only briefly plays with the idea of Ashok Kumar, the star, in a negative role by killing the bad twin relatively early in the film after he has unscrupulously effected an exchange of identities with his good twin. Even though Ashok Kumar had achieved spectacular success in an earlier negative role in *Kismet* (Gyan Mukherjee, 1943), *Afsana* chose not to risk pushing the criminal image of Ashok Kumar too far.[50] Instead, it chose the safer route of using the switched identities to have it both ways. As the surviving good twin whose identity has been exchanged with the bad twin, Ashok Kumar was able to play the part of a morally suspect character while keeping his "good" star persona intact. By means of the metaperformance required here, of having Ashok Kumar play a good character playing a bad character, the star's identity was twice removed from that of the evil twin, allowing a safe space for histrionic display.[51] But such was the prestige of multiple roles that even though this was a straightforward double role, Ashok Kumar claimed that he played "four contrasting roles" in *Afsana*, using the switch between the twins as an excuse for doubling his double role in the film.[52]

Melodrama, Stardom, and Doubling

Christine Gledhill's essay "Signs of Melodrama" is extremely suggestive for an analysis of the dynamics of stardom in the double role in Bombay films. She argues that the star text and the melodramatic text share similar characteristics because "stars function as signs in a rhetorical system which works as melodrama," conceived not as genre, but as "a mode which embraces a range of Hollywood genres." The conceptual links between melodrama and stardom include an exteriorized and hyperbolic concept of the "person," one that is dependent on spectacle and excess, and the translation of social issues into private, emotional ones. Both melodrama and stardom are invested in meaning displayed as iconic presence whose moral significance is immediately legible. Thus emotion, morality, and identity are understood in iconic, external terms, rather than as interiority: "Internalization of the social is accompanied by a process of exteriorisation in which emotional states or moral conditions are expressed as the actions of melodramatic types. . . . This double movement of internalisation and exteriorisation explains the paradoxical conjunction in melodramatic character of the emblematic and the personal, of the public and the private." It also explains the reliance on codified gesture and more generally speaking, on visual surface, whether of mise-en-scène or of the actor's physical appearance and performance.[53]

In the case of Indian cinema, melodrama is a particularly apt framework of analysis, especially in films of the late 1940s and 1950s, for both historical and textual reasons. Historically speaking, it is easy enough to trace a link between Indian cinema and Victorian English melodrama through the Parsi theater and other Indian urban theater traditions of the nineteenth and early twentieth centuries. Similarly, one can also point to references and borrowings in Bombay films from the Hollywood family melodrama of the 1950s.[54] From a traditionalist point of view, one could argue that melodrama works in ways that are similar to Indian theories of performance subsumed under the category of *rasa*. Both melodrama and the aesthetics of *rasa* place an emphasis on the stylized display of emotion, the use of characters as emotional or moral types, and a theory of performance based on codified gesture. However, the richly eclectic and hybridized nature of the Bombay film text problematizes any such project of distinguishing specific sources of influence from the West and from more "traditional" sources. Ravi Vasudevan, who has written extensively about the melodramatic configurations of the Bombay social genre of the 1950s, cautions against such attempts at "defining cultural specificity" because "when there is this kind of interaction in a colonial and post-colonial context, the positing of essences is always suspect and likely to produce orientalising results."[55]

In terms of narrative content, cinematic style, and conceptualization of characters, the melodramatic mode, broadly defined as Gledhill does, is conspicuously present in Bombay social films of the late 1940s and 1950s in the form of nonpsychological characters, a Manichean moral order, and emotional excess concentrated in song sequences, often with overtly stylized or symbolic picturization. The primary rhetorical strategies are hyperbole, coincidence, and carefully contrived narrative symmetries. Melodrama is also the primary mode of articulating anxieties regarding the modern social order, related implicitly to the formation of the new Indian state after Independence in 1947. The issue of translating old systems of morality into the uniformity of modern law recurs obsessively in social films of the 1950s. Not surprisingly, lawyers and court cases are ubiquitous in these films and often represent a benign intervention between the older moral order, usually based on affiliations of family and lineage, and the authority of the new state. Questions of gender, national, and class identity are invariably worked out in the space of the family and sometimes expressed through generational conflict. Coincidence plays an important role here by "relaying the significance of the social level to the audience. For coincidence insistently anchors figures who have a definite social function to relationships of an intimate and often familial, generational order."[56]

The paradoxical nature of the melodramatic character that Gledhill delineates, its dual expression of the "emblematic and the personal," parallels certain shared features of stardom and the cinematic apparatus itself. The fascination inherent in the cinematic apparatus, the "photo effect," as

John Ellis calls it, results from the simultaneous presence and absence of the filmed object. The star's allure is based on a similar paradox of being at once ordinary and extraordinary, intimately available and unapproachable. The source of star fascination matches the tension in melodrama between desire for plenitude of meaning and the actual inadequacies of language. A desire always deferred is therefore crucial to the pleasures of all three—the cinematic apparatus, stardom, and melodrama.[57]

John Orr's discussion of the double in Western cinema addresses a similar deferral of desire at the heart of doubling. He notes that the tradition of doubling in, for instance, the works of Hoffmann and Dostoyevski participates in the self-Other dichotomy of romantic writings where "the Other had been the ineffable of the romantic consciousness, the phantom which cannot finally be accommodated in the romantic utopia of an organic and pantheistic world." Like the workings of melodramatic excess, the Other speaks to the desire for meaning beyond the confines of the bourgeois, capitalist, and rationalist order of experience. Orr sees an analogy here with film as a medium, behind whose illusion of organic wholeness is the reality that "screen images are tantalizingly other, apart." In his view, the ultimate inaccessibility of the screen image (and, I would add, of stars and of plenitude of meaning) is an echo of "the romantic imaging of an alienated Other, a shadowing phantom." In Bombay social melodramas, in the attempt to grasp at and establish the "truth" of the actual "being" of the star, he or she was placed in double or even multiple incarnations on the screen, producing an excess of identity.[58]

Christine Gledhill's formulation of stardom as a type of melodramatic text is meant to illuminate the operations of stardom in general. But what are its implications for the functioning of star texts appearing in films that are themselves melodramas and whose narrative logic demands the multiple display of the star? In Indian cinema, the need for stars to maintain the same persona in all vehicles is tied to their function as the narrative point of entry into the film. The typecasting of stars as a form of genre identification is also closely related to the melodramatic mode's reliance on types. Recognition plays a crucial role here, with star familiarity and the moral legibility of a scenario feeding off one another. In terms of both the melodramatic needs of the narrative and the demands of stardom itself, Bombay cinema emphasizes visual excess and meaning displayed as external signs. But in films using double roles, the simultaneous articulation of stardom and melodrama produces a further intensification of meaning. When star texts and melodramatic texts come together, the effect is of a compression or shortcut in meaning. A good example of this, which I discuss in chapter 6, is when a female star plays a courtesan. Both star text and melodramatic character type here have extra-textual associations that converge in the film.

The Aesthetics of Frontality

One way of understanding the interrelated articulations of melodrama and stardom in films with double roles is through the aesthetics of frontality, which has been posed as a useful theoretical framework in recent scholarship on Indian cinema. Geeta Kapur's outline of the "formal category of frontality variously manifest in Indian popular arts" is worth quoting in full:

> Frontality of the word, the image, the design, the performative act, in several systems of address . . . means, for example, flat, diagrammatic and simply contoured figures (as in Kalighat *pat* paintings). It means a figure-ground design with notational perspective (as in the Nathdwara pictures, and the photographs which they often utilize). It means, in dramatic terms, the repetition of motifs within ritual "play," as in the *lila*; it means a space deliberately evacuated to foreground actor-image-performance, as in the *tamasha*. Frontality is also established in an adaptation of traditional acting conventions to the proscenium stage, as when stylized audience address is mounted on an elaborate *mise-en-scène*, as in Parsi theatre.

In her analysis of the 1936 devotional film *Sant Tukaram,* Kapur translates the visual dynamics of frontality into cinematic terms by focusing on instances in the film of "iconic framing" or "an image into which symbolic meanings converge and in which moreover they achieve stasis." But her reading tends to overlook the specificities of the cinematic medium—in particular, its privileging of movement. But using the conceptual framework of frontality in the sense of a "residual direct address built into the popular Indian cinema," others have offered readings of visual perception, the organization of the image, framing of the action, and narrative flow in Indian films from the silent era to the 1950s.[59]

Ravi Vasudevan distinguishes the notion of the tableau from iconic framings to discuss narrative flow and potentially also to include movement, rather than stasis. Although "both the iconic and tableau modes are often presented frontally, at a 180–degree plane to the camera and seem to verge on stasis, enclosing meaning within their frame," the tableau's "visual logic suggests an image in transit, caught between two moments." One of Vasudevan's many examples of iconic framing is in the figure of the father, Judge Raghunath, in the Raj Kapoor film *Awara* (1951). The film constructs this character as an icon, "a figure in whom meaning has come to be fixed," by placing it in relation to a range of contexts—from the extra-textual mythic references of a song sequence to the figure of his double, the villain Jagga. It is important to note here that the meaning reposing within the iconic frame usually comes from outside the frame. Here I am interested in extending the notion of frontality beyond the textual operations of "staging and narrating story events" to other arenas of meaning production in the cinema. Prasad, for example, also asserts the need to understand frontality "in the light of the individual subject's position within different political orders and the corresponding constraints and protocols of spectatorship."[60]

In my reading, we can see that in Indian cinema until at least the 1960s, stardom itself functioned through a predominantly frontal mode of address. By this, I do not mean that stars used a frontal manner of acting—namely, an overtly expressive and "presentational" performance style directed at the spectator. The opposite held true, and many of the stars who emerged in the late 1940s were lauded for their "restrained" and "natural" style of acting.[61] The aesthetics of frontality is inscribed into Indian modes of stardom. First, there is the collapsing of the metaphoric foreground and background, the surface and depth, of star identities, which is produced by a reduction in the gap between on-screen and off-screen information about them. In the studio era, this took the form of an emphasis on a star's professional identity at the cost of private, "inner" information. In the 1940s, even when there was a stated desire for private information in keeping with modes of star publicity derived from Hollywood, there was still a reluctance to constitute star personae in terms of an opposition between private and professional identity. Instead, the gossip that did circulate about stars tended to find visual and emotional *confirmation* in screen roles. The resulting tendency to conflate role and "real" identities produced stars who appeared as the equivalent of "flat" characters in fiction.

The second way in which stardom uses a frontal mode of address has to do with its connection to melodrama and its presentation through mechanisms equivalent to "iconic framing," which places and defines the star in scenarios of relatively fixed meaning. Again, this has not so much to do with acting styles per se as with the moral and symbolic meanings that accrue to the external details of a star's persona. The propensity toward types in both melodramatic narrative and star texts points to an emphasis on the external surface of meaning, on "visual rather than verbal effects." A star's persona is constructed in large part through the external display of legible and recurrent signs, such as specific bodily gestures, which then become associated with that star.[62] Sometimes, gestures are deliberately introduced to function as a kind of product identification. T. J. S. George describes the annoying trademark gesture of biting her fingers that Nargis's director, Mehboob, insisted on for the film *Andaz.* Melodramatic narrative patterns become similarly legible through morally familiar character types and exteriorized emotion and gesture.[63]

Star personae in India are constructed rather like melodramatic character types partly because of their repeated association with certain roles and, in the case of female stars, because of the severely limited options for roles—either as romantic heroine or as wife and mother. We see an instance of such a conflation of character type and star personae as early as 1932 in an article in the *Bombay Chronicle,* in which the author complains about the "imitative habits" of Indian filmmakers and their practice of modeling stars after Hollywood prototypes like Douglas Fairbanks and Jackie Coogan. Since "third-rate originality is better than first-rate imitation," he recommends making use of "the vast field in [presumably Indian] social life" to construct more authentic star identities. But in listing some potential identifying traits for Indian stars, he slips into a discussion of character types in film narratives. His examples of "the typical unemployed graduate, the typical college girl . . . the typical villager and so on" point to a complete identification between star persona and character type.[64]

The convergence of star and melodramatic personalities is to be found in the negative iconicity of the notion of the female star, concentrated in visual signifiers such as cigarettes, hair length, and clothing styles. The iconic representation of "bad" womanhood feeds into star reception as well as melodramatic narrative scenarios. The "star text" of female stardom haunts star profiles. Through negative identification of individual stars with this generalized image of the star, the discourse is maintained without implicating any specific person. For instance, we find a list of some of these assumptions in *filmindia*'s description of the things that the star Naseem *does not do:* she "has no vices. She does not drink and only smokes when it is necessary for her to do so for a film role."[65] Personal details about stars work in similarly iconic ways, drawing upon depersonalized norms of domestic ideology and consumerism, and represented through recurrent visual types, such as the star in the kitchen, the star reading a book (to counter the idea of the uneducated actress), or the star displaying her choice of home decor.

I am suggesting that the fictional world constructed by the individual film text functions like a palimpsest on which are multiple traces of metanarratives other than the primary one of the immediate film itself. In any popular cinema based on the attraction of familiar stars, the separate demands of the narrative and of stardom exist in a relationship of tension. Although the heterogeneous nature of Bombay cinema required formulaic or familiar narrative patterns, the force of the filmic narrative was still toward the illusion of a complete and self-enclosed world of unique characters and events. Certainly, the production of this illusion was never the primary motivating force behind the organization of the film as a whole, as it was in Hollywood cinema. Nonetheless, its emotional effects depended on such an illusion of self-containment. But the star text strains against the closure of a self-enclosed diegesis, its mechanisms of extra-textual recognition and memory forcing open the text and working against the production of unique characters.

Like stardom, melodrama also invokes familiar events and character types inhabiting an extra-textual universe constructed out of other narratives and culturally understood norms, all of which extend well beyond the confines of any particular diegesis. Thus, while the narrative of a film text tends toward the unique, the narrative of a star or melodramatic text tends toward the iconic, in the form of familiar and relatively fixed character types and scenarios. In Bombay films, with star identities conceived of as melodramatic scenarios, there was often an overlap between the extra-textual reference systems constituted by melodrama and by the star text. For instance, the melodramatic trope of the bad woman, usually figured in Bombay film in terms of displayed sexuality either as a courtesan or as a Westernized bar girl, coincided with the generalized star text shared by all female stars. The construction of male stars tended to adhere to certain melodramatic tropes as well. Some, like K. L. Saigal, fell into the *Devdas* (P. C. Barua, 1935) type, meaning the sensitive, passionate, alcoholic, self-destructive, artistic type who ends up forgotten, wasted, dead. Another example is to be found in a profile of the actor Premnath, which uses the lyrics from one of his song sequences to describe him as "an aimless wanderer treading his lonely way on the road of life." What is the relation between these iconic tropes of stardom and conceptions of self in the construction of individual star identities?

Authenticity and the Externalization of Star Identity

Public constructions of star identity in Bombay cinema often involved a double or contradictory conceptualization of acting. Critics writing for newspapers and magazines, for the most part, relied on an implicit notion of good acting as "an outgrowth of an essential self" or "little more than fictional extensions of the actor's true personality."[66] When evaluating film actors on the basis of such implied standards of "natural" acting, there was a desire to conflate on-screen and off-screen identities of stars. Yet almost in spite of themselves, many of the same critics would also invoke popularized, everyday notions of performance drawn from Indian traditions. In this view, the actor is a vessel (*patra*) containing the role but separate from it and transmitting it through highly codified and culturally understood gestures, which are the external manifestation of emotions. The actor not only is the vessel for the role, but also dissolves his or her identity in it. This is especially pertinent in mythological or religious roles, in which actors are understood to dissolve their "self/ego" into the role. Both these views conflate actor and role, but in opposite ways. In naturalist conceptions of acting, the star's personal life and our curiosity about it are displaced to the screen. With the star as *patra*, the role predominates and, in the case of religious or biographical roles, erases the actor's subjectivity. Both these seemingly opposing views of acting—one privileging the actor's "being," the other producing the role through external performance and costuming signs separable from the actor's "being"—feed in different ways into the aesthetics of frontality. The metaphoric background and foreground of identity are collapsed, both when the role is seen as a stand-in for inner identity and when it is understood to be constituted by external signs of costuming, gesture, and expression.

Ideas about star identity in the public mind are closely tied to issues of authenticity. Richard Dyer's brilliant outline of the mechanism by which star charisma works in Hollywood cinema shows a dialectic process of authentication by which the existing star image is countered to reveal the "true" star persona, thus producing a new authenticated image, only to have that new image countered by another "exposé." This process of authentication depends on a sense of revelation of secret and privileged knowledge about what the star is actually like. In Dyer's argument, this effect of an ongoing and infinitely receding "authenticating authenticity" is what gives a star charisma.[67]

At the heart of this account of star charisma is a concept of the self based upon surface and depth; in other words, on the difference between on- and off-screen identities. There is always the "true," usually private, identity behind the surface identity presented by a star: "The basic paradigm is just this—that what is behind or below the surface is unquestionably, and virtually by definition, the truth. Thus features of stars which tell us that the star is *not* like he or she appears to be on screen serve to reinforce the authenticity of the star image as a whole."[68]

In studio-era cinema in India, however, stars were rarely authenticated through private revelations. In the 1950s authenticity was achieved through confirmation of the star persona in film roles, rather than through the dialectic of a series of exposés designed to reveal the "truth" behind a star. In the late 1940s, even with the greater public desire for and legitimation of gossip, the movement of authentication was not from the surface of the screen to the reality behind it or off-screen, but in the opposite direction. Private information that circulated as oral gossip was at this time often acknowledged, fixed, and contained in the screen roles that replicated the gossip, with a resulting tendency to conflate star persona and film role. A striking example is the love affair of Raj Kapoor and Nargis in the late 1940s, where their on-screen identity functioned to overwrite, legitimize, and contain all extra-filmic information about them.

One of Bombay cinema's basic authenticating devices for reducing the gap between on- and off-screen identities was its use of the star's name as the character's name, thereby collapsing the distinction between the two.[69] Examples abound. Raj Kapoor's character name was invariably Raj, and Leela Chitnis, who played his mother in *Awara,* was named Leela in the diegesis.[70] In *Afsana,* the film that supposedly started the vogue for double roles in the early 1950s, the use of the double role to morally anchor the star's persona was so blatant that the good twin, the judge, was given the star's name, Ashok Kumar. A more recent variant of this practice is to give the same name to every character played by a star, such as the name Vijay for all the characters played in a series of 1970s and 1980s films by the superstar Amitabh Bachchan. More recently, of course, Shahrukh Khan has played in several films in which his different characters were all named Rahul. The practice of star and role sharing the same name also exists in the regional Indian cinemas. For instance, the Telegu-language film *Police Lock Up* (1992), which placed the star Vijayashanti in the double role of Vijaya and Shanti, made similar use of the two parts of her name. Such a widespread naming practice suggests not an imaginatively lazy way of constructing characters, but a system that works actively to integrate star and role in the public mind. The typecasting inherent in the Indian star system thus goes to its logical end of fixing even the name of the character.[71]

Even in the case of stars whose names were not used as character names, we see their identity conceived in terms of their screen names, which functioned as a frontal signifier of all the other "interior" traits of identity. Star names were, in any case, almost always a fiction and were usually chosen in the interests of corraling star identities into a homogeneous Hindu fold. Anglo-Indian stars of the silent era were given "wholesome" Hindu screen names like Sabita Devi (Irene Gasper) and Sita Devi (Renee Smith). A similar renaming took place with major Muslim stars, especially in the 1940s and 1950s when Hindu-Muslim relations were strained and Bombay's culture industry projected increasingly hegemonic Hindu identities as the unspoken norm of "Indianness." The exceptions tended to be lesser actors or stars whose roles identified them in specifically Islamicate roles. While the famous star Dilip Kumar could not remain Yusuf Khan, his less well-known brother, Nasir Khan, who was also a film actor, could keep his own name. Another interesting exception is Nargis, whose screen name was a fiction, but a Muslim name nonetheless, most likely because she started her acting career in roles that presented "an updated version of a stereotype from Islamic literature and music."[72]

The naming of Indian stars solicited different levels of knowledge about the star. Despite the frequent and routine renaming of major stars, their real names and identities were usually no secret and were reported with no sense of unexpected disclosure. Ravi Vasudevan comments on such name changes: "The transaction involved seems to have been purely symbolic. Evidence from film periodicals suggests that the true identity of such actors was mostly well known, and yet an abnegation of identity was undertaken in the development of the star personality. It is as if the screen, constituting an imaginary nation space, required the fulfillment of certain criteria before the actor/actress could acquire symbolic eligibility."[73] Arguably, the audience has the capacity to accommodate multiple contradictory identities within one star so long as the on-screen "front" is maintained. The movement of disclosure of "true" identity is from off-screen to on-screen identity, to the point that it literally takes over the star's personal identity. Although all references in the off-screen circulation of information are to "Yusuf Bhai," Yusuf Khan is now, for all intents and purposes, Dilip Kumar, and it was under that name that he became the sheriff of Bombay in 1979. Similarly, Nargis retained this screen name even after she retired from the cinema in 1958, and it was as "Mrs. Nargis Dutt" that she was nominated to the Rajya Sabha, the upper house of Parliament, in 1980.

The frontal address of Indian stardom involved the constant negotiation of identities on the surface of the screen. If the star's authentic persona was constituted through a conflation of on- and off-screen identities, a further conflation took place in films with double roles, the unfamiliar role functioning as a kind of on-screen exposé and producing a new, composite screen image of the star. Thus, with the double role, the clarification of *difference* between what the star was and was not took place not outside the screen but on it. Doubling took on the task of authenticating the star.

The drive toward monopoly inherent in the star system led to unique forms of intensification of star presence in Bombay films, involving not only the repetition of the same star across numerous texts, but also the multiple layering of star texts in the same film. In the following chapters, I discuss two such instances of layering: the double role in *Anhonee,* which layers the same star, Nargis, while authenticating her star identity; and the voice double, where the star text of the unseen playback singer, Lata Mangeshkar, is written over and authenticates the star text of the actor. In both instances of doubling, the composite star image that is worked out on screen is the product of a convergence of star identity and melodramatic character type and results in the "iconic framing" of female stardom—that is, "an organization of the image in which stable meaning is achieved."[74] Such meanings may be imported into the film text from a fluid body of extra-textual norms, values, and information, but they achieve iconic fixity only on the screen. Such negotiations of stardom show a continued investment in deflecting and managing private lives. The raw material for star analysis, the extra-textual gossip and biographical information, is channeled back to the surface of the screen.

6. *Nargis and the Double Space of Female Desire in* Anhonee

> The double's ubiquitous shadow usually signifies rebellion by the bourgeois hero[ine] against [her] . . . middle-class role and its forms of sexual constraint.
>
> —John Orr, *Cinema and Modernity,* 41

> The [Indian] social film of the 1950s . . . tends to split the woman in terms of the figuration of her desire. Legitimate figures are held close to the patriarchal hearth . . . and a more overt sexuality is displaced to another figure.
>
> —Vasudevan, "Shifting Codes, Dissolving Identities: The Hindi Social Film of the 1950s as Popular Culture," 74

Nargis was a major star for roughly a decade from 1948 to 1958, when she retired at the peak of her career at the age of twenty-nine.[1] But the public narrative of Nargis did not end with her retirement. The post-1958 Nargis star persona was one of the earliest to exemplify the paradoxical relationship between star persona and film text that is in place even today in commercial Hindi cinema. While the star persona is established, confirmed, and authenticated by specific screen roles, once that persona has been fixed in the public mind, it becomes freed of the need to be anchored in specific film texts. Stars then become public personae with little or no reference to cinema as an institution. In this way, a "star" with only one successful film can remain in the public eye for years, even without any subsequent roles. With her starring role in *Mother India* (Mehboob, 1957) and her retirement, Nargis's public persona underwent a radical and permanent shift from romantic heroine to monumentally suffering and sacrificing mother. Through her subsequent "career" as wife, mother, and member of Parliament, the interpretive framework of her publicly constructed life remained *Mother India.* Thus she was, at one and the same time, a current film star and a retired film star until her nationally mourned death in 1981.[2]

Nargis occupies pride of place in most general accounts of star dynamics in India, even though her screen career and life were both relatively short. The Nargis star text also stands out in the sparse scholarship on Indian stars, for having been the subject of several studies.[3] All the scholarly accounts of Nargis focus on the overwhelming public desire for continuity between her film role as "elemental, passionate, universal woman" in *Mother India* and her public persona after this film. Rosie Thomas teases out different strands, both written and oral, in the interlocked discourses of "female chastity, modern nationalism, and . . . morality" surrounding the film *Mother India* at the time of its release in 1958. Like Thomas, Parama Roy considers Nargis's identification with the starring role in *Mother India* (1957), but her account is "as much about Nargis dead as it is about Nargis alive," in part because of the inherently interesting crossovers between on- and off-screen events in Nargis's life. Roy examines the mechanisms of repression and emphasis by which this single role "fixes and monumentalizes a notoriously unstable star text" so that it "*literalizes* the figure of the nation to such a degree that acting itself becomes impossible after the making of a film." Roy's account pays close attention to the public construction of Nargis's Muslim identity after her retirement and the persistent analogy between her "real" relation to her son, the current star Sanjay Dutt, and her fictional relation to her son in *Mother India,* made all the more complicated because Sunil Dutt, the actor who played her son, became her husband shortly after the film was completed.[4]

In this chapter, I am interested in an earlier moment in Nargis's star persona, precisely when hers was a "notoriously unstable star text." The earlier phase of her stardom, when she played romantic young women, is still the primary mode of direct encounter with her image, because of the enduring popularity of the films she made with actor and director Raj Kapoor. Yet her public image now is completely overshadowed by her role in *Mother India* and her subsequent public identity as mother and political figure. The earlier Nargis was just as monumental and fixed a star persona as the later Mother India persona was to be. Because of her retirement after *Mother India,* Nargis was able to cross over from the "star" role of romantic heroine to the "character" role of long-suffering mother, without diminishing her star status.[5]

Nargis and Raj Kapoor in their iconic embrace in *Barsaat* (Raj Kapoor, 1949).

The logo of Raj Kapoor's RK Studios.

Nargis's pre–*Mother India* star persona was dominated by her romantic involvement with Raj Kapoor, her married costar in about seventeen films made between 1948 and 1956. Their 1949 film *Barsaat* (*Rain*) literally fixed the Raj-Nargis romance into an icon when Raj Kapoor used "an instinctive pose of intimacy they struck in a regular sequence in *Barsaat*" as the famous logo of his studio, RK Films. The open celebration and public acknowledgment of this relationship is indicative of some of the changes in conceptualizing scandal, gossip, and the private that took place in the late 1940s. Nargis's rise to stardom coincided with the public identification of her screen image, specifically as Raj Kapoor's lover, with her "private" identity. Elements of the Raj-Nargis romance that have become fixed and emblematic include the endlessly recounted story of her first meeting with Raj when he came to her house to ask her to act in his first film, *Aag* (*Fire*, 1948). The story, as told with only slight variations by both Nargis and Raj Kapoor (among many others), romanticizes the meeting by appearing to deglamorize it with the markers of domesticity. Nargis, caught unawares in the kitchen by Raj's unexpected visit to her house, appears before him with flour-stained hands, "shabby and hot from the fireplace."[6] Most famously, this event was repeated in Raj Kapoor's film *Bobby*, made twenty-five years later in 1973, with the romance still kept "in the family," as the hero was played by Raj Kapoor's son, Rishi Kapoor.[7] This mythologized first meeting between the lovers encapsulates some of the contradictory desires in this relationship. Nargis's keen desire for marriage and domesticity, fulfilled on screen but denied in reality, coexists with the public perception of the Raj-Nargis pair as the exemplary first couple representing India abroad during official trips to Hollywood (1952) and the Soviet Union (1954).

Reconstituting the Private on Screen

From the late 1940s to the mid-1950s, roughly during the period when Nargis worked for RK Studios and was involved with Raj Kapoor, she played virtually the same role across several films. As described by another star, Jairaj, this was "the now so thoroughly typed frivolous-pretty-society-college-girl role."[8] Film actor Ashok Kumar said of Nargis that "she did not look like a heroine" and that "she lacked glamour." Nonetheless, "when she was with Raj Kapoor she was absolutely inspired. Their love was legendary and that love lit up the screen."[9] While personal information regarding Nargis's tastes and consumerist preferences was spun out in magazine articles and photographs, more private details, having to do with romance and sexuality, were constituted through screen roles.[10] All the written accounts about the relationship with Raj Kapoor suggested more than they actually said, with the tacit understanding that details constituting the "inner" life of this relationship were to be found in oral gossip or on-screen. Gossip circulated knowledge about her relationship with Raj Kapoor, but the screen version of the romance gave the most visible, public face to their private, off-screen relationship, and this image predominated in the overall star persona of Nargis. More importantly, her potentially scandalous star persona was accommodated through its complete incorporation into her screen identity, with all anxieties pertaining to the legitimacy of this relationship expressed and worked out in the screen romance.[11] The paradox of Nargis's star persona at this phase was its comfortable embodiment of a range of potentially conflicting anxieties surrounding female stardom in the 1930s.

James Naremore asks, "Given the affinity between theater and the world . . . how do we determine the . . . difference between performers in everyday life and performers who are behaving theatrically?" The specific desire of stardom is to see this distinction erased as a way of grappling with the tantalizing combination of familiarity and inaccessibility that marks the experience of star power. In the non–love scenes of *Barsaat,* there was a comfortable separation between fiction and reality. But in the love scenes, the rival forces of film and star narratives were completely reconciled: "all the world could see that Nargis and Raj Kapoor were not just play-acting before the cameras. The romance they projected on the screen became so convincingly evocative because it reflected their real-life emotions." The close identification between the visible on-screen love scenes and the imagined off-screen relationship between them matches the forms of authentication involving star names that I discussed in chapter 5. T. J. S. George says that "the couple was so evidently in love with each other, so mutually complementary and so obviously enjoying themselves that they personified the adage about all the world loving a lover." Naremore's childhood question about whether actors on screen are really kissing is especially relevant to the reception of *Barsaat* and subsequent Raj-Nargis vehicles. His response—that "actors both do and pretend, sometimes at one and the same moment—hence the potentially scandalous nature of their work"—is useful in explaining why the on-screen romance elicited a suspension of moral commentary that overflowed into the off-screen romance. Arguably, the assumption that Nargis and Raj were *not* pretending rendered Nargis's performance less scandalous than the notion of a female star pretending to kiss a stranger on screen.[12]

Although the screen version of the romance worked to morally overwrite the "real" relationship, there was an uneasy coexistence of legitimacy and transgression in Nargis's star persona. She fulfilled the ideal requirement of being educated but was not, strictly speaking, from a "respectable" family. Her parents were the Muslim Jaddanbai, a former courtesan-singer who became a film actress and producer, and Mohan Babu, an upper-class Hindu. As Raj's screen lover, Nargis enjoyed a legitimate relationship with him. She played an upper-class, "modern" woman whose relationship with Raj ended in marriage and conferred wealth and status on him. In the process, she usually subsumed her modern identity under a "timeless" conception of (Hindu) womanhood, encompassing domestic virtue and sexual purity. While the legitimacy of the screen romance generated public enthusiasm for it, in her off-screen romance with Raj she was the "other" woman to Raj's wife, Krishna. The relationship had no goal in marriage, which caused Nargis great distress, and it conferred no extra status on Raj, who already belonged to the equivalent of Indian cinema's royal family.[13]

However, only after his association with Nargis, and her low-paid work in the films produced by his RK Studios, did Raj Kapoor become established as a major player in Indian cinema. His own attitude, decades after the breakup of the relationship, neatly summed up the ideology of female stardom dominant in Indian cinema since its inception. He insisted—more out of betrayed ego than anything else, according to all accounts—that "his wife was not his actress and his actress was not his wife" and that "one woman was the heroine of his films while the other was the mother of his children."[14]

In its external, visual manifestation, Nargis's star persona carried certain iconic and hyperbolic markers that served as reminders of the relationship. The most frequently noted emblem of this was her transformed taste in clothes. While Raj Kapoor's family connections with the cinema conferred an aura on him, Nargis's similar connections via her mother had the opposite effect. In descriptions of Raj's influence on her choice of clothing, we see the literal whitewashing from Nargis's persona of the negative associations of a cinematic career. After her relationship with him, she came to be known as "the woman in white" because she wore only white saris, and the "poise, dignity and sophistication" associated with this image were attributed to Raj Kapoor's own sophisticated tastes. A "close friend of Nargis'" describes the transformation as follows: "It was Raj who really groomed her and gave her that image. . . . I remember we used to see her at the Bombay Race Course with her mother after she had worked in *Taqdeer* and we remember her as dressing in 'filmi' fashion, you know, loud and common. It was only when she came close to Raj that the remarkable transformation began."[15] The oppositions here—Raj (son of the famous star Prithviraj Kapoor) and good taste on one side, and Nargis's mother (the former courtesan and film actress) and "loud and common" taste, on the other—rehearse for us the contradictory ways in which male and female stars were viewed.

These oppositions and their attendant disavowal of associations with the cinema reappear in *Anhonee* (*Impossible,* K. A. Abbas, 1952), one of two films in which Nargis played a double role. In Indian cinema, star personae become fixed, but they need constant repairs in screen role after screen role. The double role, I would argue, does a more efficient repair job than any single screen role. Using the melodramatic scenarios of the Bombay social film, the double role in *Anhonee* enabled the star text of Nargis to enact the pleasures of moral transgression, while working to separate the "authentic" Nargis persona from false versions. Further, the double role allowed Nargis to explore the visual and entertainment potential of a "bad" character without her persona being contaminated by its moral status.[16]

In *Anhonee,* Nargis plays the double role of Roop, the "beautiful, educated, but somewhat snobbish daughter" of a rich businessman, Thakur Harnam Singh, and Mohini, a dancing-girl, who turns out to be Roop's illegitimate half-sister.[17] Raj Saxena (played by Raj Kapoor), a struggling lawyer, comes to confront Roop's father, his landlord, about his extortionist rent. Instead, he meets Roop, with whom he eventually falls in love, with the father's approval. But before they can be married, Mohini comes to Raj's office one day to engage his services against her landlord. When Raj describes, in casual conversation, Mohini's surprising resemblance to Roop and mentions that she has recently arrived from Calcutta, Roop's father dies of a heart attack. His death and other clues transparently suggest a yet-to-be-revealed connection between the Thakur and Mohini.

The narrative's main interest from this point on is the unfolding of Mohini's character and her growing obsession with Raj. Two major revelations, both of which emerge after the Thakur's death, propel the characters' motivations and desires. The first, which is revealed when Mohini recognizes his picture in an obituary, is that Mohini is the Thakur's illegitimate daughter by a courtesan in Calcutta. This revelation leads Mohini to insist upon her legal rights to her father's property and to solicit Raj's help in making the claim against Roop. The second revelation, which constitutes the moral and philosophical crux of the film, is hinted at by the father on his deathbed, when he whispers the word *anhonee* (impossible). The word turns out to be the title of a book in which he has hidden a letter explaining that Mohini's mother, the courtesan, took her revenge on him for abandoning her by switching his legitimate and illegitimate daughters. This means that Mohini is actually Roop and Roop is Mohini. From then on, the plot spirals into a veritable hall of mirrors involving true, false, switched, and assumed identities in the context of a debate over whether heredity or environment has the greatest impact on identity. The film ends in madness and death for Mohini, who is symbolically killed by her father when she shoots his enormous portrait and it crashes down upon her.

As a melodrama, *Anhonee* conveys the impression of multiple moments of derailment of the narrative's apparent trajectory, constantly setting up scenarios with predictable outcomes, only to swerve unexpectedly in another direction. Clearly, certain expected avenues of conflict are forestalled in the interests of foregrounding the conflict in the double identity. For example, certain details in the opening sequences appear to set the scenario for gender and class critique. In Raj's first meeting with Roop, the servant who shows him in refers to her as "chhota sahib" (young master), which creates a moment of gender confusion until he sees her and she reacts arrogantly to his complaints regarding their exploitation of tenants. The second sequence of the film shows Raj feeling out of place at Roop's birthday party, to which her father has impulsively invited him, even though he is well below their social class.[18] Roop behaves like a spoiled rich girl and throws aside his modest gift of flowers.

With her masculine appellation, her unfeeling attitude toward poor tenants, and her spoiled behavior, Roop's character seems poised for

Nargis as Roop and Mohini in *Anhonee* (K. A. Abbas, 1952).

narrative development involving the kind of critique of the modern professional woman that other films of the 1950s routinely displayed. As with the character played by Nargis in *Andaz* (1949), such films set up and then "actively divest women characters of the modern, professional attributes which they exhibit, placing them as objects of exchange within the generational transaction."[19] However, in *Anhonee*, the last we hear of Roop as "chhota sahib" or see her displaying class arrogance is in that first scene.

Similarly, the initial reason for Raj's contact with this wealthy family seems to indicate the beginnings of a critique of the oppressive practices of urban landlords; all the more so, because the same issue is brought up again when Mohini approaches Raj for legal help against her landlord. Such a critical scrutiny of the upper classes would be no surprise from the writer and director, K. A. Abbas, who was a well-known socialist and member of the progressive theater group, Indian Peoples' Theatre Association (IPTA). But, again, no more is said in the film about the class affiliation of Roop's family; rather, it is their social class whose perspective dominates the rest of the narrative. Thus, issues of both gender and class are dropped in the very instant of their appearance, and the half-hearted social critique of wealth and fashionable society gives way to a melodramatic encounter between mirror opposites. While their real function can be read in terms of a narrative excuse for Raj to meet Roop and Mohini, such derailments can also be seen as symptoms of the heterogeneous mode of manufacture discussed in chapter 5.[20]

Another broad area of narrative derailment is in multiple situations promising a familiar melodramatic scenario of misunderstanding between lovers. Usually such moments are marked by the revelation of "unexpected" facets of the Nargis and Raj characters. When Raj goes to Mohini's house for his legal fees, in response to her challenge that he would be afraid to do so, he is inadvertently seen there by the villain.[21] The extra shot of the villain seeing Raj seems to suggest that the narrative will move next in the direction of a misunderstanding between the lovers. Instead, when Roop asks him where he was, Raj immediately tells her the truth and explains why he went to Mohini's *kotha*, and she understands. Later, when Mohini asks Raj to act as her lawyer in a court case against Roop to claim her rights, the narrative does not move on to a conflict over property between the half-sisters. Instead, the next scene shows Roop taking Mohini over to her house and giving her a share in everything, even before she has been asked to do so. The film thus repeatedly diffuses other sources of dramatic conflict to focus on the dual role itself.

A plot potentially based on misunderstanding settles down to one that plays with misidentification and relies on the extra-textual force of the Nargis star text. It is always Raj who makes the mistake, however briefly, and Mohini whom he mistakes for Roop. *We* know that they are actually the same. But by reiterating and acknowledging their physical resemblance even in the diegesis—that is, by emphasizing the obvious: their resemblance—the film persuades us to believe their difference and emphasizes the challenge of clarifying moral difference. Such difference can only be signaled through external details of gesture and costuming, which, in turn, serve as visible signs of Nargis's professional expertise in acting.

Recognition, Misrecognition, and the Double Role

Film roles play upon recognition and misrecognition of the star persona: "the star vehicle frequently places its star in a role which initially withholds the full persona."[22] The starting point of *Anhonee* is a double recognition. First, the viewer recognizes the established character regularly played by Nargis, even though this is not an RK Films production. She is Raj's love interest, wears her trademark white sari, carries herself modestly, and is the upper-class, motherless daughter of a rich patriarchal figure. Similarly, the viewer recognizes the trope of the performing woman or courtesan in Mohini, who embodies the recognizable characteristics associated not so much with a star persona or prior screen roles as with a melodramatic character type. The double role thus initially relies on the viewer's recognition of two iconic figures. Ravi Vasudevan describes a similar process of recognition in his argument that the heterogeneous elements in Bombay films, such as the comic character and the "narrational song," are reintegrated into films through their reference to an external, culturally legible set of norms: "we are both inside and outside the story, tied at one moment to the seamless flow of a character-based narration from within, in the next attuned to a culturally familiar stance from without."[23] The overlaying of star text and melodramatic associations onto the fictional characters in the diegesis of *Anhonee* opens it up to a body of overlapping, extra-textual biographical and cultural references.

The initial recognition in *Anhonee* is followed by a marked imbalance in the film's delineation of detail in the dual characters. Given Nargis's established screen identity as a character like Roop and the tendency to conflate her on-screen and off-screen identities, her role as Mohini would seem to be "acting" in comparison to the "neutral" role of Roop, which would be seen simply as a case of "being." This difference in the levels of "acting" required by the two roles is signaled by a hyperbolic style of performance as Mohini and works to effectively distance Nargis's star persona from that role. The magazine *Filmfare* made much of Nargis's performance as Mohini precisely because of its visible markers of performance. The cover of the 27 June 1952 issue was designed like a poster advertising *Anhonee.* Across a *painted* portrait of a surly-looking Nargis with cigarette in mouth were the words: "You will see a *different* Nargis co-starred with Raj Kapoor in Naya Sansar's *Anhonee* written and directed by K. A. Abbas." This cover is also an instance of the move to distance Nargis from the "bad" character by identifying her association with it in terms of entertainment value.

In Mohini's character, we see the obvious externalization of moral forces into performative modes. As Christine Gledhill observes, "Gesture reveals what words conceal" and "becomes a major link between ethical forces and personal desire."[24] In his first meeting with Mohini in his office, Raj briefly mistakes her for Roop but almost instantly realizes the difference between them. The difference is also clearly signaled to the viewer through a series of legible signs: Mohini's cigarette in hand, her chewing of *paan,* her hip-swaying gait and arms akimbo, her short hair, low-cut blouse, and flashy sari (signifying the vulgar "filmi" taste that Nargis's friend had noticed about her before her "transformation" by Raj). All these are signs that serve as a shortcut to the moral meaning of this character. They are given a hyperbolic twist the first time the film shows Mohini together with Roop after she has begun to live in her house. In this scene, because of the need to make a contrast with Roop, the act of smoking a cigarette is no longer a strong enough key to moral identification. Instead, its power is enhanced by having Mohini light the cigarette at the devotional oil lamp that Roop has just lit in front of their dead father's portrait. In one stroke, the film identifies their difference in terms of their relation to their lineage, focusing it in the external difference between lighting a lamp and lighting a cigarette. At this point, there is a double and contrary impulse in the film to entertain at the same time that it is making a moral statement. *Anhonee* builds on the entertainment potential of Nargis in such an unfamiliar role by following the obvious excess in the cigarette-lighting scene with one in which Roop tries to teach Mohini a more respectable style of walking. Nargis's performance of Mohini's exaggeratedly clumsy attempts to act respectable is accompanied by a comic, "mickey-mousing" sound track. This is one of many moments of metaperformance in the film as Nargis acts as Mohini acting "respectable." Moreover, the split screen, the protracted action, and the loose connection to the plot also point to the performative emphasis of this moment, a moment of pure star presence that exceeds the demands of the narrative.

Song and dance sequences, not surprisingly, function as key indices of moral status. The film's first two song sequences outline acceptable and unacceptable expressions of female desire. While Raj sings to Roop at her birthday party, it is Mohini who sings for Raj at her *kotha.* Both are public performances, but the first leads to legitimate romance, while the second confirms the illegitimate moral status of Mohini and the beginning of her illicit desire for Raj. Her song and dance sequence emphasizes the economic aspect of her performance, that she dances for money. At the end of the dance, she collects money from the admiring men in her audience and gives this money to Raj as his legal fees. He, in turn, clarifies his difference from the other men by throwing the tainted money back in her face. In its diegesis, *Anhonee* so stringently codifies the performance of song and dance as metonymic for fallen woman that the Roop character not only never sings in public, but also cannot be permitted even a romantic duet with Raj except over the telephone, while each of them is lying in bed. With its visible separation of space, the telephone allows for a romantic song sequence while avoiding any suggestion of similarity to Mohini.

The array of external signs and gestures distinguishing Mohini from Roop clearly identifies the double role as a simple binary opposition between a good woman and a bad woman. This view is summed up by Raj's litany of opposing traits that mark off one half-sister from the other, and is also echoed in readings of the film that see it merely in terms of "stark oppositions of good and evil."[25] When Mohini asks Raj why he cannot love her instead of Roop, given their identical appearance, his response invokes religious and class oppositions. Where Roop is a goddess, Mohini is the devil; Roop is noble, Mohini is low. Roop's heart is filled with love, truth, and compassion, while Mohini's has vice, falsehood, and lust. Mohini pounces on his description of her as low, with all its class connotations, because she can triumphantly demonstrate to him that he is wrong about her real class identity. Since she and Roop were exchanged in childhood, their "real" identity can be switched back now: "I am not low, she is! I did not grow up on the streets as Champa's daughter, she did! I am Thakur Harnam Singh's daughter!"

Anhonee is structured more literally around binary oppositions than other social films of the 1950s in which "the elements [of film narrative] are restructured into a melodramatic bipolarity, the stylistic and iconographic elements siphoned off into the world of vamp and villain, counterpointed to the realm of morality and romantic love."[26] Yet the film ends up problematizing the clean opposition between Roop and Mohini both textually, in terms of its conceptualization of Mohini's character, and intertextually, in terms of the ways in which *both* characters invoke off-screen knowledge about Nargis. The binary opposition is seriously muddied in moments where the film falters in its identification of Mohini's moral status. Is she a victim of circumstances, or is she a conscious agent of evil? The confusion stems from the nature-nurture question, which the film raises as soon as it is revealed that the sisters were exchanged at birth. *Awara,* another Raj-Nargis vehicle made a year earlier (1951), had explored this same question, and the answer there was much more ambiguous than in *Anhonee,* which makes it clear, by the end of the film, that environment rather than heredity is the decisive factor in molding identity.[27]

The ideological incoherence in the film's concept of Mohini's character becomes evident in the very moment of her introduction. When she comes into Raj's office for the first time, the cinematic emphasis is on his brief misidentification of her as Roop and on her visibly different manner from Roop. It is clearly a moment where moral commentary is suspended in favor of sheer delight in Nargis's performance. In the next scene, Mohini is obviously a scheming seductress when she tricks Raj into coming to her *kotha* to collect his legal fees. Close-ups, otherwise sparingly used in this film, function to convey to the viewer that her cunning and duplicity are consciously planned.

But in the next sequence, the film takes back this image of Mohini as a seductress. When the villain, Laddan, sexually harasses her, Mohini reveals her actual innocence, saying, "You misunderstand me. Although my songs and music may be sold in this room, I myself am not for sale," to which he responds scornfully, "You talk as if you are not a *tawaif,* but the daughter of a respectable man." The retrospective irony here is made obvious to the viewer because of clues from the start of the film concerning her identity as Thakur Harnam Singh's daughter. But again, from this point until the final moments of the film, Mohini lives up to Raj's litany of oppositions with increasing hyperbole.

Only at the climactic ending of the film is there again a confusion in the film's final statement regarding Mohini's moral status, with a contradiction between what is said and what is shown. In the final scene, an insane Mohini says to her father's portrait, "All doors are closed to me and my only place is at your feet. . . . Thanks to you and to society, I got nothing out of life." In the scene before this, when she threatens him and Roop with a gun, Raj says to her that he no longer hates her because "you are not you; you are a puppet of society. I don't hate you; I hate the society which made this puppet dance and placed the poison of greed and hatred in her."

All these statements of exoneration are undermined in the final scene by the markers of insanity in Mohini. The extreme noir lighting, canted frames, dramatic score, and the quickly edited shots alternating between close-ups of Mohini, her father's portrait, a wooden owl, a coiled rope, and a grotesque mask signify Mohini's place outside all forms of normality. This series of recurrent shots aptly illustrates a desire for plenitude of meaning straining against the inadequacies of language. The moral indictment of her dead father, uttered through Mohini's final words to him, is similarly undermined when he metes out the ultimate judgment upon her as his portrait kills her. In Hindi cinema, "the moral universe of the fiction, the figuration of guilt or innocence is always already known." Thus, the internal logic of this character and its structural position in opposition to the Roop character dictate that she must die. But at the moment of her death, the film can afford to morally recuperate her as a product of society's double standards. With the argument that Mohini's moral character is the result of upbringing rather than heredity or innate character, *Anhonee* makes social class an index of moral status. This alignment of class and moral status ties in closely with the cinema's own anxieties and concerns regarding class and the moral status of female stars. *Anhonee* seems to directly represent the complaint made in 1934 that "we cannot expect to produce a heavenly picture like 'Song of Songs' with artistes recruited from the slums."[28] The assertion of impossibility contained in this statement is echoed, not only in the title of the film, which means "impossible," but also in the final words of *Anhonee,* spoken by Roop and Raj, that "we were not able to rescue Mohini" and "we could not make the impossible possible."

At the level of obvious moral oppositions in the double role, the Roop character is clearly a stand-in for Nargis's ideal star persona, while the Mohini character is a way of negatively reinforcing and defining Nargis's distance from the modes of female performance associated with Mohini. The need for such a function is not so farfetched, given the close connection between screen performance and dancing girls in the public mind. But the extra-textual details of Nargis's public identity work equally to interrupt and blur the clean opposition between Mohini and Roop. Nargis's star persona was a complex construct comprising overt and submerged elements. Every aspect of her identity had its mirror opposite built within it, placing her always on the edge of transgression or in a state of barely recuperated legitimacy. For instance, as I mentioned earlier, Nargis was considered to be educated and was brought up in a "respectable" home, yet she was the daughter of a courtesan from Calcutta, Jaddanbai, whose association cost Nargis's father his planned medical career, his religion—he converted to Islam in order to marry her—and his ties with his upper-class family. Another set of mirror opposites emerges in her romance with Raj Kapoor. Although they were widely celebrated as a couple in screen roles and in off-screen appearances together, it was equally well known, even if submerged in her overall star identity, that Raj was already married and that his wife was extremely unhappy over this affair.

The dual role in *Anhonee* makes use of all these often contradictory elements in bewilderingly mirrored effects. Nargis's publicly known desire to marry Raj makes her relation to his wife the same as Mohini's to Roop. Raj is the object of desire standing between "wife" and "actress," in the same way that he is between Roop and Mohini. In other ways too, Nargis's similarity to Mohini's identity brings her to the edge of transgression. Like Mohini, Nargis was the daughter of a courtesan from Calcutta—even the detail of place of origin is retained in *Anhonee*—but emphatically unlike Mohini, Nargis's respectable father did not abandon her mother.[29] Mohini says that she is denied what should be hers only because her father refused to marry her mother so as to "preserve his name and face," while Nargis's father gave up all his accoutrements of class for her mother's sake. Other details, too, come dangerously close to identifying Nargis's "true" identity with that of Mohini. A very subtle example is in the scene of Mohini's first meeting with Raj, when she coquettishly, but provocatively, refuses the suffix of *bai* attached to her name because of its (Muslim) courtesan associations and insists on *devi* (literally "goddess," but used as suffix to the first names of "respectable" [Hindu] women). A faint echo is present here of the name of Nargis's mother, who was Jaddanbai, rather than Jaddandevi. She too, like Mohini in this particular scene, was no apologist for her true identity as an accomplished and celebrated singer/courtesan whom the upper classes such as her husband's family would, nevertheless, have shunned.[30]

Other moments of overlap between the Mohini character and the Nargis star text occur in scenarios of censure that invoke the negative rhetoric of female performance. Mohini herself deliberately instigates several of the moments of her misidentification as Roop—for instance, when she impersonates Roop's voice on the telephone and has Raj leave Lucknow to visit her in Mussoorie, while Roop is on her way to see him. On such occasions, Raj invariably expresses his anger when he discovers the impersonation, in terms that posit an incompatibility between true womanhood and performance. His question, "Are you a woman or a *nautanki* [theater performer]?" articulates the same opposition between wife and actress that he was to make decades later in reference to Nargis. In a 1952 *Filmfare* article, Nargis herself expressed frustration at the currency such an opposition held in the public mind: "Intruding into our public and private existence is the inevitable problem which assails every woman in film today, that of being an honest and good star and a respectable homely woman at the same time."[31] On another occasion in *Anhonee,* the extra-filmic reference to Nargis is more immediate as Raj says: "You're quite an actress! Why don't you work in the movies?" Mohini's irreverent response to this—"Then why don't we go to Bombay together?"—is spoken with performative pleasure by Nargis. Within the narrative of the film, the negative connotations of Raj's censure serve to define the Mohini character, but their obvious application to Nargis's own career as an actress works to produce the kind of textual cross-referencing that ends up temporarily problematizing the clean identification of Roop with Nargis's "true" persona. At one point in the film, when Roop expresses astonishment that Mohini feels no shame in so openly desiring Raj, her response is meant to remind Roop of the circumstances of her upbringing: "Why should I feel shame now when I didn't feel shame singing and dancing in public?" This "explanation" for Mohini's behavior at once condemns and condones it, while also potentially explaining the Raj-Nargis romance in similar terms.

Metaperformance: Identifying the "True" Nargis

In a double role, the perception of acting becomes the key to a simultaneous acknowledgment and disavowal of the absolute identity between the two roles. Only by emphasizing and celebrating performance can difference be established between the two roles. Yet only the awareness that they are, in fact, identical produces pleasure. By providing numerous occasions for the display of metaperformance, *Anhonee* acknowledges the inherent entertainment value of the double role. Metaperformance makes visible for the audience a split in the acting persona, where the same character shows a private and public face.[32] In other words, when a star is acting as a character who is acting, the audience gets a privileged view of both identities. But the other characters in the diegesis see expressive coherence rather than incoherence, unless the character is a poor actor and the act breaks down before them, as it does in a crucial dance sequence in *Anhonee.*

At a party introducing Mohini to respectable society, Roop tries to pass her off as her cousin from Gorakhpur. The villain, Laddan, who has recognized Mohini, insists, to her distress, that she sing and dance for the guests, knowing well that she risks exposing her true background when she dances. This song and dance sequence somehow failed to deliver entertainment value, as was noted in *Filmfare*'s otherwise positive review of the film.[33] The unevenness of this scene can be attributed to Nargis's complex task of acting as Mohini acting the innocent cousin of Roop. Since dance and sexuality are in a metonymic relation in this film, Mohini, the accomplished dancer and seductress, must dance in a different, more sober style as she is playing the part of a respectable woman. She begins to dance respectably enough, but to the horror of the guests and the furious embarrassment of Raj and Roop, she cannot restrain herself and slips back into her accustomed dance style.[34] She ends by dancing before Laddan and accepting money from him, in the true manner of a dancing girl.

Here Nargis's acting must signal to the viewer various levels of artifice in order to separate and clarify the moral status of the different identities involved. Nargis, the star, is presumably not a *nachnewali*, or dancing girl, herself.[35] Therefore, when she dances as one, it must be signaled as clearly a case of "good acting."[36] But Mohini, the character, is a courtesan, and a seductive dance style comes naturally to her so that she has difficulty dancing any other way. She, unlike Nargis, is not a good actress and is unable to carry off the subterfuge of pretending to be a respectable woman. Maintaining a distinction among the three identities of star, seductive character, and respectable cousin calls for a spiraling sequence of innocence-seductiveness-innocence. It calls initially for a dance form that is at once "innocent" and artificial. She begins by separating song and dance, singing without any movement at all, the lyrics to her song forming a potentially subversive commentary on the gathered elite in the drawing room: "In this respectable gathering, my heart has been stolen. Who among these upright citizens can I call a thief?" It then requires the display of a barely restrained seductiveness, which is suggested by the beginnings of dance, as she sways to the song and slowly moves around the room. At the end of the scene, this completely breaks down into the professional dance style that Mohini is accustomed to and that Nargis has already competently enacted in Mohini's first song and dance sequence. The metaperformance displayed in this sequence ends up as a sharp reminder of the impossibility of "an unacted emotional essence" that separates "Nargis" from Mohini or the cousin she is pretending to be.[37] The scene's precarious balance between respectability and seductiveness also underscores the appeal of Nargis the star, and points to the apt naming of the doubles. Together, Mohini (enchantress) and Roop (beauty) signify the totality of Nargis's star persona.

Anhonee transfers the melodramatic struggle over the tensions of bourgeois capitalism onto an emotional field, with property claims being made on Raj's affections. When Mohini discovers her lineage, her potential conflict with Roop over property is instantly diffused as Roop gives her a share in everything. Rather, the question of respectability, which is crucially tied to questions of lineage and property rights, is translated into the question of who gets Raj, who then becomes the object of exchange between the half-sisters. Mohini insists to Raj, "I have full rights to whatever is hers, including you." Yet, in the end, the actual object of exchange is Nargis, and not Raj, because he "gets" both versions of her, while neither version of her gets him. In reality, Nargis too did not get Raj because she was too much like Mohini—a mere actress to be placed in a separate category from his wife.

The battle over Raj culminates in an exchange of identities. Motivated by guilt about the accident of her privileged upbringing and concerned that Raj would not be getting the "real" Roop unless he married Mohini, Roop asks a willing Mohini to exchange identities with her just before she is to be married to Raj. Having already given Mohini a share in everything else, all that remains for Roop to do, to right an old wrong, is to share Raj. Her thinking here is based on a relational conception of identity having to do with patrilineage and heredity. According to Roop, Raj thinks he is marrying the legitimate daughter of Thakur Harnam Singh. Mohini plays upon this belief of Roop's by saying to her, "You know he would never marry you if he knew that you are the daughter of a *tawaif.*" But instead, when Raj discovers the subterfuge, he counters their notion of identity with a "modern" individualized view of identity as interiority: "I love you for your inner being, not for your outward appearance."

As long as Nargis is playing the two distinct roles of Roop and Mohini, there is no problem in clarifying difference, while acknowledging their identical appearance, because such difference becomes concentrated into a set of recognizable gestures and "accessories." That is, the inner difference in identities can be given an external counterpart. But when Roop and Mohini switch roles, the need to assert the difference between Mohini-as-Roop and Roop-as-Mohini is even more urgent because of the danger of confusing the two identities. The problem is solved by drawing attention to two *new* accessories, a mole on Roop's cheek and her long braid, as opposed to Mohini's short hair. A brightly lit close-up of Roop at the moment when she proposes the exchange of identities serves to emphasize the mole on her cheek, which is invisible in earlier portions of the film.

The switch in identities is thus effected through a very literal transference of new external traits in addition to previously established ones, such as Roop's white sari. Roop cuts off her braid and literally attaches it to Mohini's hair, while Mohini draws a mole on her cheek and Roop covers hers with makeup. The melodramatic externalization of internal moral states is taken to excess here with close-ups of the black makeup the "evil" Mohini uses to paint the mole on her cheek, and the white color the "good" Roop uses to cover her mole. Such a solution to the problem of asserting difference between them is precarious at best, not so much because of the violation of standards of "realism" and the obvious artifice involved, but because it reveals the actual impossibility of maintaining difference. During the brief sequences of the switch, especially when Mohini-as-Roop and Roop-as-Mohini share a song sequence, Nargis's performance cannot help but demonstrate that she is literally playing two roles that are absolutely identical both internally and externally. The precarious ideological implications of such a conflation of identities require that this avenue of narrative development be dropped the moment it is introduced.

This is why a plot of further misidentifications, even with its opportunity for metaperformance, quickly crumbles in yet another derailment of the film's projected direction. Before viewers can settle down to a prolonged version of the performance dynamics first seen in the dance sequence, Raj discovers the switch, and the need for such performance is dissipated. His exposure of Mohini-as-Roop's real identity is predictably based on an externalized conception of identity and an emphasis on artifice. Her mole gets smudged by her tears "of joy" after their wedding, and when he comes close to examine it, he enumerates a list of giveaway differences—"Your mole is fake . . . the smell of cigarettes on your breath."—and pulls off her false braid. Raj's misidentification of Mohini in this sequence is the longest lasting one in the film and is also the logical culmination of the tension between the two roles; yet this misidentification is also driven by the imperative to be brief. To prolong Raj's misidentification would seriously defeat the ideological function of this double role by suggesting that there might be something of Mohini in Roop.

As in other doubling films, the double role in *Anhonee* works by producing the perfect set-up for the pleasures of "misrecognition and clarification, the climax of which is an act of 'nomination' in which characters [or "authentic" star personae] finally declaim their true identities, demanding a public recognition." While *Anhonee* allows for the transgressive pleasure of momentary identifications of Nargis with Mohini, it reestablishes Roop as the legitimate point of identification in the film, first by displacing onto Mohini the troubling aspects of Nargis's star persona and then by eliminating Mohini's character. As in many other social melodramas of the 1950s, "the restitution of the bipolarities that define the moral universe of the narrative, effected by deeply contradictory operations, affords a moral confirmation after forbidden pleasures and anxieties have been experienced." The complex tangle of moral anxieties that Mohini represents is not eliminated simply because she dies. The inadequacy of a narrative resolution such as death is clear from the film's last-minute exoneration of her present behavior in terms of childhood events. A more significant form of elimination than death, this final moral recuperation serves to bring up and then explain away the negative subtext of female performance underlying the film as a whole.[38]

Transgressive Desires and the Emblematic Double Role

The only other double role Nargis played was in *Raat Aur Din* (*Night and Day,* Satyen Bose, 1967), one of the few films she appeared in after *Mother India.* (She did so as a favor to her brother, the producer of the film.) *Raat Aur Din* was a commercial failure, partly because it appeared a decade after Nargis had ceased to work in films, but perhaps also because it was so strongly responding to popular concerns in Hollywood cinema at the time. The source of the double role is a split personality, with the film engaged in the exploration of various "medical" solutions to this phenomenon, and much screen time devoted to two psychoanalysts.[39] The medical discourse also gives the film an excuse to visually emphasize the punishment of aberrant sexuality, through the spectacle of shock treatment, incarceration, and physical restraint. Early in the film, before the husband turns to medicine for an answer, the evil mother-in-law resorts to a traditional exorcist. Even as it is critiqued in the film, the exorcism scene provides yet another excuse for a fantasy of punishment for Westernized women.

While Hindi cinema is unable to imagine a female double in anything but sexualized and morally negative terms, the nature of female sexuality shows a distinct change from the late 1950s onward. Stated in essentialist terms, the difference is between "Indian" and "Westernized" conceptions of "bad womanhood." While in *Anhonee* Mohini's negative sexuality is presented in terms of the figure of a courtesan, in *Raat Aur Din* the "night" personality, named Peggy, displays Hindi cinema's conception of "Westernized" debauchery, which appears in film after film in the 1960s and beyond. The emergence of the Westernized woman as the specific incarnation of bad womanhood coincides with the post-Independence imperative to posit a pan-Indian identity to both the world of the diegesis and the ideal audience of these films. Such an identity is characterized by "the retrograde conception of an Indian-ness harking back to a phantasised, pre-colonial, edenic Indian essence to be now recovered in post-colonial times." In films of the 1960s and beyond, the essentialist figuration of identity takes place through the elimination of identifiable markers of regional or local affiliation.[40] The figure of the "Westernized" Indian woman is only rarely, as in *Raat aur Din,* actually given an Anglo-Indian or Indian Christian identity. More often, she is instantly recognizable through certain iconic traits. Alcohol, cigarettes, nightclubs, Western-style dancing with men, short hair, and Western clothes are metonymic indicators of her moral status.

However, the particular use *Raat Aur Din* makes of the figure of the Westernized woman suggests its place in the logic of a split nationalist response to the modern. Ideal Indian womanhood is unquestionably presented in the "day" personality, Baruna, who explicitly does not smoke, drink, dance, or frequent nightclubs, and who is also, above all, a devoted wife. The film's explanation for Baruna's split personality is an exemplary case of ideological doubling, of having it both ways. Since the "bad" personality, Peggy, is part of Baruna's psyche, it has to be somewhat blameless so as not to contaminate the "true" identity of the heroine and, by extension, of the star. The blame seems to be briefly transferred to her father, who confesses that in her childhood he had all the vices associated with Bombay cinema's notion of "bad masculinity": alcohol, gambling, and, somewhat unusually, wife-beating. But the film moves on quickly—without assigning blame to the father—to the real source of the problem, which was a conflict between Baruna's parents over the best way to raise a girl. The father, in keeping with forward-looking modern conceptions of progress in the new Indian nation, wants to give her an education and raise her in contact with the rest of society. The mother, who turns out to be the negative center of the film, expresses the worst kind of premodern, "traditional" values, insisting that Baruna receive no education and be raised in the equivalent of *purdah,* in complete isolation from other people. The film emphasizes the mother's values as emphatically wrong by having her be a "bad" wife and leave her husband in order to follow through on her ideas. Baruna, living with her mother, is locked up all day and given no education. She finds an escape in her secret friendship with her neighbor, Peggy, who goes to school and is being raised presumably as Baruna's father would have wanted. Baruna's night personality then takes on the identity of Peggy.

There is an absolute contradiction here between the "good" values of the father with regard to the raising of girls and the "bad" womanhood represented by the adult Peggy, who has been raised according to those values. The film resolves this contradiction by deflecting all blame onto the figure of the mother, whose role "interrupts" the irreconcilable logic that states that if you educate your daughter, she will become a Peggy, while if you isolate her, she will become a Baruna. In this split logic resides, on the one hand, a positive approach to the modern, which embraces education, and by extension, technology—that is, all those externals of modern life in which the West excels.[41] On the other hand, where it impinges on the inner domain of morality and notions of "traditional" womanhood, the modern has nothing to offer. From this point of view, the mother of Baruna is certainly not a genuinely traditional woman, having left her husband, even though she may advocate outmoded norms of traditionality for her daughter.

The double role in *Raat aur Din* works much more simply than in *Anhonee* to provide a point of recognition of the "true" identity of Nargis, clarifying its moral contours through a rigorously delineated mirror opposite in the "bad" double. With Nargis's retirement from the cinema and with her star persona safely established as a Mother India figure, the task of reiterating a positive screen image was redundant. The double role in *Raat Aur Din* could thus function primarily as a safe venue for showcasing Nargis's versatility as an actress. In contrast, the function of the double role in *Anhonee* was to manage, contain, and morally clarify the disparate and contradictory knowledge that constituted the Nargis star persona at the time of the film's release in 1952. This containment took place not in the realm of public relations or of authenticating exposés of the "real" Nargis behind the screen image. Rather, the screen itself became the arena where various levels of authentication were played out.

The emblematic nature of melodrama and stardom results from their similar function in articulating repressions in social reality. In the Indian context, one example of such an articulation is the contradictory response to female stars, in which the avid consumption of female performance coexists in a state of tension with moral condemnation. It is equally possible to read the characters of Mohini and Peggy against the grain. If Mohini and Peggy provide the moral and narrative interest of the films they appear in, they are also the performative centers of these films. In the frequently expressed pleasure of seeing Nargis in such roles, it is possible to see these characters not only as articulating transgressive desires, but also as providing alternative readings of the Nargis star text. In the public enthusiasm for the Raj-Nargis romance, one way of reading the Nargis text was as a celebration of female desire outside the confines of marriage and social norms of ideal womanhood.

Richard Dyer's ideas on authenticity—where a star's "true" nature is established through a series of dialectical revelations about the "star-as-real-person" with regard to the "star-as-image"—are translated in Indian films with double roles onto the plane of performance. In such films, as in *Anhonee,* the "star-as-real-person" is replaced by a second "star-as-image," the twin role, which is eventually revealed to be false. So the entire authentication process is carried out on-screen, even when the roles might be framed in terms of extra-filmic information regarding Nargis. But in the end, "emblematic monopathy" is the goal of the star text, and the reestablishment of the "fixed" star persona can only involve a demonstration and then a denial of histrionic ability. The excessive star presence associated with the post-1950s Indian "star system" is specifically gendered in the different ways in which the double role serves male and female star identities. A sign of market value and a type of curriculum vitae for male stars, the double role becomes, for female stars, an essential space of metaperformance that undertakes the task of morally clarifying both generalized and particular rumors about female sexuality.[42]

7. *The Embodied Voice*

SONG SEQUENCES AND STARDOM IN BOMBAY CINEMA

> The power of movies to recontextualize detail is so great that a single role frequently involves more than one player.
>
> —James Naremore, *Acting in the Cinema,* 25

Thus far I have considered the implications of the public circulation of the female body in star discourses in India cinema. The demands of a cinematic form that privileges song sequences produced the imperative to technologically separate singing voices and acting bodies. In this chapter I turn to the implications of the circulation of the female voice for star discourses in India. I examine the operations of stardom within song sequences and the dynamics of aural, as opposed to visual, stardom. Focusing on the voice of Lata Mangeshkar as a monumental and singular site of stardom and displaced interiority, I argue that her star power draws on the negotiated identities of the dual star text produced by the combination of her voice and various actresses' bodies. If in European modernity the human voice is associated with interiority, truth, and authenticity, in Indian cinema the female singing voice became another site of externalized displacement for anxieties about the true nature of actresses. The role of the female voice in Indian cinema is deeply implicated in the history of sound's impact on commercial cinema and in the recording technologies developed in response to specific concerns of performance and music.

In 1931 the first sound film in India, *Alam Ara,* established the dominance of song sequences, frequently combined with dance, in the Indian film form. Early hits like *Indrasabha* (1932), which included seventy-one songs, indicated enthusiasm for this new attraction in cinema, allowing these "all talking, all singing, all dancing" extravaganzas to quickly intersect with the music business. The first film song was released on gramophone record in 1934, and since then, until the last decade, film songs have been exclusively the popular music of India. In 1985 film music accounted for about 80 percent of total record sales, in contrast to Indian classical music, which accounted for only 20 percent.[1] Songs reconfigured the economic parameters of film production: "on the film song depends the popularity of the film, that is, its repeat value and box office returns."[2] Thus, film and popular music have long been parallel and intersecting components of the entertainment industry in India. This connection was first solidified in the late 1940s.

Film songs and song sequences became the first mass-mediated forms of Indian popular culture to permeate everyday life through official and unofficial circuits of distribution and transmission. Their circulation, initially via gramophone records and radio, adapted quickly to new technologies, including television, audio and video cassettes, CDs, and DVDs. Unofficially, they are represented in everyday life through amateur singing, stage shows, games such as *antakshari,* brass bands, and myriad other forms of informal appropriation.[3] Film songs have permeated the aural environment of India's public spaces, from markets and festivals to long-distance buses and trains. But it was primarily through radio and, later, audio cassettes and television that film songs reached a wide audience.[4] Soon after Indian Independence in 1947, All-India Radio (AIR) tried to ban all film music from its programming in order to promote a national identity based on the "pure" forms of traditional and classical music.[5] But by 1957 competition from Radio Ceylon in Sri Lanka, which did air Indian film songs, forced AIR to establish a separate station, Vividh Bharati, solely for the broadcast of film songs.[6] Since then, radio has become the most widely accessible source of film songs and hence a standard medium of advertising for films. For example, an advertisement for the film *Tezaab* (N. Chandra, 1988) starts with the sentence: "Tune in to Vividh Bharati tonight and every Saturday night at 9:45 p.m. for the radio programme of *Tezaab.*"[7] The importance of song sequences to the advertising of films is also evident in the prominence they typically give to the name of the music director, which is second only to that of the film's stars.

Film songs have become free-floating signifiers whose original narrative context is often forgotten or overlooked, even while they remain attached in popular memory to particular stars. This is because they have been frequently repackaged in television programs, video cassettes, and DVD compilations in the form of a chain of song sequences unified by theme, era, singer, music director, or actor. Film music is created with "the desire . . . to compose an item that is self-sufficient in its melodic draw and which can therefore be received, reproduced and remembered in isolation, i.e., irrespective of the filmic situation in which it is intended to appear." Since the 1950s, "radio listener request programmes and a weekly 'top hits' chart . . . determined the most popular Hindi film songs on a regular basis." Given their presence in everyday life in India, film songs became one of the most important vehicles of star construction, since song sequences epitomized the most spectacular aspects of star performance.[8]

Song sequences are a potent star vehicle not only because of their infinite repeatability in other contexts, but also because, as Richard Dyer suggests with respect to the Hollywood musical, they are the site of the film's utopian impulses and therefore frequently represent the most idealized aspects of star presence. Their utopianism derives not so much from the actual song content, which may very well be tragic, but from the formal construction of the scene and the emotional appeal of the music: "utopianism is contained in the feelings it embodies . . . it thus works at the level of sensibility." With song sequences produced separately under the heterogeneous mode of production, their "spectacular and emotional excess" dominates the film and is "privileged over linear narrative development." The idea that the song sequence is a film's predominant site of emotion shapes its placement and function in films. The seemingly extravagant claim that songs are capable of "expressing every shade of emotional reverberation" is true insofar as the hybrid forms of film music and dance are also associated with classical Indian performance theories and the *raga* system of Indian classical music, which is structured according to a "predetermined correspondence between musical stimulants and audience effects." The formal construction of song sequences also contributes to their utopian sensibility. The disregard for continuities of time and place in the editing allows for changes in location and costuming from one shot to the next, thereby producing for the spectacle an idealized setting that does not really exist within the diegesis. Thus, performance techniques, the music itself, and the "artificial geography" produced by the editing all contribute to the intensified emotion that characterizes the utopianism of song sequences.[9]

Voice Monopoly

Since the mid-1940s, the songs in Hindi cinema have been sung by so-called playback singers. The song sequences, or "song picturizations," are then filmed with actors lip-synching to the prerecorded voice of the singer. Until the early 1990s playback singing was the monopoly of a very small number of singers, who became stars in their own right.[10] In the case of the female singing voice, this monopoly went to the extreme of excluding virtually all other voices except the voice of Lata Mangeshkar and, to a lesser extent, that of her sister Asha Bhosle.[11] This has meant that, for almost five decades, every major film actress borrowed the same singing voice, that of Lata Mangeshkar. Since the mid-1990s Mangeshkar's voice no longer monopolizes film music, but she continues to sing playback. However, as Bhaskar Chandavarkar observed in 1989, "Today it is difficult to imagine a female voice that is not Lata Mangeshkar's."[12] Given the extreme degree of voice monopoly in the case of the female singer, it is easy to overlook the fact that there was only a slightly larger number of male playback voices, including those of Mukesh, Talat Mahmood, Mohammed Rafi, and Kishore Kumar. If voice monopoly characterizes the mode of aural stardom in post-Independence Hindi cinema, this has important consequences for the relation between aural and visual pleasures. It involves the repetition, one might say during the entire lifetime of the Indian nation, of the same female singing voice as the ideal norm of aural femininity across numerous female bodies.[13]

A sequence from the 1981 film *Naseeb* (Destiny), directed by Manmohan Desai, provides a convenient point of entry into the dynamics of stardom in Hindi cinema's song sequences. In this sequence, one of the heroes of the film is distracted from his daily jog by the streetside filming of a commercial for throat lozenges. In the commercial that is being filmed, the heroine of the film, who is a singer-star, is endorsing the throat lozenges. She attempts to sing, clears her throat, takes one of the lozenges, speaks about its therapeutic potency, and then sings a flawlessly executed line of melody ("*mere naseeb mein . . .*") in which no musical accompaniment overshadows the pure tones of her voice. Shots of the singer are intercut with close-up reaction shots of the hero, whose face wears what can best be described as the direct *gestus* of fandom. Even at the overt level of the narrative, the subject of this sequence is clearly star power itself. The hero experiences the pleasures of recognition, desire, and identification with the star, all of which are basic to the experience of stardom. While the narrative context here draws viewers into a fictional individual's experience of star power, another level of star fascination is simultaneously at work here. Viewers of the film would themselves immediately recognize Hema Malini, the actress who is *playing* the singing star. They would also be equally aware that the voice emerging from her throat belongs not to her, but to the playback singer, Lata Mangeshkar.

Although this sequence does not develop into a full-blown song sequence, it nevertheless epitomizes the way in which Hindi cinema's song sequences simultaneously draw upon two different star texts, those of the singer and of the actor. Putting together the ideal voice with the ideal body results in a cinematic construct, a composite star who is the visual-aural equivalent of what is frequently the Kuleshovian artificial geography of the song sequence's setting. The two intersecting star texts of the singer and the actor exist in a symbiotic relationship, appealing simultaneously to two sets of pleasures, the aural and the visual. While the disembodied voice of the playback singer attaches itself to the body of the actor and thereby acquires visual presence, the actor's figural gestures similarly acquire an aural dimension through the borrowed voice of the singer. Responding to the voice-body pairing of Lata Mangeshkar and Madhubala in the film *Mughal-e-Azam* (1960), one fan describes it as "the most beautiful voice in the world going on the most beautiful woman in the world." In its ideal matching of marketable voice and visually alluring body, Hindi cinema is no different in its cinematic imperatives than the Hollywood musical of the 1950s and 1960s.[14] However, what this voice-body combination *means* in the context of Hindi film culture is strikingly different, especially with respect to two interrelated issues: the primacy of the visual over the aural, and the masking of technology as a means of conveying the authenticity of the performance.

The Authenticity of Song Performance

Because of the star status of playback singers in Hindi cinema, the question of the authenticity of the song performance is cast in terms that are different from those of Hollywood. The Hollywood prototype is the situation in *Singin' in the Rain,* where the film narrative is concerned with revealing the technological artifice behind the experience of a musical, making "the exposure of song dubbing the climax of the plot." Yet, as Jane Feuer and others have argued, the film reclaims its status as "magic" by itself making use of such artifice in "invisible" ways. Rick Altman shows how the rhetorical structure of *Singin' in the Rain* must work to reverse "the illegitimacy of a 'lying' sound track" in which "Debbie Reynolds's voice does not emanate from the mouth portrayed by the image." Important to discussions of *Singin' in the Rain* is a central irony in the climactic moment. We are shown that the "true" source of Jean Hagen's voice is Debbie Reynolds, and we are meant to accept this fictional revelation as a statement about the authenticity of the *actress* Debbie Reynolds's voice; but when Reynolds dubs Hagen, her voice is, in fact, being dubbed by a third singer, who remains uncredited in the film.[15]

Both in the film's diegesis and in the extra-textual information about the film, concerns of authenticity center on the question of the morality of voice dubbing. As early as 1929 a *Photoplay* article took the tone of an exposé in describing the trickery involved in voice doubling: "There are voice doubles in Hollywood today just as there are stunt doubles. One is not so romantic as the other, perhaps, but certainly just as necessary. Those who create movies will probably not cheer as we make this announcement. In fact, they may resent our frankness."[16] Anxieties about vocal authenticity in the Hollywood context may also be interpreted in terms of the status of the human voice as a key to interiority or to the "true" self of the speaker in Western thought.[17] Because of the voice's association with interiority and true identity, voice doubles are more troubling than body doubles in stunt sequences. Thus, in Hollywood cinema, as in the examples of *Singin' in the Rain* and the *Photoplay* article, authenticity of performance is cast in terms of the audience's assumption of an actual match of voice and body. Further evidence of this assumption is the denial of an Academy Award nomination to Audrey Hepburn for her role in *My Fair Lady* once it was revealed in the press that she did not actually sing her own songs.[18]

In the sequence from *Naseeb* various devices work to visually embody the voice of the singer. We literally "see" the voice as it emerges from its point of origin, as Hema Malini strokes her throat, and we also see its visceral effect on the hero as he swoons with delight on hearing her sing. Two apparently contradictory mechanisms are at work here. At one level, the sequence illustrates a basic observation of theories of film sound, that the function of sound synchronization is to mask the operations of technology so as to produce the effect of the organic unity of voice and body, and of a natural, rather than a technologically constructed, performative space. The smooth transition in this sequence from the singing voice to the speaking voice and back again serves to reiterate the seamless conjoining of voice and body, and to mask the different sources of the two sounds. The clearing of the throat is the point of transition between the two voices, and it could be coming equally from Lata Mangeshkar or Hema Malini. While this masking of technology is similar to constructions of authenticity in Hollywood cinema, it is complicated by the viewer's recognition of, and pleasure in, the dual star reference of the song. The viewer's awareness of the true source of the singing voice tends to pull in precisely the opposite direction, becoming a *reminder* of the workings of technology. This is similar to the effect, in the film as a whole, of the extra-textual mechanism of star recognition, which puts a strain on the illusion of a self-contained narrative world with its own unique characters. Vocal substitution, in this context, can be framed not in terms of deceit, as it might be in Hollywood, but in terms of a displacement of the very *question* of interiority, as represented by voice, onto a second star text. Thus, to put it somewhat hyperbolically, the excess by which the new economy of the Indian "star system" is characterized serves, in this case, as another form of deflection away from interest in private identities.

Singing Stars

The question of the authenticity of the experience of song sequences has been vital to their history in Indian cinema. Roughly speaking, there have been three, often overlapping, phases. In the 1930s, during the first decade of sound cinema, song sequences were performed by singing stars, actors who sang their own songs, so that the question of authenticity was cast in terms similar to those of Hollywood cinema. As fan magazines of the period will testify, the audience's pleasure derived from their knowledge that the singer they were watching was really singing the song. Yet, technologically speaking, even in this phase there was a disjunction between voice and body, because the playback technique, which was first used successfully in Nitin Bose's 1935 film *Dhoop Chhaon,* was already in place.[19] In *Street Singer* (Phani Majumdar, 1938) there is a sequence in which the two main characters, Bhulwa (K. L. Saigal) and Manju (Kanan Devi), perform a song outside the house of a theater director who listens appreciatively to their music. There is a similar dynamic of star fascination here as in the sequence from *Naseeb.* Here, too, there is an internal audience for the song, whose awestruck response is meant to match that of the film audience. In this case, however, viewers would know that the actress Kanan Devi is actually singing the song, and furthermore, that she is being accompanied on the harmonium by K. L. Saigal, the most popular singing actor of the time and still a prototype of the ideal male singing voice in the movies. While there is no question here of the source of the singing voice, the film recasts in other terms the question of the authenticity of the performance.

As in the Hollywood musical, a hierarchy is set up between the spontaneity and immediacy of the popular music of the streets and the staged performances of the theater, between amateur and professional singing. This sequence in *Street Singer* is the first moment of the meeting of the two worlds. The response of the lascivious theater director, who listens to the music with awestruck greed, is meant to characterize the decadent values of the theater and its impulse to commercially exploit the natural talent of singers. The known star persona of K. L. Saigal strongly relied on a similar implicit hierarchy between the "natural" and the "trained" voice, emphasizing his lack of formal musical training and his innate gift.[20] Both musically and morally, the film shows the world of itinerant singers to be superior to that of the theater, which is clearly a stand-in for the world of cinema. Furthermore, while the film's viewers would recognize the "true" star here as K. L. Saigal, their narrative pleasure would lie in seeing the morally questionable theater director fail to notice him and pay greater (and misguided) attention to the lesser star, Kanan Devi. The film interweaves multiple star texts and derives its narrative power partly through the audience's recognition of a mismatch between real and fictional star.

The Relation of Sound and Image

The question of the authenticity of song performance in Hollywood cinema is related to the primacy of image over sound. According to Marsha Siefert, "the illusion that the voice belongs to, as well as emanates from, the image on the screen requires [the] assumption of an image's natural authority." In Indian cinema, by contrast, the use of the term *song picturization* to describe the production of song sequences already shows a certain tendency toward defining the image in the terms set out by the song. Even in the 1930s, when studios used actors who sang their own songs, the star's identity was primarily constructed in terms of the voice rather than the body. Since all sound films contained song sequences, this meant that histrionic ability in all major actors was understood to include musical ability. Film critic Bunny Reuben observes in 1970 that "ours is probably the only country where [in the 1930s] the ability to sing was the prime qualification for the permission to act." The exclusive use of singing stars at this time inevitably put a strain on the authenticity of song sequences and of other performances because of the frequent mismatch of acting and singing abilities.[21]

K. L. Saigal's star status was mainly centered on his singing ability rather than on his acting skills or physical presence. A snide reply to a letter to the editor in *filmindia* in January 1941 makes note of this:

Manju (Kanan Devi) and Bhulwa (K. L. Saigal) in *Street Singer* (Phani Majumdar, 1938).

Bhulwa at the theater director's office in *Street Singer* (1938).

"[Saigal's] views on acting should not be taken seriously. New Theatres [the studio for which he worked] took him up for his voice which is a gift not a talent."[22] A self-confessed fan of Saigal wrote in 1940 that although "everyone of us is his fan" because of his singing voce, "that is all [there is] about him. His face is pudding-like, his hair is always badly dressed."[23] Conversely, physically attractive actors were often derided in *filmindia* if they were not good singers. A letter to the editor in 1940 asks: "Wouldn't it be better for Ashok Kumar to stop singing in pictures? His effort doesn't sound like singing."[24]

The primacy of the aural over the visual in song sequences in Hindi cinema parallels the relation of spectacle and narrative in the films themselves, which Lata Mangeshkar pithily describes: "In India, cinema is an excuse for music."[25] Indian films of the 1930s and 1940s similarly tended to represent fictional stardom in aural rather than visual terms, with a star's fame predicated upon musical talent. In films about the world of performance, the "star," almost invariably female, is conceptualized not so much as an actor as a performer of music and dance. The primacy of aural over visual forms of stardom is also evident in the implicit hierarchy among different forms of stardom. For instance, *Street Singer* represents two kinds of stardom placed in a clear moral hierarchy that is also gendered. Bhulwa (K. L. Saigal) and Manju (Kanan Devi) start out as street singers of equal talent, although it is made clear for us that Bhulwa is Manju's teacher, which makes her talent "learned" while his is "natural." At the beginning of the film, though, they are morally and musically equivalent in their sharp difference from the commercialized world of theater music. But the rest of the film is about Manju's rise to stardom at the expense of Bhulwa, whom the viewer recognizes as K. L. Saigal, the "true" star of the film. Discovered by the decadent world of theater, Manju becomes a singing star who is visually available to the public not only in the theater but also on billboards. Bhulwa meanwhile achieves a quieter moment of fame as a radio singer whose voice alone is sufficient to identify him.

In detailing Manju's rise to stardom, the film marshals many of the tropes of female stardom current at the time. She is subject to the lecherous attentions of the theater bosses, she neglects her home and her friendship with Bhulwa, she becomes increasingly urban in her tastes and musical preferences as she becomes wealthy, and she gradually becomes contaminated with innuendos of a relationship with the theater director.[26] Because of such associations given to the specific mode of fame Manju attains, in *Street Singer*, as in film magazines of the time, stardom of the spectacular kind is imagined as being inherently female. Manju's star status is cinematically visualized through the use of her written name in multiple star-shaped frames superimposed over her stage performance. Bhulwa is not visible to his audience and also chooses to withhold his name from his radio audience and sings anonymously. In emphasizing the modest nature of Bhulwa's moment of fame in the film's narrative, *Street Singer* is clearly relying on the actual star status of K. L. Saigal to make its statement on the contrast between his musical and moral values and those into which Manju strays.

The climactic moment of this film, not surprisingly, centers on a song ("Babul Mora") and the two versions in which it is performed. In Bhulwa's original version, the song (though composed specifically for *Street Singer*) is meant to be a traditional song. Rewritten for Manju's theater performance, the new version is to be seen as a commercialized debasement of the original song. The musical betrayal here corresponds directly to the moral betrayal at the heart of the film's representation of Manju's rise to stardom, and the two versions of the song serve as musical reminders of the entire edifice of oppositions upon which the film is structured. The irony, of course, is that the "traditional" version of the song, which became a major hit, is the exact equivalent, in commercial terms, of the theatrical version in the film's diegesis.

As in *Street Singer*, other films until the mid-1940s also represented radio stardom as a more respectable, if less spectacular, form of stardom, particularly for women, because of its limitations on the public circulation of the body. In *Khazanchi/Cashier* (Moti B. Gidwani, 1941) there is an interesting example of the function of radio stardom in films of this period.[27] The hero (Kanwal) and heroine (Madhuri) first express their romantic interest in one another through the medium of a song sequence. Unusually, however, the declaration takes place in the presence of Madhuri's father, who asks her to turn on the radio to entertain their guest, Kanwal. The romantic song sequence is therefore a radio song that expresses Madhuri's feelings, but is not sung by her. We not only hear the song, but also see the female singer singing in the radio station, accompanied by musicians. Moreover, we recognize the singer in the radio station to be Kanwal's sister, who is one of the secondary characters in the film. The song sequence intercuts shots of the singer with shots of the expressions of Madhuri and Kanwal, suggesting, in no uncertain terms, that the lyrics are a direct statement of Madhuri's feelings for Kanwal.

At the end of the song sequence, while Kanwal presumably recognizes his sister's voice and says nothing, Madhuri expresses fannish admiration for the singer and vows to find out her address in order to

Poster of *Khazanchi* (Moti Gidwani, 1941).

visit her. Beyond providing a narrative excuse for having Madhuri show up at Kanwal's house the next day in search of his sister, the radio song seems to serve no other purpose. Clearly, the film is not trying to avoid having the heroine perform at all, since later in the film she has her own romantic song sequences with the hero. Moreover, the film does nothing more with the sister's identity as a singing star. Narratively speaking, the radio scene might seem merely gratuitous, but it functions in multiple ways as a moral buffer that diffuses overt suggestions of sexuality in either the heroine or the hero's sister. To play the role of an upper-class, respectable woman in love, the actress playing the heroine has to be distanced from the act of performing such feelings at the initial moment of expressing them; hence the use of a radio song to express her feelings. By having the hero's sister sing the song, the film works hard to simultaneously contain and express female sexuality. The heroine is not singing this song, and the woman whose song she "borrows" is not just any other woman, but her future sister-in-law, the safest possible vehicle for expressing romantic feelings in this context. At the same time, by making the sister a radio singer, the film provides her with a less questionable form of performance. In the shots of her singing in the radio station, her performance is markedly sober, with the emphasis on the aural rather than visual aspects of her performance. Likewise, the only fan of hers that the film represents is another woman, Madhuri, rather than any men.

Ghost Voices and Playback Singers

When playback singers began to be used in the early 1940s, there was considerable anxiety regarding the industry's deception in using what were then called "ghost voices." During this second phase, studios used voice-casting, or the use of a singing voice that matched both the speaking voice and the personality of the actor. Yet, despite voice-casting, the audience's knowledge of a split between singing voice and acting body was a source of discomfort. For example, in the December 1944 issue of *filmindia,* a reader asks, "Isn't the system of using ghost voices harmful? The film-goer soon finds out the trick and the song loses its charm." The editor's attempt at a reassuring reply is that, although this system "lends to the crow a cuckoo's voice, [it] is an artistic fraud which the producers practice on the film-goers with the good intention of giving them maximum entertainment. Though this procedure does interfere considerably with the emotional worship of the average film-fan, it is still a blessing."[28] Similarly, the tendency of repeating the same "ghost voices" receives an extremely negative response because of the obvious disjunction between voice and face, and the technological impression made by such a voice: "These wholesale singing machines like Rajkumari and Amirbai get on people's nerves. . . . They have been repeated too often and whosoever's the face, experienced film-goers spot the voice as belonging to one of these two. Once the identification has been done, where is the emotional thrill in the music? . . . Everyone knows that our Madhuris and Sabitas don't sing. Where then is the sense in selling a falsehood? It is just bad business!"[29] A 1946 fan letter goes so far as to say that "we prefer to hear songs from a gramophone record or a radio instead of from the pictures because we know that the singer on the screen is not really singing."[30]

Aadmi (V. Shantaram, 1939) parodies the use of ghost voices, which the film can safely indulge in because its own heroine is played by the singing star, Shanta Hublikar. In this scene, a woman stands in front of a curtain, performing a song for a male audience in a brothel. But the shot is framed so as to show us a servant boy, the actual singer, hiding behind the curtain. In a comedic performance, the woman merely lip-synchs to the boy's song, while surreptitiously passing coins to him to keep him from revealing her deception to her audience. In the end, the audience sees through the act, as the exchange of money inadvertently reveals the boy to them and they angrily chase after him. As implied in this example, at this point in the history of playback singing, the question of the authenticity of the singing voice is discussed in terms of the morality of vocal substitution and the effect this knowledge has on the viewer, terms similar to those of Hollywood cinema.

How, then, did the split between the voice and the body come to be not only accepted but even to be the desired norm, to the point where voice-casting was no longer practiced? With only a handful of voices dominating the aural environment of Hindi cinema by the end of the 1950s, what mattered in this third phase was no longer whether the voice and body matched, but whether the singing voice was recognizable in and of itself. By the 1960s, in comic song sequences similar to *Aadmi*'s ghost voice parody, it is the film's hero, rather than a minor character, who borrows someone else's voice.[31] With the acceptance and establishment of playback singing, song sequences have simultaneously appealed to a seemingly contradictory set of pleasures, encompassing both knowledge and disavowal of technology. Knowledge of the use of technology enables the recognition of the singing voice as that of the playback star and not the actress, while the willful disavowal of technology allows the pleasure of watching this well-known voice embodied in the physical presence of another star. Song performances are here authenticated precisely through knowledge of the star persona of the singing voice. The morality of vocal substitution becomes irrelevant when the dual star reference makes it equally a question of borrowing a body or of borrowing a voice. That song sequences address both types of pleasure is evidenced by the fact that they are marketed in two ways. One can buy CDs and DVDs titled, for example, either "Golden Hits of Lata Mangeshkar" or "Hits of Hema Malini." In the latter case, the title is legitimate even though everyone knows that Hema Malini is not, in fact, the singer of these songs, but merely embodies their performance. Similarly, the immensely popular stage shows featuring film stars can be either live performances of song sequences by acting stars, while lip-synching, or straightforward musical concerts by playback stars, who may or may not have a strong stage presence.[32] Thus, the marketing of song sequences caters to fan identification geared primarily toward either the aural star or the visual star. This is clearly unlike Hollywood cinema where the practice of anonymous voice dubbing "may rob the singer of the opportunity to reclaim his or her voice in live performance and may prevent the non-singing actor or actress from gaining full credit for the screen performance."[33]

The shift to the dominance of a few recognizable voices is explained in the Bombay film industry as a monopoly engineered by shrewd individuals such as Lata Mangeshkar, who were able to take advantage of the migration of several singers (such as the equally popular Noorjehan) to Pakistan after the partition of India in 1947. In the 1940s war profiteering brought large sums of money into the film industry, causing the demise of the studio system and the rise of independent producers. Since then, Bombay cinema's general tendency toward monopolization also affected the status of playback singers. The heavy odds against commercial success in Bombay films, caused by the punishing tax structure imposed upon it and by the heterogeneous mode of manufacture, dictated the repeated use of "proven" stars, which translated as the most recent box office successes.[34] This imperative toward a "risk free" production system was extended to playback singers as well.

While acting stars have aged over the last five decades and been replaced by others, playback singers have continued to have commercial success, and public taste with respect to their voices has remained unsated. The enduring dominance of a mere handful of singers is also related to their shift to star status, which is indicated in a change in the terminology referring to them: as "ghost voices" they were unacknowledged in credits and relatively unknown to the public, but as "playback singers" they received credit and developed star personae. A further, and ironic, indication of their stardom is their contrast with anonymous "dubbing artistes." Like acting stars, playback singers in high demand also sign on innumerable films simultaneously, which has resulted in the practice of having dubbing artistes "record a song when the actual playback singer is not available and then dubbing it all over again when she is free to record."[35]

The Dynamics of Aural Stardom

One of the earliest song sequences to establish Lata Mangeshkar's star identity was "Aayega Aanewala" (the one who is to come will come) from the film *Mahal* (Kamal Amrohi, 1949), in which she is playback singing for the actress Madhubala. In this sequence, the hero enters an empty mansion following the sound of a beautiful singing voice, which is later revealed to belong to the ghost of the former owner's mistress. Here, both narratively and technologically, we hear a ghost voice, and at both levels the emphasis is on the lure of the disembodied voice. This song is now

Poster of *Mahal* (Kamal Amrohi, 1949).

more closely identified with the star persona of Lata Mangeshkar than with the character played by Madhubala, although Madhubala's death at an early age certainly adds resonance to it. But the song's aural associations are stronger than the visual or narrative context of the film in which it appeared. In the fan discourse on Lata Mangeshkar, it also provides a kind of myth of origins for her identity as a playback star. The record of the song was originally released with the name of the narrative character, Kamini, credited as the singer, but it became so popular that "thousands of requests for the song used to pour in at the radio station along with a request to mention the name of the singer while playing the record. The radio officials approached HMV to find out who the singer of this runaway hit was. As a result of this, Lata's name began to be announced over the radio. It was only with the film *Barsaat* [Raj Kapoor, 1949] that names of the playback artistes began appearing on the records and on screen." In *Cassette Culture,* Peter Manuel observes that, by virtue of their association with cinema, "singers and composers of Indian popular music are not stars themselves. There is no aura of fantasy and glamour woven around the leading singers, who remain invisible voices singing for the actors." Underlying Manuel's observation is a visual conception of stardom based on popular notions of what stars are, so that playback singers cannot be stars because they are invisible and no glamor attaches to their image. It is necessary, however, to theorize an aural conception of stardom to account for the dual pleasures and recognitions in song sequences. This needs to be a concept of stardom in which even the absence of glamor and the invisibility of playback singers can be regarded as defining features of their star personae. In the context of Indian cinema, aural stardom is constituted by voice recognizability, the circulation of extra-textual knowledge about the singers, and the association of certain moral and emotional traits with their voices, which then has an effect on the voice-body construct in song sequences. In a 1967 article marking the twenty-fifth anniversary of Lata Mangeshkar's career, Gangadhar Gadgil waxed hyperbolic on her aural stardom: "To me, and, I believe, to every Indian, Lata Mangeshkar is not so much a person as a voice—a voice that soars high and casts a magic spell over the hearts of millions of Indians from the Himalayas to Kanyakumari." A single voice unites the imagined nation of India. Aural stardom is predicated upon the awareness, and even celebration, of the workings of technology and its ability to embody the star voice.[36]

Lata's song from *Mahal* may be said to mark the transition from "ghost voices" to the aural stardom of "playback singers," a transition forced by fans. The transition to stardom is evident in the different terms in which film magazines write about playback singers within the span of a few years. A 1948 article critiquing the stranglehold of the star system upon the industry complains that, in unjust contrast to the stars, the vast majority of film workers remain unknown and unacknowledged. The article cites, as an example, the contrast between the playback singer and the actor who gets all the fame on the basis of the singer's work.[37] But by 1952 an editorial in *Filmfare* magazine could remark upon Lata's growing hold on the medium, even while mentioning the starlike appeal of other popular playback singers: "In more than ninety out of every hundred films since produced, Lata Mangeshkar has given the playback for all feminine songs. Geeta Roy, Talat Mahmood, Shamshad, Mukesh, and Lata have been as much a draw at the box office as the leading stars."[38] While the tendency toward the monopoly of a few voices is unquestionable in Hindi cinema, this monopoly has itself come to constitute a defining feature of the aura of playback stardom. For fans, the numbers game of who sang how many songs is a subject of enduring and passionate interest. The publication of Har Mandir Singh's four-volume *Hindi Film Geet Kosh* (*The Encyclopaedia of Hindi Film Songs*) in the 1980s added fuel to this pastime and settled many old debates, such as the controversy over Lata's entry in the *Guinness Book of World Records*.[39]

Aural stardom has also been differentiated along gender lines. The female singing voice, being limited primarily to the voices of the sisters

Lata Mangeshkar and Asha Bhosle, cut across any association with a specific acting star. Remaining constant over time and across numerous bodies, the voice of Lata Mangeshkar easily lent itself to appropriation as the norm of ideal femininity, while that of her sister became associated with "oozing sensuality . . . a compelling come-hitherness, which makes her slotted only for the cabaret and disco numbers."[40] In the case of the male voice, with at least three major playback singers between the 1940s and the 1980s (Mukesh, Mohammed Rafi, and Kishore Kumar, all since deceased), the masculine voice tended to be somewhat more varied than the feminine voice. For example, Kishore Kumar's star persona was defined entirely in terms of an eccentric, madcap genius, whose noncomformist and outright lunatic antics provided unending fodder for fan consumption. In terms of its moral traits, the male equivalent of Lata Mangeshkar's voice was that of Mohammed Rafi. The recurring motif in his extra-filmic star persona was his moral uprightness and religiosity. The traits read into male voices also often resulted from their association with specific acting stars, as was the case with the voice-body pairing of singer Mukesh with actor Raj Kapoor, who consciously cultivated a Chaplinesque persona. The distinctions among male voices are less based on gender stereotypes than those of the two main female voices, which soon were divided into the conventional feminine dichotomy of virgin and vamp.

While Lata Mangeshkar provides a case study in playback stardom, in a crucial sense she is more than just an example. By virtue of her five-decade dominance in Indian cinema, she has come to be regarded as synonymous with playback stardom in India. Hence any analysis of the workings of stardom in song sequences must center upon her star persona. In this regard, it is relevant that discussions of Lata's voice emphasize its affinity to the microphone. She exists only as a recorded voice, a voice mediated by technology. Music director Datta Davjekar says, "When it is time to record, you don't have to tell her how far to position herself from the mike, at what angle to hold her face, at what points to turn away slightly to avoid over-emphasis, or how to tackle very high and very low notes or how to control breath. She really knows how to use the microphone. The microphone is her friend."[41] Even being in her presence makes no difference to the mediated nature of her voice, as R. D. Burman recalls. When she was recording for his famous father, S. D. Burman, he tried to listen to her: "I . . . hung around in the singer's booth. The recording started after a while, but it seemed to me that she was only moving her lips, not singing. So I went a bit closer, but it still seemed as if she was not singing at all. . . . And then, I heard the 'terrific voice', sounding exactly as it did in the records. So I asked Baba, 'She's not singing in there, so where is this voice coming from?' And Baba explained, 'That is her style—she appears to be singing so softly, but her voice carries such tremendous power and is so appropriate for the microphone, that the results take your breath away.'"[42] Given this reiteration of the inherent connection between her voice and the technology of playback singing, Lata has come to epitomize playback stardom in Indian cinema. Moreover, in this response to her physical presence in the studio, we see yet again the dominance of voice over body as she is disembodied even in the very act of recording her voice.

Implicit in the dual star reference of female song sequences is a moral hierarchy between the female *voice* and the female *body*. Unlike the voice, the body is available for visual consumption and lends itself more easily to scandalous associations. While technology allows the filmic illusion of a unity of voice and body in the song sequences, their actual division is indicative of a basic contradiction between the two star texts, which is further paralleled by an ideological contradiction in post-1950s Hindi films over the issue of national and feminine identity. Just as the songs themselves are a hybrid of Western and Indian musical forms, the films, too, are ideologically divided. They espouse "traditional" Indian values, while at the same time visually representing Western lifestyles as desirable. This contradiction between traditional India and modern Westernized India recurs at various levels, the most obvious being the simple narrative opposition between "good" (traditional) values and "bad" (Western) values, as represented by characters, settings, clothing, and education. Post-Independence Hindi films have overtly moralized about the values associated with the West, which Rosie Thomas describes as follows: "evil or decadence is broadly categorized as 'non-traditional' and 'western,' although the West is not so much a place, or even a culture, as an emblem of exotic, decadent otherness, signified by whisky, bikinis, an uncontrolled sexuality and what is seen as lack of 'respect' for elders and betters, and (from men) toward womanhood."[43] At the same time, it is precisely the visual potential of this "decadence" that is exploited in some song and dance sequences.

The attempt of post-Independence Hindi films to negotiate the contradictory values of material consumption (associated with the West) and austerity (associated with traditional Indian values) can be seen as the general principle behind the dual star text indicated in the voice-body split in female song sequences. The star image of actresses is based on their visual presence both within the films and in extra-filmic sites such as fan magazines and billboards. When it comes to the lives of acting stars, the emphasis in post-1960s fan magazines has been on scandal and decadence. Rosie Thomas notes that "although the Indian audience is very conservative and easily shocked, this same audience is very eager to be shocked in certain contexts, if one is to believe the evidence of the network of gossip that surrounds the scandals in the lives and loves of film stars in India."[44] Gossip about female acting stars is based on overt sexuality, the flouting of conventions of traditional Indian society, and an emphasis on conspicuous consumption. All of these are values that the narratives in the films themselves equate with the decadent West. Emphasizing public visibility and spectacle, photographs in film magazines display female stars in flamboyant, nontraditional clothing, visually echoing their spectacular presence in the song sequence. All these filmic and extra-filmic visual signs work together to signify and confirm the longstanding association in Indian cinema and theater of female performance with uncontrolled sexuality. The female body, while made available for visual consumption in song sequences and other texts, thus remains subject to moral and nationalist discourse. The female voice, however, as constituted in song sequences, lends itself more to notions of idealized femininity, especially because of its singular nature.

Mary Ann Doane notes that the separation of voice and source, as in the voiceover, carries the risk of "exposing the material heterogeneity of the cinema," which, she says, is masked in the case of synchronous sound, as in the case of playback singing. "As soon as the sound is detached from its source, no longer anchored by a represented body, its potential work as a signifier is revealed."[45] With playback singing, even though the sound is synchronous, the cultural work that produces knowledge of the playback singer serves to undermine the techno-psychic mechanisms of synchronicity as Doane describes it. The uncanny quality of the unanchored voice is indicated in the original name "ghost voice" given to playback singing. But the shift in terminology from ghost voice to playback singer signals a shift in perception of the unanchored body, where it is knowledge of the separation of voice and body and their moral hierarchy that produces a *cultural* anchoring of the female body on display, thereby more than compensating for the potentially disturbing exposure of material heterogeneity of the filmic apparatus.

Lata Mangeshkar and the Idealized Female Voice

In contrast to the Westernized and overtly eroticized persona of the female acting star, Lata Mangeshkar's star persona is defined precisely by the absence of physical beauty and glamor. The recurring trope here is of the ugly woman with the beautiful voice.[46] By extension, this gives rise to clichés about the beauty of the soul rather than of the body with its implicit reference to acting stars. For example, the journalist Khushwant Singh says: "Lata is beautiful. Not in the conventional vulgar film sense, but what the word means to *me.* She is slight, dark, faintly pockmarked. She radiates an aura of goodness, humility. Her *namaskar* is a distant bow. Her eyes never rise to meet you." In Lata Mangeshkar's star persona, the perceived purity of her voice is extended to her moral character. According to Gangadhar Gadgil, Lata's voice is "ageless, pure, vibrantly alive . . . [and] really belongs to a temple or ashram." Thus, Lata is frequently compared to the medieval singer-saint Meera, a parallel that is reinforced by Lata's own attribution of her success to *tapasya* (religious dedication). Her first recording of Meera *bhajans* (devotional songs) came out in 1968. But even before this, in 1967, Gadgil says, "it would have been . . . appropriate if a voice such as Lata's had sung exclusively the ecstatic bhajans of Mirabai . . . [which] are an expression of total surrender to God. They are a quest which can only be expressed by a voice such as Lata's."[47]

In keeping with her "Meera-image," fan discourse about Lata Mangeshkar emphasizes the austerity of her lifestyle, despite her fabulous wealth, while representing her in traditional familial roles. Describing a visit to her home, one reporter writes, "it is not the glittering home of a superstar which the chance visitor would expect to walk into. The last expectation for glamour evaporates when Lata enters the room. Dressed in her habitual off-white sari, peering hard through her stern reading glasses, she is mending her school-going nephew's shirt." He describes her apartment as having "an austere decor. . . . The drawing-room has no paintings, no objet d'art. The only intruder from the modern age is an electric clock."[48] One sees the clear ideological construction of her image in terms of traditional Indian religious and familial values in the fact that no sexual scandal attaches to her image, despite actual food for gossip in her life: articles about her make no more than a passing reference to her longstanding "association" with Rajasthan prince Raj Singh Dungarpur. Thus in direct contrast to the overt sexuality in the representation of visual stars, Lata Mangeshkar is completely desexualized. Describing the effect of this on individual song sequences, Partha Chatterjee says, "The picturisation got past the stringent Censor Board of the time because the innocent manner in which the song was sung (in playback) . . . served to deflect the message so clearly present in the tall, shapely dancer's movements."[49] Not surprisingly, a visual indicator of her public persona is that Lata Mangeshkar is invariably to be seen in a white sari. That star personae are not fixed, but develop over time, is indicated by the fact that some elements of her current public persona are taken from the early years of her career, before her separate star identity was established. Her visual identification with a white sari has its origins in the formative years of her career when she was often paired with the acting star Nargis, who was also known as "the woman in white."[50]

Despite Lata's monopoly, her image was not always fixed into the Meera type. In the 1950s, for instance, when playback singers were only newly regarded as stars, her star persona was based on a different kind of opposition to the acting star. Instead of an implied moral difference between voice and face, Lata's image allowed the inscription of the ordinary in the extraordinary. The democratic assertions underlying the Hollywood ideology of stardom promised the possibility of class mobility in stories about actors who rose from ordinary circumstances to stardom by means of their talent, hard work, or luck. Given the anxieties surrounding social class and public performance in India, the discourse of stardom not only avoided narratives of class mobility but insisted on its opposite, that the lower classes would only demean this new medium. During the 1950s Lata's star persona relied on its difference from the acting star, based on appearance. When she was the voice of Nargis and other major female stars, she helped to anchor the glamorous and potentially slanderous aura of the acting star in the ordinary and the unglamorous. Articles on Lata routinely stressed her ordinary, even ugly appearance, her poor choice in clothes, her awkward manner, and her lack of sophistication.[51] Likewise, profiles of acting stars also stressed their ordinary human nature. This body of characteristics in Lata helped to democratize the acting star, not through narratives of class mobility, but merely through difference in appearance and manner.

The Hindi film song sequence's ideological investment in the split between the eroticized female body and the pure female voice is well illustrated in the history of the film *Satyam Shivam Sundaram*, released in 1978. The director, Raj Kapoor, was supposedly inspired by Lata's voice to make a film about an ugly woman with a beautiful voice. Even though Lata remained the playback singer for the lead role, the actress chosen to play the ugly woman was Zeenat Aman, a fashion model and winner of beauty contests, including the 1970 Miss Asia contest. The irony of his choice of actress was not lost upon critics or upon Lata, who then failed to turn up for her recording sessions and stalled the final production of the film by months.[52] In the public eye, the film, which was a box office flop, failed to negotiate the contrary desires for a moral fable regarding the emptiness of physical beauty and for the eroticized spectacle of scantily clad Zeenat Aman.

Zeenat Aman in *Satyam Shivam Sundaram* (Raj Kapoor, 1978).

Because of the decadence ascribed to the world of cinema and the logic of the split between pure voice and eroticized body, fan discourse stops just short of denying Lata's connection with the cinema. For example, the 1967 article marking her silver jubilee observes, "It is incongruous that Lata should have almost exclusively devoted herself to singing songs for films." Writing about Lata's film career in 1995, Partha Chatterjee says: "Perhaps an early exposure to the duplicity and moral degradation within the film industry made her turn away from worldliness and seek emotional sustenance in a less troubled private world. The result of this experience was startling: her singing had an innocence and naiveté that was completely at odds with the trying world she had lived in. Thus when she sang (playback) for adult heroines in films, her songs, in retrospect, were a surreal counterpoint to the amorous desires of the actresses concerned."[53] Lata has herself participated in this distancing from the world of cinema by repeatedly expressing regret at an aborted classical music career. In a two-part interview on Zee TV after receiving the 1999 Padma Vibhushan, India's highest national honor, she again mentioned this regret and spoke of her desire to spend the rest of her life singing religious and classical music: "In my career this is the only vacuum which bothers me. If I would have started it earlier it would have been better as it is very tough now."[54] This aspect of Lata's star persona was reinforced by her refusal to sing songs that she considered to be "vulgar."[55] Such songs often became associated with her sister's voice, which the music director Naushad described as having, in contrast to Lata's voice, a tinge of the bazaar in it.[56] Between the two sisters, there-

Lata Mangeshkar. From the author's collection.

fore, they met both the ideological and the commercial requirements of the entire market for the female singing voice. As Raju Bharatan puts it, "The elder [sister] picks up all the soft and lilting pieces while the younger wraps up all the hot numbers."[57]

A popular slogan, "Lata is Meera, Meera is Lata," while identifying her with the medieval singer-saint, also echoes the 1970s political slogan, "Indira is India, India is Indira."[58] Like Indira Gandhi, Lata Mangeshkar is perceived as a tough woman who has handled her career with shrewd business acumen. This aspect of her reputation also works to effectively reinforce the desexualized nature of her star persona. She was the first playback singer to fight for a share in the royalties of film songs, instead of a flat fee for each song. This led to a much publicized dispute with Mohammed Rafi and others in the film industry.[59] In the context of her shrewd career moves, most of the gossip about her centers on her relationship with her sister, Asha Bhosle, who is outspoken about being a victim of Lata's monopolization of the female playback industry. The assumption that Lata has the ultimate monopoly is, arguably, itself something of a construct, because her dominant position in the playback industry has more to do with her place in the public imagination than with the actual number of songs she has recorded. Her star persona is also, in part, defined by her now controversial entry in the *Guinness Book of World Records* as the world's most recorded singer, a claim that was disputed by her male rival, the late Mohammed Rafi, and also by her sister.[60] One strand of popular discourse condemns Lata for her voice monopoly, but that monopoly, in the form of popular taste, was also shaped by the regulation of the female singing voice in arenas outside cinema, with an array of administrative and cultural changes that were designed to cleanse aural traces of courtesan culture in the actual pitch of women's singing voices. In classical music, the respectable voice was shaped in the context of the emergence of upper-class women in vocal public performance where "the natural voice and the chaste female body were linked." In this context, one can read Lata's monopoly in terms of the "clean" lines of her thin, higher pitched voice replacing other voices, such as those of Noorjehan and Shamshad Begum, who had a greater density and lower pitch to their voices. Explanations for Lata's voice monopoly are by no means exhausted by the contradictory, but recognizably gendered explanatory frameworks of cutthroat manipulation, sisterly maneuvering, business acumen, piety, and natural talent.[61]

Some of these issues pertaining to the aural stardom of Lata Mangeshkar are illustrated in the continuation of the sequence from *Naseeb* with which I began this discussion. The lozenge commercial is being filmed in London, and the director of the commercial tries to persuade the fictional star to wear a bikini while filming it. When he grows insistent and she continues to refuse, the hero intervenes. Reminding the expatriate director of the values of his native land, he says, "Listen, you foreign crow, the women of our country are beautiful by wearing clothes, not by taking them off." The film distances itself from its own primary mode of stardom, by making the fictional star a singer rather than an actress. Furthermore, the fictional singer borrows her austerity from the known star persona of the actual singer. Here, questions of national identity are neatly conflated with norms of femininity and foreground the dichotomy between the singing voice and the displayed body. At this point, the gender connotations of the dual star text of the singer-star are also reinforced as she is "rescued" by the hero. Accompanying the rescue is a reversal in the direction of looks with which this sequence started. Now it is Hema Malini who is looking at the hero, her admiring glances confirming both his masculinity and his national identity. The film's preferred mode of stardom is represented by the values given to the fictional character played by the actress Hema Malini. In refusing to wear a bikini, which is Hindi cinema's ultimate symbol of decadent modern femininity, both the fictional and the real-life star verbally distance themselves from associations of the body, while suggesting its erotic potential. They borrow not only the voice of Lata Mangeshkar but also traits of her star persona—specifically, her identification with traditional values. The resulting construct is Hindi cinema's notion of the ideal woman whose sexuality is both suggested and contained. She is visually beautiful in accordance with the changing tastes of the time, but her familiar and unchanging voice signifies a traditional purity that transcends the female body on the screen.

Since the 1990s, the voice monopoly of playback singers has given way to multiple voices, especially with the older generation of male singers all deceased. In the mid-1990s Lata and Asha were understood to have graciously "permitted" new voices, the idea being that their popularity was still so enduring that nothing short of a voluntary stepping aside would make room for others. While multiple voices indicate less development of a clear-cut star persona for new singers, this has had the effect of adding new layers to the aural stardom of Lata and Asha. Since they continue to sing playback for the occasional film, Asha more so than Lata, and with the same consistently high level of commercial success, the "ageless" quality of their voices is stressed—the woman over seventy playbacking for the sixteen-year-old. With age, the moral gap between the voices of Lata and Asha is also closing, as demonstrated by many articles "reassessing" Asha's career in terms of her missed opportunities and the real affinities between her vocal qualities and those of her sister. Similarly, Lata's Meera image began to acquire overtones of the elder guru.[62] Younger singers invariably made a public point of seeking her blessings, even while making veiled references to her grasping hold over the industry.[63] Music videos and independent recording artists have now significantly altered the relation between film song and popular music in India. With the music video, the nature of the public's encounter with the singing voice has changed. The voice is no longer the invisible, immediately recognizable, aural entity. Instead, through the music video, it acquires a visual dimension beyond its embodiment in an actor or actress, so that now even Asha Bhosle herself appears in music videos. While song sequences remain a central feature of Hindi cinema and playback remains its predominant technology, with all these changes and above all, with the multiplication of the singing voice, the female voice and body are undergoing new and varied forms of commodification. Even as song sequences appropriate the look of music videos, the non-film music video is once again producing singing stars whose voice and body are unified.

In focusing on the 1930s through the 1950s, this book has tracked first a lack and then a proliferation of star discourse. This initial "lack" was not only a paucity of research materials, but also a characteristic of the discourse of cinema stardom in India, which evaluated Indian stars in terms of a lack of technical expertise and moral standing. Around the late 1940s, lack changed to its opposite when an intensified star discourse began to dominate film magazines, and the Indian star was no longer measured against Hollywood and other international standards. The 1950s marks the point of transition into the proliferation of star presence inherent in the Indian "star system," and also into a reconstitution of the star in terms of private information, looking forward to the emphasis on star lives in contemporary Indian and Bollywood star discourse.[64] In the 1950s,film magazines begin to discuss stars less in terms of their cinematic roles, and more as fascinating private beings. In ending this book in the early 1950s, I might have offered further case studies of individual female stars, such as Meena Kumari or Madubala. Instead, I chose to focus on a vocal star, Lata Mangeshkar, whose long career has allowed me not only to point out broader trends in Indian forms of stardom, but also to bring the book to the present in a still-unfinished account of her ongoing star career. An equivalent study might have included a star analysis of Cuckoo, the actress who routinely played dancing girls from the late 1940s through the late 1950s. She was replaced by Helen, who had an even longer career playing Westernized cabaret girls, from her first uncredited roles in the early 1950s, including *Awara* (Raj Kapoor, 1951), up to the early 1980s.[65] The "star system," as defined in the specific context of Indian cinema, emphasizes the inherently ephemeral nature of stardom, especially for female stars, producing a structure of intensive capitalization of what is understood to be a fast-depleting resource. In this context, one cannot overestimate the structural importance of the enduring careers of figures who might not ordinarily be considered stars, such as Lata Mangeshkar or Helen. While the central female star might have quickly worn out her welcome on the screen, it was the seemingly peripheral players, such as the playback singer or the vamp, who remained in place and provided, through their staying power, a stability and familiarity of structure that the Hindi film might otherwise have lacked.

The history of the economics of the star system in India is dominated by a dialectic of impermanence and stability. Top stars, fearing the transience of stardom, appeared in as many films as possible in a given year, creating a rhetoric of excess and insecurity. At the same time a structure of stability and continuity emerged through recurrent supporting stars, such as playback singers, stunt stars, cabaret performers (such as Cuckoo and Helen), and comic actors (such as Johnny Walker), who enabled the emergence of a recognizable and enduring cinematic form. In the numbers game, it is the peripheral stars who win: like top stars, they performed in countless films per year, but as secondary performers, their stardom was won by their sheer durability and the number of years in which they continued to play the same role. Lata Mangeshkar's half-century career was possible partly because it was her voice rather than her body that became the focus of her stardom. Other supporting stars similarly had far more years on the screen than most top stars, whose careers tended to swiftly dwindle into the dreaded lower status of "character actor."

The current star who seems to combine these two aspects of the star phenomenon in India—durability as well as intense visibility—is Amitabh Bachchan. By the early 1990s he seemed to have traversed the typical top star trajectory: multiple film roles per year over the course of a decade (the 1970s), followed by fewer and fewer films per year in the next decade. The prognosis was that his career would continue in occasional appearances, rather than the character actor destiny of an earlier generation of stars, such as Ashok Kumar, who was a top star in the 1940s and a character actor from the 1950s until the 1990s. Instead, Bachchan has had a second stardom starting in the early 2000s and continuing up to the present. And along with his second decade of stardom, in which his age is acknowledged but seemingly makes no difference to his primary billing in films, there has also been a shift in the dynamics of permanence in Hindi cinema stardom. Rather than bet on stable peripheral stars whose familiarity might provide a structural permanence in the face of changing stars, Hindi cinema now has found a different form of stability in the immortal genealogies of star dynasties, with dozens of second- and third-generation stars stepping in to take the place of their mothers, fathers, cousins, uncles, and aunts. In the case of Bachchan again, and paralleling the political dynasties by which independent India has been ruled, especially in the case of the dynastic Gandhi-Nehru family, the concentration of star power and permanence has been extended to the star's son Abhishek Bachchan. Star monopoly was further solidified and kept all in the family with Abhishek's much publicized marriage to Aishwarya Rai, one of the top female stars. Yet, even today, star durability has a gendered division of voice and body. Bachchan, the male star whose eternally young, but aging, body is visibly celebrated on screen, now has had more than thirty years of stardom, while for the female star, the only avenue to permanence remains the voice, and in that arena Lata and her sister Asha have continued to be unrivaled.

If in the early decades of cinema in India, social and "cultured" status were the most coveted qualities in film stars, this has now been replaced by star genealogy. Still markedly different from the Hollywood ideology of social mobility through stardom, the class-based discourse of education and culture in earlier forms of stardom has now been replaced by an equally class-based ideology centered on ancestry. This analysis of the star system as inherently dynastic in contemporary Hindi cinema is sharply implicit in the 2007 blockbuster homage to Bollywood, *Om Shanti Om* (dir. Farah Khan), whose hero, Om, starts out as a minor actor in the 1970s. The film hyperbolically demonstrates the impossibility of a Hollywood-style dream of rising from humble beginnings to fame, by having Om lack any means to realize his dreams of stardom except through death and reincarnation as the son of a top Bollywood star. Yet in the best tradition of Hindi cinema, this analysis is also placed in the entertainment context of a euphoric celebration of three decades of star fascination, with numerous cameo appearances by stars, primarily in a sequence celebrating the talentless Om's success in winning the "best actor" prize in the *Filmfare* awards. In having the reincarnated Om remember his past self and reconnect with his humble roots, the film underlines the fantasy scenario of the availability of stardom to anyone who desires it strongly enough, even if that desire can only be fulfilled in the next life. Yet in having Shahrukh Khan play Om, the film also slyly points to the possible viability of ordinary dreams of stardom, since Khan is a notable exception to the dynastic rule of star families, having no connection to any other star.

Equally perceptive is the film's different treatment of the star aspirations of its male and female protagonists. Through its tribute to a long list of stars, the film removes reincarnation from a religious context to one of cinema history, serving as a reminder that this is indeed the current generation's revenge, through self-reflection, on past generations of film producers who famously drove iconic female stars like Meena Kumari to their death. Om dies midway through the film, but more important perhaps for the narrative, Shanti, the actress with whom he falls in love, also dies, murdered by her producer-husband. Their trajectories take opposite directions, for Shanti is already a top star in the 1970s when she is murdered. Significantly, the film does not have Shanti reincarnated like Om in the 2000s. Instead, a lookalike (played by the same actress) with significantly diminished acting skills shows up in the 2000s and is used by the reincarnated Om in an elaborate revenge set-up to play the ghost of Shanti so as to get a confession from her murderer. Thus Shanti's experience of stardom is not only brief and shortlived, but also takes place one generation earlier, while the film shows Om attaining his star aspirations in this next generation exclusively through birth, rather than talent. In this gendered difference between who gets to be reincarnated, the film deftly acknowledges the historical truth of the ascendance of the male star over the female star in contemporary Hindi cinema.

NOTES

Introduction: Translocating Hollywood Stardom in India

1. Lakshmanswaroop Tripathi, "What Do They Want? Serious Advice from Cinema Viewers to Film Producers," *Rangbhoomi,* annual issue, January 1933, 106–9 (my translation and paraphrase). Since I refer to so many magazines and newspapers, for the convenience of the reader I have included a fuller identification of each magazine in the Works Cited. I hesitate to use the term *fan magazine,* and prefer *film magazine* instead, to describe these journalistic sites because the concept of "fan" is so closely tied to that of "star." Until the end of the 1930s, when trade newspapers and magazines began to appear, there was no formal separation between film magazines and trade journals. But even in the 1940s, most film magazines continued to address film professionals as well as film audiences. What the film weekly *Filmfare* was to say in its first issue in 1952 thus applies to most film magazines until then: "It is from the dual standpoint of the industry and its patrons, who comprise the vast audience of movie fans, that 'Filmfare' is primarily designed" (Editorial, *Filmfare,* 7 March 1952, 3). Most magazines carried, in addition to film-related articles and screenplays, items of general interest, such as fiction, poetry, song lyrics, and social commentary. Some, like *Sound,* also carried political news and analysis.

2. *filmindia,* December 1937, 4. This monthly magazine used an affected lowercase form for its title.

3. Hughes, "Is There Anyone Out There?" 29–30; Rajadhyaksha, "Neo-Traditionalism," 24.

4. Rajadhyaksha, "Phalke Era," 56; Rajadhyaksha, "Neo-Traditionalism." For a discussion of such transmutations in Indian calendar art and commercial design, see Jain, "Figures of Locality and Tradition." See also Christopher Pinney's argument against the canonization of Ravi Varma as the founder of modern Indian art (*Photos of the Gods,* 60–71).

5. Gutman, *Through Indian Eyes,* 15; Pinney, *Photos of the Gods,* 24.

6. India's first feature-length film is now acknowledged to be R. G. Torne's *Pundalik,* released on 18 May 1912 (Rajadhyaksha and Willemen, *Encyclopaedia of Indian Cinema,* 243).

7. Phalke's own account of how his interest in filmmaking was aroused has subsequently been read by film historians as the originary moment in the awakening of nationalist film aspirations in India. Phalke recounts how, at a 1910 screening of *The Life of Christ,* he was fired by the exciting possibility of creating "Indian images on the screen." He says, "I experienced a strange indescribable feeling . . . at the sight of the noble incidents in Christ's life. While the life of Christ was

rolling before my physical eyes, I was mentally visualizing the Gods, Shri Krishna, Shri Ramchandra, their Gokul, and Ayodhya" ("Indian Cinema—I," 88).

8. Chabria, *Light of Asia,* 20. In its brief history of Indian cinema, the editorial in the 1934 annual issue of *Moving Picture Monthly* mentions the source of popularity of the stunt genre: "The average Indian picturegoer wants stunts and magic and thrills in a picture. This vogue was started in India by the success of *Thief of Bagdad* and Rudolf Valentino pictures" (rpt. in Bandopadhyay, *Indian Cinema,* 17–29). Likewise, the *Report of the Indian Cinematograph Committee* in 1927–28 states that "the most popular film ever shown in India was 'The Thief of Bagdad,' with Douglas Fairbanks in an Oriental setting" (21).

9. See Hansen, "Mass Production"; and Zhang, *Amorous History,* xv. See also Jennifer Bean and Diane Negra's edited collection, *A Feminist Reader in Early Cinema*; and *Camera Obscura*'s two special issues, no. 48 on early women stars and no. 60 on new women of the silent screen.

10. On the point that Hollywood provides the paradigmatic norm for stardom, see also Babington 3; and Gledhill, "Screen Actress," 193.

11. M. Hansen, "Falling Women, Rising Stars, New Horizons," 14; M. Hansen, "Mass Production of the Senses," 340–41; Russell, "Naruse Mikio's Silent Films," 60.

12. On the "Modern Girl," see Barlow et al., "Modern Girl around the World."

13. M. Hansen, "Mass Production," 341.

14. See Bruno, *Streetwalking on a Ruined Map.*

15. See Majumdar, "Film Fragments."

16. Studlar, *This Mad Masquerade,* 2.

17. Regarding star analysis, Dyer notes that "one needs to think in terms of the relationship . . . between stars and specific instabilities, ambiguities and contradictions in the culture" (Dyer, "Charisma," 58). The "real" person refers to Dyer's notion of "authenticity" as discussed in "*A Star is Born.*"

18. I want to clarify here that the focus of this book is on North Indian cinema and that an important and equally complex articulation of star discourses existed in the South Indian cinema and in the Madras studios in particular.

19. Gledhill, "Screen Actress from Silence to Sound," 199.

20. Chakrabarty, "Nation and Imagination," 29, 43.

21. Knight, "Star Dances," 390; Babington, "Introduction," 4. See Lucy Fischer's discussion of Garbo as art deco design, and Hastie, *Cupboards of Curiosity.*

22. See Bean, "Technologies of Early Stardom and the Extraordinary Body"; Fischer, "Greta Garbo and Silent Cinema."

23. See Rajadhyaksha, "'Bollywoodization' of Indian Cinema," for a discussion of the independent development of cinema as a culture industry in India outside state support.

24. See Kaushik Bhaumik's exhaustive and original research on this shift in "Emergence of the Bombay Film Industry."

25. Rajadhyaksha, "'Bollywoodization' of Indian Cinema," 126.

26. See Huyssen, *After the Great Divide.*

27. See Sinha, "Nationalism and Respectable Sexuality in India."

28. James Clifford, *The Predicament of Culture* (quoted in Niranjana, *Mobilizing India,* 3).

29. For some recent works on Indian silent cinema, see Bhaumik, "Emergence of the Bombay Film Industry"; Dass, "Outside the Unlettered City"; and Jaikumar, *Cinema at the End of Empire.*

30. The earliest analysis of Amitabh Bachchan was by Vijay Mishra, Peter Jeffery, and Brian Shoesmith in "The Actor as Parallel Text." They proposed a mode of star analysis that took into account the formal and cultural specificities of post-Independence Indian cinema. Mishra has extended those ideas to an analysis of fanzine discourse around Bachchan in his *Bollywood Cinema.* Other significant readings of the Bachchan star text include those of Sumita Chakravarty, Ranjani Mazumdar, and Ashwini Sharma. I discuss others' readings of Fearless Nadia and Nargis in chapters 4 and 6, respectively.

31. The Indian Cinematograph Committee (ICC) interviewed more than a thousand respondents in Bombay, Calcutta, Madras, Lahore, and Burma during 1927 and 1928. The *Report* is their summary and recommendations based on the interviews and written questionnaires. The committee also published the five-volume *Evidence,* which is a transcript of the "Oral Evidence of Witnesses and Their Written Statements" (hereafter cited as *ICC: Evidence*). For a discussion of the conflicting interests represented by the committee, see Jaikumar, *Cinema at the End of Empire.*

32. See Hughes, "Is There Anyone Out There?" 80. The ICC is rife with discussion of the undesirable lower classes and their cinematic tastes. For an overview of the ICC's discussion of class, see Dass, "Outside the Unlettered City."

33. "This Stardom Racket: Overnight Glamour Products," *filmindia,* October 1942, 45–46.

1. The Split Discourse of Indian Stardom

1. "Making of Stars," *Filmland,* Puja issue, November 1932.

2. Editorial, *filmindia,* December 1937.

3. Leo Braudy's history of fame takes as one of its starting premises the ordinary individual's dream of fame and urge toward achievement in Western culture (*Frenzy of Renown,* 7). My interest is not so much in the dream of fame, as in the forms of circulation of fame.

4. We find similar uses of the English word *star* in early French cinema, including Méliès's Star Film Co. (Vincendeau, *Stars and Stardom in French Cinema,* viii).

5. *Times of India,* 27 July 1927 (rpt. in Subramaniam, *Flashback,* 59); Chabria, *Light of Asia,* 19.

6. See the entry on Madan Theatres in Rajadhyaksha and Willemen, *Encyclopaedia of Indian Cinema,* 139.

7. *Times of India,* 27 January 1920 (rpt. in Subramaniam, *Flashback,* 40). See also Garga, *Art of Cinema,* 163.

8. Biswabasu Ray Chowdhury, "A Saunter through Screen-dom in Bengal," *Varieties Annual,* 1 January 1934, 13.

9. Paragraphs 88–92 of the *Report of the Indian Cinematograph Committee 1927–1928* were devoted to "complaints regarding Madans' alleged monopoly" (43).

10. There is as yet no published history of fame in India. However, the following works are relevant. Ranajit Guha's chapter on "Transmission" in *Elementary Aspects of Peasant Insurgency in Colonial India* analyzes "the correspondence between the public discourse of rumour and the popular act of insurrection" (259). Rimli Bhattacharya and Kathryn Hansen discuss actresses of the Bengali and Parsi theaters, respectively, while Tanika Sarkar takes up notoriety rather than fame in her work on scandals.

11. deCordova, *Picture Personalities,* 24; Nasir, quoted in K. Hansen, "Different Desire," 177. Similar forms of passion are referenced in what happened to Janaki Bai, a popular singer and dancer of the 1920s and 1930s who was stabbed fifty-six times by an admirer when she refused to be his exclusive paramour (Tharu and Lalitha, *Women Writing in India,* 384).

12. See Fuller, *Motion Picture Story Magazine*; and Stamp, *Movie-Struck Girls.*

13. There was similarly no fan discourse in terms of merchandise in Shanghai, but there was fan-actress interaction in the form of personal encounters as, for example, when "hundreds of fans" went to meet a star at the train station (Chang, "Good, the Bad, and the Beautiful," 135–36).

14. See Banerjee, *Parlour and the Streets.*

15. P. Chatterjee, *Nation and Its Fragments,* 138–39. On the oral aspects of Gandhi's renown, see, for instance, Amin, "Gandhi as Mahatma."

16. See Christopher Pinney's discussion of lithographs of Khudiram's execution in "Nation (Un)Pictured?" 855–60, and of both Khudiram and Bhagat Singh in *Photos of the Gods,* 117–28.

17. See, for example, Knizkova, *Drawings of the Kalighat Style,* 79. Some of the popular topics of these paintings, included in Knizkova's book, are men and women embracing, women beating men and vice versa, ridicule of men dominated by women, dancing women and prostitutes, and the lifestyle of Europeans. See also R. Chatterjee, "Representation of Gender in Folk Paintings of Bengal."

18. The most extensive discussion of this event is to be found in Tanika Sarkar's "Scandal in High Places," which reads the Tarakeshwar scandal as an event that "knits up the everyday with the grand themes of a historical period," in particular, debates over gender norms, law, domesticity, and ideal Hindu womanhood (36). See also Banerjee, *Parlour and the Streets,* 132; and Archer, *Bazaar Paintings of Calcutta.*

19. Archer, *Bazaar Paintings of Calcutta,* 12. This street culture is described by Banerjee, *Parlour and the Streets.*

20. Sumanta Banerjee suggests one explanation for this association of prostitution with female public performance of any sort. He argues that it was Western-educated, middle-class "disapproval of the style of popular female singers" that led to "an attempt to brand them as prostitutes, so that they could be driven out from the streets under the anti-prostitution law" ("Women's Popular Culture in Nineteenth Century Bengal," 153). See also S. Joshi on the successful takeover of courtesan culture in Lucknow. R. Bhattacharya, Introduction to Binodini Dasi, *My Story and My Life as an Actress,* 13.

21. In her autobiography, Binodini describes the print reviews as follows: "Needless to say, my acting was discussed extensively in print. Naturally, the criticism comprised both praise and censure." But the criticism "had nothing to do with

my acting. They censured me saying that it was a sin for people of my sort to even act the part of such lofty characters" (*My Story and My Life as an Actress,* 99, 100).

22. R. Bhattacharya, introduction to Binodini Dasi, *My Story and My Life as an Actress,* 22 (emphasis in original). See S. Chatterjee, "Colonial Stage(d)," for a detailed discussion of the debates around the use of actresses to play female roles in nineteenth-century Bengali urban theater.

23. K. Hansen, "Making Women Visible," 135–36.

24. R. Bhattacharya, introduction to Binodini Dasi, *My Story and My Life as an Actress,* 16. Calcutta's first film screening took place on the premises of the Star Theatre (Kaul, *Cinema and the Indian Freedom Struggle,* 12).

25. Binodini Dasi, *My Story and My Life as an Actress,* 89. Analyses of this event include S. Chatterjee, "Colonial Stage(d)," 241; and P. Chatterjee, *Nation and Its Fragments,* 151–55.

26. The conventional date for the beginnings of the star system in Hollywood is usually 1910, when the story about the death of Florence Lawrence was circulated. See Staiger, "Seeing Stars," for a historiography of this event.

27. I am using *discourse* in Richard deCordova's sense (derived from Foucault) of "discursive practice," which, in the star system, includes "both a set of *positions* from which statements about stars can emerge and the *statements* themselves" (*Picture Personalities,* 10; my emphasis). The two main positions deCordova identifies are the films themselves and film journalism, which provided the institutional setting for most of the discourse. In the case of Indian cinema, as I will argue, the network of oral gossip that functioned at the margins of the institutionalized discourse of journalism is a third position, which, however, can also only be accessed through references in print journalism.

28. The same can be said about the studio or the director/producer, both of which were early rivals to the stardom of actors.

29. This is based on the filmography of Indian silent cinema in Chabria, *Light of Asia.* Given the absence of direct and recorded evidence on the films, these numbers must remain tentative, as they are derived, for the most part, from censorship data and refer only to released (and therefore publicly available) films. The *Encyclopaedia of Indian Cinema* mentions fifty-nine films in 1924 (32).

30. Dharamsay, "Introduction: Indian Silent Cinema 1912–1934," 77. Chabria, *Light of Asia,* 19, lists nine genres: the mythological, the devotional, the social, the historical, the costume movie, the stunt movie, the comedy, the literary adaptation, and the crime movie. Most other accounts omit the literary adaptation and comedy as separate categories. See, for example, Ojha, *75 Glorious Years of Indian Cinema.*

31. Concerning the "social" genre, in a 1950 dissertation on Indian cinema, Panna Shah writes that "in the language of the Indian film industry, 'social' is still used to describe a film in which the atmosphere, setting and costumes are modern, as distinct from a mythological or historical film" (30). In other words, in the Indian context, the primary film genres of the mythological and the historical set the terms for all subsequent genre identifications, such as the "social," even though the mythological had become a marginal genre by 1950. One should note, too, that the social as a generic category had been used in theater as well.

32. A more common way of distinguishing between these two categories of genres

was in terms of realism, both in the context of cinema and in other media, such as theater and literature. See Chakrabarty, "Nation and Imagination," for a discussion of debates over realism in Bengali literature based on generic categories.

33. *ICC: Evidence*, 22–23.

34. deCordova, *Picture Personalities*, 23. Patience Cooper's films included *Nala Damayanti* (1920), *Behula* (1921), *Laila Majnu* (1922), and *Noorjehan* (1924), all of whose titles refer to characters famous in mythology or history, the boundaries between these two categories often being blurred.

35. S. Chatterjee, "Colonial Stage(d)," 250; K. Hansen, "Making Women Visible," 133; Gargi, *Folk Theatre of India*, 100.

36. Information extrapolated from Chabria, *Light of Asia*, 76–78.

37. Information extrapolated from Chabria, *Light of Asia*, 93–99.

38. deCordova, *Picture Personalitities*, 23 (my emphasis); *ICC: Evidence*, quoted in Kaul, *Cinema and the Indian Freedom Struggle*, 21; S. Chatterjee, "Colonial Stage(d)," 226; editorial, *Moving Picture Monthly*, annual issue, 1935 (rpt. in Bandopadhyay, *Indian Cinema*, 17–29).

39. Some examples: *Andhare Alo* (*The Influence of Love*, 1922); *Lady Teacher* (1922); *Marriage Tonic* (1922); *Pati Bhakti* (*Devotion to Husband*, 1922); *Matri Sneh* (*Mother's Devotion*, 1923); *Kanya Vikraya* (*Sale of Daughter*, 1924); *Swapna Sundari* (*Dream Damsel*, 1925). None of these films (like the vast majority of Indian silent cinema) has survived.

40. Orsini, "Reading a Social Romance," 187–88. We also see other signs of this self-image of "maturity." Already in 1932, in just the second year of sound production in India, the July issue of *Rangbhoomi* presents the "three ages" of Indian cinema, although the metaphor slips somewhat as it moves from "childhood" and "middle age," not to old age but to "sound films" ("Bharatiya Chitrapat ka Itihas," *Rangbhoomi*, 31 July 1932, 5, 18).

41. See entries on these three films in Rajadhyaksha and Willemen, *Encyclopaedia of Indian Cinema*. I discuss *Cinema Queen* at greater length in chapter 4.

42. Rajadhyaksha and Willemen, *Encyclopaedia of Indian Cinema*, 247; advertisement for *Indira* (featuring Sulochana) in *Bombay Chronicle*, 19 October 1929.

43. The *Report of the Indian Cinematograph Committee 1927–1928* noted Western cinema's fulfillment of "a natural desire to see something of the life of the West which, to the unsophisticated at any rate, is full of novelties" (23).

44. In 1931, the year of India's first sound film, thirteen out of twenty-four sound films belonged to extra-cinematic genres.

45. The switch from silent to sound film is quite dramatic. In 1931, 24 sound films were made, compared to 207 silent films; by 1934 silent film production had dwindled to a mere 7 in comparison to 120 sound films.

46. deCordova, "Emergence of the Star System," 17; deCordova, *Picture Personalities*, XX. See also note 26, above.

47. deCordova, "Emergence of the Star System," 25–26; Chang, "Good, the Bad, and the Beautiful," 133; deCordova, *Picture Personalities*, 98–99, 102; Macnab, *Searching for Stars*, 4.

48. "By 1926, 85 per cent of playing time in India was used by foreign films, of which 9 out of 10 were American. . . . In a year like 1937, 395 imported films

(79 percent of them American) were shown in the country as against only 180 Indian films" (A. D., "America Abroad," 91). However, Hollywood was not the only model of filmmaking available to Indians. In 1932, for example, the Hindi magazine *Rangbhoomi* carried a series of articles on the history of Russian cinema. There were also articles on Italian and British cinema in other journals of the time. But no other cinema received regular features or was referred to as frequently and casually as Hollywood.

49. Patel, "I Was The Only Paper That Counted," 66. Older magazines could easily turn up in *raddi* shops where old reading material, such as newspapers, magazines, and books, could be bought and sold as both reading and packaging material. See P. Joshi, *In Another Country,* for an engaging account of public libraries and the circulation of popular reading material at this time in India.

50. Ellis, "Stars as Cinematic Phenomenon," 91; Wada-Marciano, "Imaging Modern Girls in the Japanese Women's Film," 24, 36.

51. Star profiles: Alice White (April 1932) and Billie Dove (September and October 1932). Hobbies: see the April 1931 issue. Near-miss accidents: Robert Montgomery and Lawrence Gray, "My Greatest Thrill before the Camera," May 1931, 29. Career recommendations: Desmond Kirkpatrick, "Blonde or Brunette? Which Has the Better Chance of Breaking into the Movies?" July 1932, 26–27. Speculative pieces: E. Stephens, "Will Garbo Retire?" August 1932, 27. Events: Erdine Stephens ("*Cinema*'s Los Angeles correspondent"), "A Premiere—A Movie Fan's Supreme Thrill," August 1932, 21–22, proclaiming that "no other city in the world has the number of stars that one of Hollywood's premiere openings brings forth."

52. Sheikh Iftikhar Rasool, "Screen Beauties I Have Known," *The Cinema,* November–December 1932, 13–15.

53. *The Cinema,* April 1932.

54. *Rangbhoomi,* 21 May 1933.

55. *Filmland,* June 1932; *Varieties Weekly,* 11 November 1933.

56. An example is a feature on the secrets of Jean Harlow's success in the 19 January 1934 issue of the Hindi film magazine *Chitrapat.*

57. Ishwariprasad Mathur, "Acting in the Cinema," *Cinema Sansar,* 8 April 1933, 66–69.

58. deCordova, *Picture Personalities,* 107, 117.

59. Fazalbhoy, *Indian Film,* 55–57. Baburao Patel mentions that some film magazines, such as the Gujarati weekly, *Mouj Majah,* "had to exclusively depend on the advertisements of film producers" because they did not get any other advertising ("I Was The Only Paper That Counted," 67).

60. Quoted in Garga, "New Look at an Old Report," 69.

61. Fazalbhoy, *Indian Film,* 58.

62. I do not wish to suggest any kind of unbroken continuity between the aesthetic practices underlying cinema and those of classical Sanskrit drama. Rather, I refer to *rasa* theory in the popular everyday sense (even if ultimately derived from classical texts), which "enters . . . vocabulary as habit, as part of [one's] habitus . . . as an element of the embodied cultural practices that inform [one's] experience of nationalism" (Chakarabarty, "Nation and Imagination," 43). Roughly speaking, *rasa* is the emotional flavor of an aesthetic text. Angelika Heckel compares

rasa to the tasting of juice (which is what *rasa* literally means) but emphasizes its relational quality: "it is realized in the relation and as the relation between audience [or reader or viewer] and stage" (36). Just "as the taste of a juice is generated by the mixture of its ingredients," the *rasa* of a specific text can be one or more dominant emotions/*rasas* or, ideally, a balanced blend of all nine principal *rasas* ("*Rasa*," 37).

63. However, such a focus on facial expression and emotion also seems to have been a wider response generated in the early years of cinema. Béla Balázs, for example, emphasizes facial expression and the play of emotions visible in close-ups when describing "the whole gamut of appropriate emotion . . . displayed in [Asta Nielsen's] face" ("Close-up," 260). Balázs also points to the importance of physiognomy and "microphysiognomy" as modes of communicating subtle information in silent cinema.

64. S. Ramamurthy, "Profile of Miss Zebunissa," *Varieties Weekly,* 16 September 1933, 17–18.

65. *Varieties Weekly,* 7 October 1933, 21 October 1933, 4 November 1933; *Moving Picture World,* 5 April 1913, quoted in Slide, *Lois Weber,* 59.

66. Vinodini Mehta, "Mrs. Khote and Her Art," *Rangbhoomi* (undated; front page missing), 3, 15 (my translation).

67. B. R. Rawal, "Film Acting," *Rangbhoomi,* 14 August 1932, 20 (my translation).

68. See Pearson, *Eloquent Gestures*; and deCordova, "Emergence of the Star System."

69. Gledhill, "Screen Actress" 196; Kaul, *Cinema and the Indian Freedom Struggle,* 14; Prafulla Mookerjee, "Characteristic Features of Cinema-Acting," *Filmland,* 4 June 1932, 112.

70. Novel W. Silverstein, "Manorama (alias Miss Winnie Steuart)," *The Cinema,* August 1931, 23, 28.

71. "Editor's Mail," *filmindia,* November 1939.

72. Sarkar, *Hindu Wife, Hindu Nation,* 56. See Amin, "Gandhi as Mahatma," for an analysis of how rumor was politically mobilized to construct the "Mahatma" out of Gandhi.

73. Editorial, *filmindia,* May 1936.

74. Michael Chang shows a similar double reputation of actresses in Shanghai cinema in the 1920s, where individual actresses were praised for talent, virtue, and sincerity, but were also linked to the general category of "movie actress," which was "characterized as degenerate, corrupted, and deceptive" ("Good, the Bad, and the Beautiful," 129). The split discourse about Indian actresses, however, did not include discussion about individual virtue or sincerity, and unlike Shanghai star identities, was not understood in terms of a private and interiorized "self" that was accessible in screen roles (130).

75. See, for example, the advertisement (on page 74) accompanying Siddharth Kak's essay on Devika Rani, "Colossus and the Little Flower from India."

76. "Buck Up Devika Rani" in "Bombay Calling," *filmindia,* July 1940, 10.

77. Manto, *Stars from Another Sky,* 1. Manto was a screenplay writer for the studio Bombay Talkies and also a film journalist and writer of short stories (in Urdu), who moved to Pakistan after the partition of India in 1947. His career exemplifies the close connection between film journalism and the film industry.

78. "Pimps and Prostitutes," editorial, *filmindia,* May 1940.
79. deCordova, *Picture Personalities,* 119, 105–6.
80. The 1932 *Rangbhoomi* editorial also promised biographies of actors in its planned new format, but this never materialized in subsequent issues, possibly because of the unwillingness to present information on the biographies and private lives of actors.
81. *Times of India,* 21 February 1936 (rpt. in Subramaniam, *Flashback,* 109).
82. Some examples are "star" directors, such as Pramathesh Barua and V. Shantaram.
83. "Notes and News," *filmindia,* August 1939, 21.
84. S. Rangaswamy, "Film and Star Publicity," *Varieties Annual,* January 1934, 16–17.
85. Ghanshiam U. Vaswani, "At the Cinema in 1930," *The Cinema,* August 1931, 21–22.
86. "Editor's Mail," *filmindia,* December 1937, 15.
87. "Cinema Star in Court/Alleged Assault," *Times of India,* 11 February 1928 (rpt. in Subramaniam, *Flashback,* 61).
88. P. Chatterjee, *The Nation and Its Fragments,* 138; Chakrabarty, "Postcoloniality and the Artifice of History" 350; Arnold and Blackburn, "Introduction: Life Histories in India," 13–14.
89. Orsini, *Hindi Public Sphere,* 15. First-person confessional literature provided a space for "taboo-breaking sincerity [and] the voicing of 'prohibited' feelings" (Orsini, "Reading a Social Romance," 202). See also Gupta's discussion of lowbrow literature in *Sexuality, Obscenity, Community.*
90. Orsini, *Hindi Public Sphere,* 15 (emphasis in original); Orsini, "Reticent Autobiographer," 73, 80; Chakrabarty, "Postcoloniality and the Artifice of History," 352.
91. Manto, *Stars from Another Sky,* 205 (my emphasis).
92. "False Stones" in "Bombay Calling," *filmindia,* May 1936.
93. "Editor's Mail," *filmindia,* April 1937, 11.
94. "Editor's Mail," *filmindia,* August 1938, 21.
95. "Editor's Mail," *filmindia,* August 1937.
96. The 3 November 1941 issue of the American *Time* magazine had a brief item about this aspect of *filmindia*: "In Bombay's movie fanpaper, *Filmindia* [*sic*], Editor Baburao Patel conducts an unusually piquant question-&-answer department. Last week Hollywood learned how Editor Patel does it" ("Foreign News [India]," "Such a Thing," 25).
97. In "Veteran Journalist Shocked by Film Journalism" (*Mirror,* 14 May 1939), *filmindia*'s "Question and Answer" section is the specific target.
98. "Editor's Mail," *filmindia,* December 1939.
99. Sulochana, "Love," *Filmland,* Puja issue, 1934 (rpt. in Bandopadhyay, *Indian Cinema,* 101–2).
100. Quoted in P. Chatterjee, *Nation and Its Fragments,* 154.
101. S. Chatterjee, "Colonial Stage(d)," 257–58; Nadkarni, *Bal Gandharva,* 64.
102. Manto, *Stars from Another Sky,* x–xi.
103. P. Chatterjee, *Nation and Its Fragments,* 138.

2. The Morality and Machinery of Stardom

1. Ravi Varma's work is discussed in Guha-Thakurta, *Making of a New "Indian" Art*; Kapur, "Ravi Varma"; Pinney, "Indian Magical Realism"; and Pinney, *Photos of the Gods.*

2. See Rakesh Solomon for similar strategies in Marathi theater. Rimli Bhattacharya's discussion of the nationalist inspiration of Bengali theater points out that "the turning back to the past was inspired in part by the publication of such works as Tod's *Annals and Antiquities* (1829–32), which probably had the single most effect on literary output in subsequent decades" ("Notes on the Bengali Public Theatre," 167).

3. V. Shantaram's *Dharmatma* (1935), whose original title was *Mahatma,* is a case in point. Ostensibly about the Marathi saint-poet Eknath, the historical character and events had enough similarity to current political realities that it attracted censorship.

4. "Editor's Desk," *Varieties Weekly,* 18 November 1933, 1. See also Kaul, *Cinema and the Indian Freedom Struggle,* for a full overview of cinema's direct and indirect engagements with the national movement.

5. *Rangbhoomi,* 10 September 1932. The *swadeshi* movement, starting in 1895, was a "nationalist programme for the boycott of all foreign manufactures and, by extension, a spur to self-reliance and 'Indianness' in education, the arts, technology, etc." (Rajadhyaksha and Willemen, *Encyclopaedia of Indian Cinema,* 225).

6. See, for example, the section on "Cinema as a National Issue" in Bandopadhyay, ed., *Indian Cinema,* which reprints an open letter by K. Ahmad Abbas to Gandhi (*filmindia,* October 1939), protesting his negative attitude to cinema. The January 1940 issue of *filmindia* severely took Gandhi to task for the same reason, saying that "when he talks on subjects about which he knows nothing, he makes himself . . . ridiculous" ("Editors Mail," 18). On the viewing habits of the Indian elite, see, for example, Jyotsna Nath Chanda, who complains that "a good many number of Indians . . . would, without discrimination, prefer any foreign film to the best of our own" ("The Difficulties We Face," *Varieties Annual,* 1 January 1934, 21).

7. The "What's Wrong with Indian Cinema?" genre continues even into the present in film portals such as Upperstall.com, which has a page by that title that critiques and analyzes the shortcomings of contemporary Indian cinema under headings such as "Very Little Originality," "Identity Crisis," "Lack of Appreciation of Good Films," and "Star Power," which cites the prevalence of stars over scripts in selling a film to producers: http://www.upperstall.com/wwic.html. Accessed on 18 May 2007.

8. Journalistic efforts to evaluate national cinemas were not confined to India. In Germany, for example, similar "debates over the relative merits of German and American motion pictures" took place in the early 1920s, with Hans Siemsen a major voice in this debate (Saunders, *Hollywood in Berlin,* 91–96).

9. Guha, *Dominance without Hegemony,* 30–31; Chakrabarty, "Difference-Deferral," 55. Many of these issues are crystallized in the controversy over Katherine Mayo's *Mother India,* which Mrinalini Sinha analyzes in "Reading *Mother India.*"

10. P. Chatterjee, *Nation and Its Fragments,* 10, 7; testimony of Anthony

Soares, principal of Anthony de Souza High School in Bombay, *ICC: Evidence,* 1:380.

11. Quoted in Chakrabarty, "Difference-Deferral," 56.

12. Editorial, *Rangbhoomi,* 22 May 1932, 3 (my translation).

13. Editorial, *Rangbhoomi,* 15 May 1932, 4.

14. See Viswanathan, *Masks of Conquest.*

15. We find a similar tendency in English colonial theater traditions in India. Rakesh Solomon quotes the *Bengal Gazette* describing an English actor in Calcutta as "the Garrick of the East" and mentions the usage of the "Indian Drury" to refer to the Calcutta Theatre ("Culture, Imperialism, and Nationalist Resistance," 339).

16. Chabria, *Light of Asia,* 20; *filmindia,* January 1942.

17. "Editor's Mail," *filmindia,* January 1939, 19.

18. Profile of Master Vithal, *Rangbhoomi,* 2 July 1933, 27. This has echoes in the contemporary discomfort with the term *Bollywood* among Indian film stars such as Ajay Devgan (see Prasad, "This Thing Called Bollywood," 1).

19. For a discussion of the utopian, scientificist, and rationalist discourse underpinning Americanism, see Wollen, "Cinema/Americanism/The Robot," especially 43 (quote).

20. Brigsby, *Superculture,* 16–17; Saunders, *Hollywood in Berlin,* 2–3.

21. See also Arora, "'Imperiling the Prestige of the White Woman.'"

22. Reported in *Times of India,* 9 November 1927; rpt. in Subramaniam, *Flashback,* 78.

23. Garga, "A New Look at an Old Report," 67. See also Jaikumar, *Cinema at the End of Empire.*

24. The title page of the book describes the author as "Proprietor, International Pictures Corporation."

25. Dalvi, *New Profession,* 2–3, 48. One example of this is Saadat Hasan Manto's account of how the male star Ashok Kumar got his first major role through his brother-in-law (*Stars from Another Sky,* 1).

26. Edward Schellorn, "Don't Envy the Movie Stars," *filmindia,* May 1936.

27. Tom Gunning's famous formulation borrows the term from Sergei Eisenstein's usage in the sense of circus attractions, to refer to the kinds of spectator-oriented pleasures of early cinema, in which "theatrical display dominates over narrative absorption" ("Cinema of Attractions," 59). Indian films with a similar formula became increasingly popular with hits like *Khazanchi* (Moti Gidwani, 1941) and films produced in the studio Filmistan.

28. Fazalbhoy, *Indian Film,* 53–61, especially 60 (quotes).

29. Both K. T. Dalvi and Y. A. Fazalbhoy, for example, devote much space to star salaries in their books.

30. "India Has No Stars," Editorial, *filmindia,* December 1937.

31. "John Stewart and Unusual Letters," *Rangbhoomi,* 8 May 1932, 16.

32. S. Rangaswamy, "Film and Star Publicity," *Varieties Annual,* 1 January 1934, 16–17.

33. Charu Roy, "Making of Stars," *Filmland,* Puja issue, November 1932.

34. For example, the April 1932 issue of *The Cinema* promises (in a half-page advertisement) "3 color plates of Sulochana together with 2 colour plates and single colour plates of many Indian and foreign stars" in its forthcoming annual

issue (8). (The numbers refer not to the number of photographs, but to the technique of reproducing color.)

35. See the photographs of matchboxes in Siddharth Kak, "Editorial." My evidence for such star postcard series is from online auctions, where, for example, a postcard of Sabita Devi in *Lagna Bandhan* (Kaliprasad Ghosh, 1936) was for sale along with several other star postcards. It was numbered 375 in the "Sharda Indian Cinema Star Series" printed by S. S. Picture Co. in Calcutta.

36. According to Somaaya, the first actress ever to star in an advertisement was Leela Chitnis in 1955 in *Screen* magazine (*Story So Far,* 53). But Lux soap advertisements featuring stars had already begun in 1943, as seen in a Lux ad featuring Manorama in *filmindia* (July 1943). By 1966 another Lux ad could say: "every star that dazzled the country in this golden era of cinema has been featured in a Lux ad" (quoted in Somaaya, *Story So Far,* 79).

37. Hughes, "Is There Anyone Out There?" 31; Dass, "Outside the Unlettered City," 32.

38. The 1928 *Report of the Indian Cinematograph Committee* devotes a section to the problem that "with a few exceptions . . . the actors and actresses are not drawn from the cultured classes. The actresses are mainly recruited from the 'dancing girl' class" (33).

39. Michael Chang discusses a similar hierarchical discourse linking morality, education, and upper-class status in Shanghai in the 1920s and 1930s ("Good, the Bad, and the Beautiful," 140–41).

40. For an overview of the intellectual history of the nineteenth-century identification of woman and nation in India, see Zutshi, "Women, Nation and the Outsider in Contemporary Hindi Cinema."

41. Sultan Mirza, "Overflow from the Pen of a Sufferer," *Filmland,* 14 February 1931; rpt. in Bandopadhyay, *Indian Cinema,* 67.

42. See P. Chatterjee, "Nationalist Resolution"; and Sinha, "Reading *Mother India.*"

43. P. Chatterjee, *Nation and Its Fragments,* 117. See also N. Bhattacharya, "Notes towards a Conception of the Colonial Public," 152–53.

44. Chakrabarty, "Difference-Deferral," 63, 60; P. Chatterjee, *Nationalist Thought,* 130. In her autobiography, the 1940s star Renuka Devi (Khurshid Mirza) notes that when she first started working in the movies, she "was pleasantly surprised at the congenial and professional atmosphere at Jayant Desai Studios. Jayant Bhai was a family man, and most of the young boys he employed were educated and from respectable homes" (Kazim, *Woman of Substance,* 148). Renuka Devi herself was already married, and her husband accompanied her on the sets everyday.

45. Orsini, "Reticent Autobiographer," 65.

46. Miss Wahida Aziz, "Society on the Indian Screen," *PicturPost,* 15 May 1943, 24 (emphasis in original).

47. Joshi, *Fractured Modernity,* 57, 7.

48. Prasad, *Ideology in the Hindi Film,* 100, 93, 98.

49. Kuhn, *Cinema, Censorship and Sexuality, 1909–1925,* 120; M. Hansen, "Adventures of Goldilocks" 51–72; M. Hansen, "Early Silent Cinema," 155. See also M. Hansen, "Early Cinema, Late Cinema."

50. There is a discussion of the British fears regarding Hollywood's representation of white women as being "dangerously suggestive for Indian men" in chapter

6 of Stephen Putnam Hughes's dissertation on silent cinema audiences in South India, "Is There Anyone Out There?"

51. Sister Nivedita, "The Function of Art in Shaping Nationality," *Modern Review,* January–February 1907; quoted in Guha-Thakurta, *Making of a New "Indian" Art,* 187. Sister Nivedita (formerly Margaret Nobel), was an English disciple of Swami Vivekananda and a significant art critic.

52. Quoted in Bahadur and Vanarase, "Personal and Professional Problems of a Woman Performer," 25.

53. Orsini, "Reticent Autobiographer," 55.

54. K. Hansen, "Making Women Visible," 143. I discuss this process further in chapter 4.

55. K. Hansen, "Making Women Visible," 140.

56. Sarkar, *Hindu Wife, Hindu Nation,* 89. We find examples of this attitude in writings on nineteenth-century Bengali theater as well. For example, one commentator insists that "it is not possible for an uneducated young woman to remain unmoved when listening to [sexually suggestive] episodes like Raas [Krishna's dance with the milkmaids] or Krishna's escape with the clothes of the milkmaids." Quoted in Banerjee, "Women's Popular Culture," 151.

57. Dhiren Ganguly, "Bengal Needs Real Artistes," *Filmland,* Puja issue, 1934; rpt. in Bandopadhyay, *Indian Cinema,* 94–95.

3. *Real and Imagined Stars*

The title of this chapter borrows from Rajeshwari Sundar Rajan's book *Real and Imagined Women,* which argues that "the problems of 'real' women cannot lie outside the 'imagined' constructs in and through which 'women' emerge as subjects" (10).

1. Bhudev Sharma, "Chitrapat," *Rangbhoomi,* 12 March 1933.

2. Rpt. in Subramaniam, *Flashback,* 60.

3. A previous report on this case had said that Ermeline's real motive for suing the studio was that "she wanted a justification for her backing out of her contract of service and joining a new Company which she was immediately starting" (*Times of India,* 27 July 1927; rpt. in Subramaniam, *Flashback,* 59)

4. Rpt. in Subramaniam, *Flashback,* 60.

5. Rpt. in Subramaniam, *Flashback,* 63.

6. Harishchandra Vidhyalankar, "A Few Words with Miss Ermeline (Sudhabala)," *Rangbhoomi,* annual issue, 1933, 145–52 (quote on 152).

7. A Lady Artiste, "Should Respectable Ladies Join the Films?" *Filmland,* 26 September 1931; rpt. in Bandopadhyay, *Indian Cinema,* 108–10.

8. Sabita Devi, "Why Shouldn't Respectable Ladies Join the Films," *Filmland,* 7 November 1931; rpt. in Bandopadhyay, *Indian Cinema,* 111–13.

9. Snehaprabha Pradhan, "Oh A Mere Actress! A Plea to Cast Off Hypocrisy!" *filmindia,* February 1941, 39–41.

10. For more on Hollywood stardom and the American dream, see Dyer, "Stars as Stars," in *Stars,* 33–46.

11. Sindhu Gadgil, "A Snob's Reply to a 'Mere Actress'" *filmindia,* March 1941, 41–42.

12. "Social Status of Stars," *filmindia,* February 1940, 8–9.

13. K. Ahmad Abbas, "Fans! Where Are Your Manners? A Plea for Less Vulgarity in Expressions of Admiration," *filmindia,* March 1940, 43–45.

14. Baburao Patel, "Sandhya—The Prostitute-Actress! Is a Star Born in the Producer's Bed?" *filmindia,* December 1940, 21–27.

15. For example: "That's how the stars are received in India. Mammoth crowds welcomed Ashok Kumar and Leela Chitnis when they arrived at the Lahore Station" (22).

16. "Editor's Mail," *filmindia,* February 1941.

17. *Stars from Another Sky.* See also Reuben, *Follywood Flashback,* for a more recent example of the same phenomenon.

18. For instance, *Bombay Chronicle*'s "Stars Speak for Themselves!" 1 February 1940, carried an item about Patel's visit to Hollywood. Manto, *Stars from Another Sky,* also devoted an entire chapter to Patel.

19. For instance, Kamini Kaushal "prefers English pictures. In fact, she hadn't even seen an Indian picture until she acted in one" ("An Interview with Kamini Kaushal," *Sound,* April 1949, 48–52 [quote on 52]).

20. The Bengali-language version of this film, released in the same year, was *Bhagya Chakra.*

21. The similarity here between the actor and the role is an instance of the aesthetics of frontality, which I discuss in chapter 4.

22. The *Encyclopaedia of Indian Cinema* has the following comment on *My Sister*'s treatment of the female star: "The film passes an unusually harsh judgement on Rekha, notwithstanding the convention of damning 'liberated' women in the Indian cinema of the time" (Rajadhyaksha and Willemen, 302).

23. Devika Rani was the grand-niece of Nobel laureate Rabindranath Tagore. The *Encyclopaedia of Indian Cinema* lists her many accomplishments: "studied at the Royal Academy of Dramatic Arts and at the Royal Academy of Music (London); degree in architecture and successful designer of Paisley textiles. . . . In Germany . . . Rani was able to see Fritz Lang, G. W. Pabst and Sternberg at work and assisted Marlene Dietrich on the set of *Der blaue Engel* (1930). Also worked briefly with Max Reinhardt" (Rajadhyaksha and Willemen, 192).

24. *filmindia,* March 1940.

25. See Khote's own account of her experience filming *Amar Jyoti* (*I, Durga Khote,* 51).

26. Rajadhyaksha and Willemen, *Encyclopaedia of Indian Cinema,* 256, 263.

27. Sudipto Chatterjee's comment on mythological and historical narratives is relevant here. Their "characterization, in general, was thinner in psychological complexity" than in social plays "where the subjects were closer to contemporary reality" ("Colonial Stage(d)," 226).

28. Vinodini Mehta, "Mrs. Khote and Her Art," *Rangbhoomi,* 1932, 3, 15 (my translation).

29. See Khote, *I, Durga Khote,* 62–77.

30. This defense exactly parallels the actual circumstances by which Khote, a good wife and mother, was forced to take up acting as a profession. See Khote's autobiography, *I, Durga Khote.*

31. Review of *Aadmi* by K. A. Abbas, *Bombay Chronicle,* 13 September 1939.

32. Review of *Aadmi* by K. A. Abbas, *Bombay Chronicle,* 13 September 1939.

Abbas's comment on Moti in his review was: "Yes. He is a coward. A social coward. But then many of us, Indian youths, are like him. His weaknesses are the weaknesses of a generation. On the other hand, he is far more genuine, his reactions are far more natural, than most 'heroes' of the screen."

33. A major factor in *Aadmi*'s popular and critical success was its songs. An advertisement for the film acknowledged this by saying "Hear Song Hits from 'Aadmi' on Young India Records" (*Bombay Chronicle,* 2 October 1939).

34. There are clear overtones, in the disrobing of the Anglo-Indian actress, of a central episode in the epic *Mahabharata,* in which Draupadi, the wife of the Pandava brothers, is publicly humiliated and disrobed by the Kauravas. Draupadi epitomizes ideal Indian womanhood and valiantly resists the disrobing to the point that Krishna comes to her aid by miraculously transforming her unfolding sari into an endless length of cloth. The Anglo-Indian actress is made to bear a negative comparison with Draupadi, as she not only does not resist public shame, but herself takes the action of disrobing publicly. In her case, there is certainly no divine rescue to be expected. (Thanks to Dr. Tony Stewart for pointing out this connection.)

35. Abbas, review of *Aadmi, Bombay Chronicle,* 13 September 1939.

36. Despite the song's popularity, Devika Rani was not considered to be an accomplished singer. Saraswati Devi, the music director at Bombay Talkies, had this to say about Devika Rani's musical abilities: "Towards the end of '36, Himansu Rai asked me to teach Devika Rani music. That was quite difficult because it was beyond her ability" (Kinkar, "Lasting Lady, Khurshid-Saraswati," 71).

37. Jawaharlal Nehru reportedly wrote a fan letter to Devika Rani after seeing her in *Achhut Kanya* (Kaul, *Cinema and the Indian Freedom Struggle,* 40).

38. "'Life is for Living'—And Laughing!" *Bombay Chronicle,* 4 October 1939.

39. K. A. Abbas, "Mainly about 'Life's for Living,'" *Bombay Chronicle,* 13 September 1939. *Devdas* (P. C. Barua, 1935) was a highly successful film that gave rise to innumerable imitators. It featured a clichéd prostitute with a golden heart who sacrifices her own happiness for the hero.

40. K. A. Abbas's review of the three major studios in the May 1939 issue of *filmindia* acidly attributed the meteoric rise of Bombay Talkies to Devika Rani, "the only star they have got" ("These Three! Prabhat—New Theatres—Bombay Talkies," *filmindia,* May 1939, 45–54 [quote on 53]).

41. The *Encyclopaedia of Indian Cinema* says that "in *Achhut Kanya,* her arched eyebrows, beads and vaguely Rajasthani-style, knee-length dress of the Untouchable, defined the 'village belle' for Hindi cinema" (Rajadhyaksha and Willemen, 192–93).

42. "In social-cultural terms the advantages with which Devika Rani started would prove detrimental to her in the end. She remained the 'Westerner' she had become by upbringing, the Indianness she acquired through her first marriage [to Bombay Talkies founder Himansu Rai] dissipating with her second [to Russian painter Svetoslav Roerich]. Her alienation would stand out pathetically in her old age when she became confined to a hotel suite, her considerable wealth a subject of acrimony among avaricious contenders. By contrast, Nargis was wholly Indian in her culture and outlook" (George, *Life and Times of Nargis,* 10).

43. Shantaram's statement, "I would be a film critic if I could live again," was reported by Abbas, review of *Aadmi, Bombay Chronicle,* 13 September 1939.

44. "Leela Chitnis Excels in Bombay Talkies' 'Kangan,'" *Bombay Chronicle,* 2 November 1939 (emphasis in original).

45. Hublikar's rise from unknown actress to star is indicated in Bal Chitale's "One Fine Morning She Found Herself Famous! The Romantic Story of Shanta Hublikar's Rise to Fame," *Mirror,* 31 December 1939.

46. This is an example of *bricolage* in the sense that Jane Feuer uses it in the context of the Hollywood musical (*Hollywood Musical,* 3–7).

47. There were frequent questions in film magazines of the 1930s about the "nationality" (meaning regional affiliation) of a particular Indian star. In the movies, national identity had not yet become fixed into a homogeneous "Indianness" as it was to be from the late 1940s onward. One has only to compare the construction of "Indianness" in *Aadmi* with a later film like *Amar Akbar Anthony* (Manmohan Desai, 1977), whose title may suggest a diversity of religious groups in India, but whose notion of "Indianness" is a homogenizing Hindu one.

48. The mother even talks admiringly about a religious figure, Chintamani, who "was a *sadhvi* [holy woman], even though she was a prostitute."

49. The *Encyclopaedia of Indian Cinema*'s entry on V. Shantaram mentions Abbas's view that *Aadmi* was Shantaram's finest film (Rajadhyaksha and Willemen, 214).

4. Spectatorial Desires and the Hierarchies of Stardom

1. See my discussion of genre and stardom in chapter 1.

2. None of Sulochana's 1920s and 1930s films has survived.

3. *Punjab Mail* advertisement, *Bombay Chronicle,* 9 March 1929.

4. See, for example, "India Has No Stars," editorial, *filmindia,* December 1937.

5. Karnad, "Glorious Gohar," 23.

6. *ICC: Evidence,* 5:5.

7. *Filmland,* 18 June 1932.

8. Vikramaditya S. Nigam, B.A., "Our Versatile Star," *Filmland,* 10 December 1932.

9. See Bhaumik, "Emergence of the Bombay Film Industry," 64–65.

10. Rajadhyaksha and Willemen, *Encyclopaedia of Indian Cinema,* entry on *Cinema ni Rani*; Bhaumik, "Emergence of the Bombay Film Industry," 88.

11. V. S. Nigam, "Cinema Queen Miss Sulochana," *Rangbhoomi,* annual issue, 1933.

12. Bhaumik, "Emergence of the Bombay Film Industry," 88.

13. *Filmland,* Puja issue, 1934. Although the silent version of *Indira M.A.* was subsequently referred to as *Indira B.A.*, its original title, as seen in an advertisement in *Bombay Chronicle,* 19 October 1929, was *Indira.*

14. "Your Fan," "An Open Letter to Sulochana's Soul," *Moving Picture Monthly,* September 1934; Dushyant Chaubey, "Screen's Beloved," *Moving Picture Monthly,* June 1934.

15. Wadia, "Those Were the Days," 20; Dushyant Chaubey, "Screen's Beloved," *Moving Picture Monthly,* June 1934.

16. V. S. Nigam, "Cinema Queen Miss Sulochana," *Rangbhoomi,* annual issue, 1933.

17. F. Mohamed, "Siren Sulochana," *Varieties Weekly*, 28 January 1933.

18. "Your Fan," "An Open Letter to Sulochana's Soul," *Moving Picture Monthly*, September 1934.

19. The kiss became informally censored from the 1930s to the end of the 1990s. See Prasad, *Ideology of the Hindi Film*, 88–92, for a discussion of this prohibition.

20. *Bombay Chronicle*, 9 June 1934.

21. *filmindia*, 1943.

22. See, for example, Charu Gupta on redefinitions of obscenity in literature specifically to control female sexuality and to redefine it as "passionlessness" (*Sexuality, Obscenity, Community*, 46–48).

23. List extrapolated from Wadia, "Those Were the Days," 119–20.

24. "Those Were the Days," 116. Evans, who was of Scots-Greek parentage, grew up in Peshawar and Bombay, but with no connection to Indian languages or culture. See Wenner, *Fearless Nadia*, for further information.

25. *Bombay Chronicle*, 2 July 1932. The only surviving silent-era stunt film, *Diler Jigar/Gallant Hearts* (Agarwal Film Co., 1931), fits this review's description of stunts in earlier films in the genre.

26. "When I decided to call my film *Hunterwali* there was concerted opposition in the studio. The Pundits said that I was combining 'Hunter' which was English [but meaning whip] with 'wali' which was Hindustani thus coining a hybrid and massacring the language" (Wadia, "Those Were the Days," 119).

27. See Wenner, *Fearless Nadia*, 166.

28. As a sign of their popularity, JBH Wadia mentions merchandise associated with the films, such as "Hunterwali whips, belts, matchboxes, playing cards etc. etc. Had I only patented the word I might have made a fortune earning royalties. Hunterwali started a cycle of stunt films and producers added their films with suffix 'wali' such as Cyclewali, Chabukwali, Motorwali" (119).

29. *filmindia*, July 1935.

30. See Fuller, "*Motion Picture Story Magazine*," for a discussion of similar hierarchies between big-city and small-town values in American cinema in the 1910s.

31. *filmindia*, May 1936.

32. P. L. Seth, "Morality and the Indian Screen," *Mirror*, 26 November 1939.

33. An early reappraisal of Fearless Nadia by Rinki Bhattacharya appeared in *Filmfare* (29 April–12 May 1977). One of the earliest memoirs was by Girish Karnad in *Cinema Vision India*. Other memoirs include JBH Wadia's own unpublished manuscript, "Those Were the Days," excerpts from which were also published in two issues of *Cinema Vision India*. The groundbreaking scholarly account of Fearless Nadia was Behroze Gandhy and Rosie Thomas's 1991 essay "Three Indian Stars," which Thomas has more recently elaborated in her ongoing research and publications, such as "Not Quite (Pearl) White." The resurgence of interest in Nadia may be attributed to the 1993 documentary film *Fearless: The Hunterwali Story* made by her grand-nephew, Riyad Wadia. The film's success at international film festivals led to the German-language biography by Dorothee Wenner, published in English translation in 2005 (*Fearless Nadia*). Wadia's documentary and Wenner's biography are also the source of many of the oral memoirs about Nadia's star status. Until recently, there were also rumors of a biopic about

Nadia in the making, with Shekhar Kapur and Vishal Bharadwaj variously cited as the director.

34. Homi Wadia continued to make stunt and action features under the banner of his new studio, Basant Pictures.

35. *filmindia,* June 1935.

36. Thomas, "Not Quite (Pearl) White," 48–50.

37. Wadia, "Those Were the Days," 10; Bean, "Technologies of Early Stardom," 406.

38. Wadia, "Those Were the Days," 77; Bhaumik, "Emergence of the Bombay Film Industry," 61; Wenner, *Fearless Nadia,* ix, xv; K. Hansen, "A Different Desire," 171; Thomas, "Not Quite (Pearl) White"; K. Hansen, "Virangana in North Indian History."

39. Wadia, "Those Were the Days," 140; publicity programme quoted in Wenner, *Fearless Nadia,* 68.

40. *filmindia,* September 1940.

41. Khanderao Kelkar, quoted in Wenner, *Fearless Nadia,* 79.

42. See Eco, "Myth of Superman."

43. Karnad, "This One Is for Nadia," 86. The *Diamond Queen* footage opens Riyad Wadia's documentary on Fearless Nadia. My discussion of sequences in Nadia's films is based on clips included in Riyad Wadia's *Fearless,* and viewings of *Hunterwali, Miss Frontier Mail,* and *Diamond Queen.* Although many of Fearless Nadia's films have survived, they are not in wide circulation.

44. See Sinha, *Colonial Masculinity*; and Roselli, "Self-Image of Effeteness."

45. Chapman, *Sandow the Magnificent,* 156; Ray, "Calcutta Women in the Swadesh Movement," 172. While wrestling has a long history in India, bodybuilding did not take hold until the 1930s, even though Sandow made a deep impression on middle- and upper-class Indians when he visited India in 1903. With the Hercules Gymnasium in Bangalore, established in 1935, and the books and courses of Professor K. V. Iyer, bodybuilding became mainstream (Chapman, *Sandow the Magnificent,* 159–60). See also the Web site *Bodybuilding and Muscle Control in India*; and Mujumdar, *Encyclopedia of Indian Physical Culture.*

46. *Bombay Chronicle,* 27 December 1924, 23 March 1929, 4 April 1934.

47. Joseph Alter notes that bodybuilding, unlike wrestling, was modeled on Western notions of hygiene, health, and body, and had no religious or philosophical overtones (*Wrestler's Body,* 50–57).

48. Wadia, "Those Were the Days," 127–28, 118; Wenner, *Fearless Nadia,* 40.

49. Wadia, "Those Were the Days," 122. Both car and horse had their debut performance in the Wadia production *Jai Bharat* (1936), which did not feature Fearless Nadia.

50. See Bean, "Technologies of Early Stardom," 420–21. Durga Khote was also famous for her screen companion, a cheetah, in *Maya Machindra* (V. Shantaram, 1932) (Khote, *I, Durga Khote,* 66–67).

51. Bean, "Technologies of Early Stardom," 419–20. Numerous accidents are reported in Wenner, JBH Wadia, and *Fearless: The Hunterwali Story,* and clearly provide an interpretive frame of authenticity and competence.

52. Wenner describes Nadia as a "pioneer in the Indian fitness craze. . . . In

various magazines you saw Nadia pictured winking as she performed particular exercises" (*Fearless Nadia*, 233–34).

53. I discuss these changing norms further in chapter 5. The columnist Hyacinth, who regularly lampooned Indian stars whom she found unattractive, made unflattering remarks about Nadia's weight in *filmindia*, April 1942 (quoted in Wenner, *Fearless Nadia*, 75–76). When the Prabhat Studio star Shanta Apte went on hunger strike to protest the terms of her contract, a parody article asking "what would happen if some of the other artistes follow in [her] footsteps?" referred to Nadia in terms that suggested manliness, overweight, and physical aggression (*Mirror*, 1 August 1939). At the same time, there was equally a discourse of Nadia's unashamed sexuality: "Then in another scene she was being sold in the Slave Market. The slave dealer drags her on the dais dressed in scanty clothes revealing her limbs in no uncertain terms. He describes her beauty limb by limb and I took close-ups of her legs, her buxom torso, her pearly teeth, her sparkling eyes etc. Vasant Jagtap was my cameraman" (Wadia, "Those Were the Days," 117).

54. "Not Quite (Pearl) White," 55. There were enough historical figures, such as Sister Nivedita and Annie Besant, to fit this model.

55. *ICC: Evidence*, 5:3–4.

56. Quoted in Wenner, *Fearless Nadia*, 50.

57. See K. Hansen, "Making Women Visible."

58. See Dyer, *White*, 89–103.

59. Singer, *Melodrama and Modernity*, 102, 91; M. Hansen, "Fallen Women," 12, 16. See also M. Hansen, "Mass Production of the Senses."

60. Quoted in Wenner, *Fearless Nadia*, 14.

61. Wadia, "Those Were the Days," 8.

62. Pinney, "Indian Work of Art in the Age of Mechanical Reproduction," 359, 356; Pinney, *Photos of the Gods*, 194.

63. Assadullah, *Film in India*, 7.

64. Wadia, "Those Were the Days," 7, 116–17; Wenner, *Fearless Nadia*, 49. "The effect of mimicry on the authority of colonial discourse is profound and disturbing," says Homi Bhabha, referring both to the closeness of mimicry and mockery, and to the threat it poses to "'normalized' knowledges and disciplinary powers" (*Location of Culture*, 123). In the stress Bhabha puts on "ambivalence" lies the difference from the Wadias' practice, because the ambivalence of colonial mimicry comes from its imperfect, "partial," and "inappropriate" form (121–23). While contemporary camp responses to Nadia's films, at least in the West, might seem to support a reading of these films as colonial mimicry, such a reading does not adequately account for the responses of the films' original audiences.

65. Wenner, *Fearless Nadia*, 106–8; Wadia, "Those Were the Days," 132–33. I am drawing on the work of Henry Jenkins and Barbara Klinger for my notion of participatory fan culture. See also Shefrin, "*Lord of the Rings, Star Wars,* and Participatory Fandom."

66. M. Hansen, "Falling Women, Rising Stars, New Horizons," 12; Karnad, "This One Is for Nadia," 89.

5. Monopoly, Frontality, and Doubling in Postwar Bombay Cinema

1. *filmindia,* June 1945, 13.

2. Here are some sample figures for the years 1948 to 1952. Nargis appeared in 4 films in 1948, 5 in 1949, 11 in 1950, 5 in 1951, and 6 in 1952. Raj Kapoor appeared in 3 films in 1948, 4 in 1949, 6 in 1950, 1 in 1951, and 4 in 1952. It should be noted that the numbers given here take into account only films that were released. There is no way of accounting for the innumerable unreleased films that most major stars have worked in. Nargis, for instance, mentions working in eighteen films simultaneously in 1950 ("If I Were to Live My Life Again," *Filmfare,* 28 May 1954, 10–12).

3. For instance, Cuckoo appears in film after film in the 1940s and 1950s in the role of dancing girl. She appeared in 11 films in 1948, 17 in 1949, 27 in 1950, 19 in 1951, and 10 in 1952. Her numbers are so high because she was indispensable in song and dance sequences. Such figures also demonstrate the monopoly of playback singers that I discuss in chapter 7.

4. Such interchange between *star* and *hero* or *heroine* continues in contemporary film terminology in India. For example, a recent discussion of a star aspirant who ended up becoming a cameraman in Bombay describes him as "a teenage runaway who came to Bombay to become a hero" (Sengupta, "Reflected Readings in Available Light," 125).

5. A growing number of voices in the 1950s began to critique the labor conditions of film extras. See, for example, "Tragedy of the Extras: A 'Filmfare' Symposium," *Filmfare,* 11 July 1952.

6. "Dimpled Duse of the Indian Screen," *Filmfare,* 23 July 1954, 10.

7. Interview in Vasudev and Lenglet, *Indian Cinema Superbazaar,* 253.

8. "Glamour Boys or Garbage Men?" *filmindia,* January 1943, 11.

9. Interview in *Sound,* April 1951, 41–44 (quote on 43).

10. "Trade Winds," *Sound,* March 1950, 37.

11. Quoted in Rajadhyaksha, "'Bollywoodization' of Indian Cinema," 126–27.

12. The following quotation is representative: "Our stars have borrowed Hollywood shirts and Hollywood hair-dos—but not Hollywood punctuality, efficiency and conscientiousness!" ("Love and Irony," *Sound,* February 1951, 13).

13. "Bombay Calling," *filmindia,* January 1943, 14.

14. "This Stardom Racket: Overnight Glamour Products," *filmindia,* October 1942, 45–46.

15. Purohit, *Profile of the Hindi Hit Movie,* 16–17.

16. "Though filmmaking was neither an industry, nor a respectable profession for the educated, working in the old 'silents' had a charm all its own. We worked and behaved like a family, and a happy one at that!" (Jairaj, "The Magic World of the Movies . . . As I Remember It," *Sound,* August 1949, 33, 35 [quote], 37). We find a similar "paradise lost" version of cinema history in the memories of film personnel interviewed in Sengupta, "Reflected Readings in Available Light," 130.

17. Rajadhyaksha and Willemen, *Encyclopaedia of Indian Cinema,* 23. See Rajadhyaksha, "'Bollywoodization' of Indian Cinema."

18. Hemen Gupta, "Films and the State: An Analysis of Their Relation and Function," *Sound,* April 1951, 11–13 (quote on 13). Another commentator notes, too, that "it is a fact that no other industry is taxed so heavily. Our film industry enjoys all the handicaps and humiliations you can think of, but none of the privileges that are extended to our other industries" (S. Khalil, "What Price Stars?" *Sound,* November 1959, 25–28 [quote on 27]).

19. For the rest of this chapter I will refer to commercial Hindi cinema of the late 1940s and 1950s as Bombay cinema. At this time, commercial Hindi films became much more formulaic and geographically localized, with most studios now concentrated in the Bombay area. During the previous decade of the studio era, Hindi films had also been produced in studios located in different parts of the country. Their films had distinctive features based often on the studio's particular regional affiliation. This is not to say that regional cinemas ceased to be productive after a more homogeneous Bombay film formula fell into place. Rather, the distinction between regional cinema and Bombay cinema became much more absolute, with the former now exclusively in regional languages as opposed to the routine dual-language releases of the studio period.

20. Review of *Kismet* in *Star and Style,* January–June 1970.

21. Rajadhyaksha and Willemen, *Encyclopaedia of Indian Cinema,* 231. "Filmistan's style arguably had the largest impact of any studio on later independent commercial film-making in Hindi" (96).

22. Prasad, *Ideology of the Hindi Film,* 32, 43, 45; Bharat Bhushan, "Your Ticket to Stardom," *Filmfare,* 28 November 1952, 10–11. More recent complaints by stars about the difficulties of acting under such conditions include the following statement by actress Sharmila Tagore: "I have this one grouse against the Hindi film industry. . . . You come to the sets and you are told you are 'Miss Rekha' or 'Miss Meena.' Now what on earth does that mean? Why can't I have a clearer understanding of who she is? Is she Muslim? Is she Hindu? . . . What is her family background like? Why can't I have a clearer understanding or more lengthy data on her background? . . . Nothing is personal, so it is very difficult to give a personal touch to your style" (quoted in Bawa, *Actors and Acting,* 132).

23. K. T. John, "The Art of Film Editing," *Sound,* November 1950, 29–31 (quote on 29).

24. Review of *Barsaat, Sound,* May 1950, 45–46.

25. Vasudevan, "Melodramatic Mode," 45; "Sexuality and the Film Apparatus," 196–97.

26. Vasudevan, "Melodramatic Mode," 30. However, in the case of genres other than the social film, it is possible that the identification worked in the opposite direction, with a star's identity being understood entirely in terms of a preexisting genre, as was the case with Bharat Bhushan and the saint film genre. In an article in *Filmfare,* 9 July 1954, Bharat Bhushan wrote humorously about the perils of being so completely identified with the saint genre.

27. Pfleiderer and Lutze's study of rural audiences (*Hindi Film*) showed that those who were unfamiliar with the stars had a lot of difficulty following the intricacies of the narrative.

28. The contents of the January 1942 issue of *filmindia* gives a sense of the sudden increase in the number of articles promising "private" information: "Naseem Thinks Santaram Wonderful! Spends Thousands on Saris and Perfumes!

Beautiful But Terribly Shy Star" (31–33); "Give Us Publicity with Pep—Tell Us about Private Lives" (37–39); "Blackmailed Interview of Mazhar Khan—Blushing Confessions of a Famous Actor" (47–49); "These Glittering Stars! How Do They Look at Home?" (65–69); and "Round the Town with Zabak: Death of Popular Producer—Slandering Stars—Studio Pests—Neena's Mystery Parcel" (76–78).

29. "Give Us Publicity with Pep—Tell Us about Private Lives," *filmindia,* January 1942, 37–39.

30. "A Dirty Racket" (in "Bombay Calling"), *filmindia,* March 1942, 15. Only in the pages of Saadat Hasan Manto's *Meena Bazar* (1968), translated as *Stars from Another Sky,* do we get the full details of the events sparking these posters (103–5).

31. *filmindia,* January 1942, 31.

32. Raj Kapoor, "Audience Reaction," *Filmfare,* 4 January 1957, 23.

33. "The Big Three in the Dock: Three top-notch stars of the Indian screen reply to the common charges levelled against them," *Filmfare,* 25 October 1957, 52–55 (quote on 55).

34. Kishore Sahu, "How to Overcome the Star Famine," *Filmfare,* 13 September 1957, 32–35, 43.

35. "Editor's Mail," *filmindia,* March 1944, 29.

36. "Bombay Calling," *filmindia,* August 1944, 7.

37. Dyer, "Star is Born," 135.

38. "While it was sufficient to have one or two top stars last year, now it has become de rigueur to have as many as possible in one picture. . . . And yet, it is also a fact that most of the all-star cast films have proved to be the biggest flops. In fact, it would be correct to say that the more the stars the greater the chances of failure" ("Trade Winds," *Sound,* March 1950, 37). The most famous of the successful multi-starrers from this period was *Andaz* (Mehboob, 1949) starring Nargis with the two top male stars, Dilip Kumar and Raj Kapoor. It is interesting to note, though, that Raj Kapoor's name appeared five lines lower in advertisements than the names of Nargis and Dilip Kumar. *Anmol Ghadi* (Mehboob, 1946) offered a different type of multiple star attraction by including three of the major singing stars of the period: Suraiya, Noorjehan (who was also a playback singer and ended up moving to Pakistan after partition and Independence), and Surendra.

39. Examples are the Bombay Talkies star teams, Ashok Kumar and Devika Rani, and Ashok Kumar and Leela Chitnis. Perhaps to maintain some degree of product differentiation, Ashok Kumar sported a mustache while playing opposite Devika Rani and appeared clean-shaven next to Leela Chitnis.

40. For example, most accounts of Binodini, the nineteenth-century Bengali stage actress, admiringly mention her seven roles in Michael Madhusudhan Datta's *Meghnadbad Kavya.* The stigma against female performance led to the first double role in Indian cinema when the male actor Salunke played both the hero, Ram, and the heroine, Sita, in Phalke's mythological *Lanka Dahan* (1917). A catalogue of double roles in silent cinema would also include Sulochana's eight roles in *Wildcat of Bombay* (Mohan Bhavnani, 1927).

41. Parameshwari Lal Gupta, "Reasons for the Failure of the Talkies," *Rangbhoomi,* 10 September 1932, 8–10 (my translation).

42. *Sound* (November 1949, 47) mentions *Rajtarang* (1928), starring Master Vithal, as "the first successful double role produced in this country," while *Film-*

fare ("This Fortnight in Films," 7 March 1952) mentions Gohar's triple role in *Vishwamohini* (Chandulal Shah, 1933) as "the pioneer of this vogue in the film industry." The *Encyclopaedia of Indian Cinema* states that Patience Cooper's double roles in *Patni Pratap* (J. J. Madan, 1923) and *Kashmiri Sundari* (Madan Theatres, 1925) were "perhaps the earliest double roles in Indian film" (Rajadhyaksha and Willemen, 80).

43. Jimi Hafizi, "The Double Role—Status Symbol for Footage-Hoggers?" *Filmfare,* 7–20 January 1977, 52. Here are some informal statistics pointing to the boom in double roles for male stars of the 1960s onward: Amitabh Bachchan played double roles in 9 films; Rajesh Khanna in 8; Dev Anand in 3; Dilip Kumar in 3; Sanjeev Kumar in 3. Among female stars, too, everyone worth the name has been seen in a double role. Of even greater prestige to the star are films involving more than two roles. Some examples are Rajesh Khanna's nine roles in *Chhaila Babu* (1967) and Sanjeev Kumar's nine roles in *Naya Din Nayi Raat* (1974). According to Ashis Nandy, "there have been many more versions of *The Prisoner of Zenda* (Anthony Hope's novel about a prince and his double) in Hindi than in the language in which the novel was written" ("Double in Hindi Cinema," 8).

44. Reported in *Varieties Weekly,* 16 September 1933; reported in *Filmland,* 19 November 1932.

45. Even in 1950, a dissertation on Indian cinema observes, "The general trend of the argument is that films are not a respectable profession; that the moral standards of studios are very low and that anyone wishing to join the profession is morally depraved" (Shah, *Indian Film,* 157).

46. Schechner, *Performative Circumstances,* 95; Nandy, "Popular Hindi Film," 95; Gopalan, *Cinema of Interruptions,* 54, 57.

47. "This Fortnight in Films," *Filmfare,* 7 March 1952, 5. *Nishan* (1949), based on Alexandre Dumas's *Corsican Brothers,* was a Tamil film (with Telegu and Hindi versions as well) made by S. S. Vasan of *Chandralekha* fame. The moral dualism in *Nishan* seemed less remarkable to reviewers than its technological and performative aura. A review in *Sound,* November 1949, explained the pleasure of dual roles in terms of "the remarkable acting feat . . . [of] creating two strikingly different personalities before your eyes," and also noted its competent use of the split screen. *Nishan* was a runaway success in its Tamil version (*Apoorva Sahodarargal*) but did not do as well in its Hindi version, perhaps because the star playing the double role in Hindi was relatively unknown. Other notable dual-role films of the 1950s included *Neel Kamal* (Kidar Sharma, 1947), with Begum Para playing mother and daughter roles; *Chamki* (J. K. Nanda, 1952), with Shekhar in a double role; *Ghungroo* (Hiren Bose, 1952), with both Om Prakash and Sumitra Devi in double roles; and *Paapi* (Chandulal Shah, 1953), with Raj Kapoor in a double role.

48. Jimi Hafizi, "The Double Role—Status Symbol for Footage-Hoggers?" *Filmfare,* 7–20 January 1977, 52.

49. Naremore, *Acting in the Cinema,* 76, 72.

50. "The hero's character must never be 'negative.' He must never be involved in situations which will present him in an unsympathetic light to the audience. If he is 'bad,' he must be so only temporarily" (Raj Khosla, "Logic in Our Films—or Lack of It!" *Filmfare,* 1 August 1958, 28–29).

51. Reviews tended not to share Ashok Kumar's own enthusiasm regarding his

ability to incarnate different identities in this film. While he strongly implied in an interview in *Film Pictorial,* March 1951, that this was his "greatest role," a review in another magazine judged his acting to be "ham" and "somewhat weak" (*Sound,* March 1951).

52. "This Month in Movieland," *Film Pictorial,* March 1951, n.p.

53. Gledhill, "Signs of Melodrama," 207, 210.

54. See Vasudevan, "Melodramatic Mode and the Commercial Hindi Cinema," 30–31.

55. Vasudevan, "Melodramatic Mode," 31.

56. Vasudevan, "Shifting Codes, Dissolving Identities," 73.

57. Gledhill, "Signs of Melodrama," 210; Ellis, "Stars as Cinematic Phenomenon," 97.

58. Orr, *Cinema and Modernity,* 36–37.

59. Kapur, "Revelation and Doubt," 20, 82; Vasudevan, "Cinema and Citizenship," 13. See, for instance, the work of Ashish Rajadhyaksha, Christopher Pinney, Ravi Vasudevan, and Madhava Prasad.

60. Vasudevan, "Shifting Codes, Dissolving Identities," 60–61; Vasudevan, "Sexuality and the Film Apparatus," 202, 199–200; Prasad, *Ideology of the Hindi Film,* 20.

61. Both Dilip Kumar and Nargis, considered to be top stars of the 1950s, were praised for their low-key style of acting, while Raj Kapoor was often critiqued for "overacting."

62. Gledhill, "Signs of Melodrama," 211. See James Naremore's discussion of the biological aspects of stardom and of the construction of star personae through the body of the star (*Acting in the Cinema,* 20, 65).

63. George, *Life and Times of Nargis,* 77. The following observation by actor Vinod Khanna, made in the late 1970s, exemplifies the close connection between star personae and melodramatic character types in Bombay films: "After a while you can play the hero blindfold. You know what his actions are and how he is expected to behave. It nearly always falls into a set pattern. . . . You know, the revengeful character . . . or the poetic singer. . . . But then you begin to realize that you've got to please your public. That they come again and again to see you, Vinod Khanna, on the screen" (quoted in Bawa, *Actors and Acting,* 165).

64. A. Bhaskar Rao, "The Indian Cinema Suffers from Superlatives," *Bombay Chronicle,* 27 March 1932, 10.

65. "Naseem Thinks Santaram Wonderful! Spends Thousands on Saris and Perfumes!" *filmindia,* January 1942, 31–33 (quote on 33).

66. Naremore, *Acting in the Cinema,* 19.

67. Dyer, "A Star Is Born," 133–37.

68. Dyer, "A Star Is Born," 136.

69. "Bombay cinema . . . collapses all distinctions between actor and character. A star like Raj Kapoor or Amitabh Bachchan is only rarely . . . other than himself as a composite being, sets of expectations, created by the audience" (Mishra, "Decentering History," 141). Recent examples of the desire for continuity between on- and off-screen star identities are plentiful. For instance, stars who do not themselves sing the songs in their song sequences will maintain a continuity with their cinematic persona by lip-synching, even when performing stage shows of their song sequences.

70. Like many other Raj Kapoor films, *Awara* also collapses the distinction between character and star by having Prithviraj Kapoor, his father in real life, play his father in the diegesis.

71. In Hollywood, the conflation of star and character names seem to have been limited to B movies, such as Westerns featuring Gene Autry and Roy Rogers playing characters with the same names. The cultural meaning of such conflation is clearly different in Hollywood and Indian cinema. The reiteration of the same character name across a number of films is mostly the prerogative of major stars in Indian cinema. Since the repeated character name may or may not be identical to that of the star, it seems to function as a secondary tier of stardom. Thus, for example, there is the primary star text of Amitabh Bachchan and the secondary star text of Vijay, where there are cross-textual similarities and references that produce a coherent extra-textual persona for the Vijay characters. For audiences and filmmakers alike, star identity in Indian cinema seems to overwhelm and threaten any pretense at producing fictional roles for the star.

72. Rajadhyaksha and Willemen, *Encyclopaedia of Indian Cinema,* 161. Nargis's real name was Fatima Rashid.

73. Vasudevan, "Addressing the Spectator," 322.

74. Vasudevan, "Shifting Codes, Dissolving Identities," 61.

6. *Nargis and the Double Space of Female Desire in* Anhonee

1. "By the mid-1950s Nargis began commanding fees in excess of her leading men" (George, *Life and Times of Nargis,* 109).

2. For a production history and textual analysis of *Mother India,* see G. Chatterjee, *Mother India.*

3. See Thomas, "Sanctity and Scandal"; Gandhy and Thomas, "Three Indian Film Stars"; and Roy, "Figuring Mother India: The Case of Nargis," in *Indian Traffic,* 152–73.

4. Abbas, *Mad, Mad, Mad World of Indian Films,* 41; Thomas, "Sanctity and Scandal," 13; Roy, *Indian Traffic,* 154 (emphasis in original).

5. Because of the divide between the status of star and character actor roles available to women, "a great deal of courage is necessary for an Indian heroine to make the transition to character roles" ("Dimpled Duse of the Indian Screen," *Filmfare,* 23 July 1954, 10). Many stars of the 1930s, such as Durga Khote, Leela Chitnis, and Ashok Kumar, went on to become character actors in numerous films.

6. Reuben, *Raj Kapoor,* 87; George, *Life and Times of Nargis,* 86; Nargis, "It's *Good* to Be a Star," *Filmfare,* 4 April 1952, 8–9, 19, 21.

7. *Bobby* is described as a "very successful kitschy teenage love story" (Rajadhyaksha and Willemen, *Encyclopaedia of Indian Cinema,* 416).

8. Jairaj, "Nargis: Ambitious and Pretty! Intelligent as She Is Lovely!" *Sound,* February 1949, 51.

9. Quoted in George, *Life and Times of Nargis,* 86.

10. For instance, the 18 April 1952 issue of *Filmfare* carried a detailed description of the "furnishing and fittings" that Nargis chose for her new flat ("This Fortnight in Films").

11. Ravi Vasudevan makes a similar observation when he says that "speculations about Nargis's family background and suspicions of her chastity following her affair with Raj Kapoor seemed to repetitively feed into, and be resolved within, a host of films from *Andaz* to *Bewafa/Faithless* (M. L. Anand, 1952), *Laajwanti/Woman of Honor* (Rajinder Suri, 1957) and *Mother India*" ("Addressing the Spectator," 323).

12. Naremore, *Acting in the Cinema*, 22, 22n; George, *Life and Times of Nargis*, 91, 93.

13. See George, *Life and Times of Nargis*, 117–21. Raj's father, Prithviraj Kapoor, was a highly respected star of the 1930s, and with Raj and his brothers, a dynastic empire was in the making, which is strong to this day.

14. George, *Life and Times of Nargis*, 129–30. Like most other details about this relationship, Raj Kapoor's notorious statement about wife and actress has been repeated so many times that it has become a free-floating item of mythology, with no writer feeling the need to provide a specific context or date for it. Bunny Reuben, Kapoor's biographer, mentions in passing that Kapoor made this statement to a journalist in 1973 (*Raj Kapoor*, 118).

15. Quoted in Reuben, *Follywood Flashback*, 21.

16. After the final shot of *Anhonee* was filmed, "while dinner was in progress, Nargis disclosed that she always wanted to play a bad girl and an old mother. Her desire to portray a bad girl has now been fulfilled" (*Filmfare*, 25 July 1952, 9).

17. Plot summary of *Anhonee* in *Filmfare*, 8 August 1952, 27–29 (quote on 27). The difficulty of summarizing this typically convoluted plot is indicated by the three-page length of *Filmfare*'s summary. "Dancing-girl," "courtesan," or "prostitute" are all inexact translations of *tawaif*. A *tawaif* is a professional female singer and dancer who performs in private homes for the pleasure of men and is also often a prostitute. A *tawaif* performs a highly codified and pedigreed style of music and dance. See also Kesavan, "Urdu, Awadh and the Tawaif."

18. The heroine's birthday party has been a staple in Hindi films ever since the 1950s. Its appeal goes beyond the screen to magazine accounts of (female) stars' birthday parties. It is the quintessentially modern celebration that formally places the adult female character in society. It also functions as an acceptable communal space for the beginnings of romance.

19. Vasudevan, "Shifting Codes, Dissolving Identities," 74.

20. Ravi Vasudevan observes a similar derailment in *Awara*, where "the narrative 'forgets'" its earlier critique of "rigid, inegalitarian conceptions of the social order associated with [the hero's father] Raghunath" when it presents the criminal Jagga as a "villain, pure and simple" ("Sexuality and the Film Apparatus," 213n6).

21. Mohini's house is the *kotha*, which is not a private home but a communal space inhabited by other women like her. The English word *brothel* doesn't quite work, because the *kotha* is also a space of performance where the visible function of the women is to sing and dance for the entertainment of men. "At its best, it combined the creative brilliance of dancers, singers and poets to produce an entertainment style of high quality" (George, *Life and Times of Nargis*, 23).

22. Gledhill, "Signs of Melodrama," 212.

23. Vasudevan, "Addressing the Spectator," 320.

24. Gledhill, "Signs of Melodrama," 210.

25. Chakravarty, *National Identity in Indian Popular Cinema,* 142.

26. Vasudevan, "Shifting Codes, Dissolving Identities," 66.

27. See Ravi Vasudevan's discussion of *Awara* in "Sexuality and the Film Apparatus" and "Addressing the Spectator."

28. Vasudevan, "Shifting Codes, Dissolving Identities," 65; Amar Das Mullick, "1934 Heralds a Brighter Dawn: Renaissance of Bengal's Motion Picture Industry," *Varieties Annual,* January 1934, 7.

29. An account of Nargis, first published in a 1956 book of star portraits, presents the meeting between her parents as having taken place in a hospital where Jaddanbai was a patient and Mohan Babu was "a brilliant medical student" (Bhooch and Doyle, *Star-Portrait,* 101). This account places their meeting in Mohan Babu's more respectable space, the hospital, as opposed to Jaddanbai's space, which, according to other accounts, is where their meetings took place. By this means, it bypasses the need to mention explicitly what was already well known. The entry on Raj Kapoor in this book also gives the lie to gossip by making no mention of Nargis except as his costar. Instead, it presents him as "happily married in 1946 to Krishna Mehra, the charming sister of Premnath" (Bhooch and Doyle, *Star-Portrait,* 130).

30. T. J. S. George refers to K. L. Saigal, the famous singing star, admiringly "describing [Jaddanbai's] singing as classical in character enriched by 'rustic charm' and 'melodious voice'" (*Life and Times of Nargis,* 25).

31. "It's *Good* to Be a Star," *Filmfare,* 4 April 1952, 8–9, 19, 21 (quote on 8).

32. Naremore, *Acting in the Cinema,* 75.

33. "The all-important dance number where, as Mohini, [Nargis] performs to her own shame, exposing herself to the contempt of the sophisticated society she finds herself in, fails to rise to the expected climax" ("Nargis Gives Dazzling Performance in *Anhonee,*" *Filmfare,* 5 September 1952, 26).

34. The dance style performed by a *tawaif* is not a "personal" expression but the product of rigorous training and has a pedigreed lineage.

35. The male actor Nawab "filed a defamation case against an outrageous and vulgar Sethia who had dubbed him and all other artistes as ignorant *nachnewale* [derogatory term for dancers]. Nawab retorted, 'We are not *nachnewale,* but your educators,'" thereby countering this negative view of entertainment with learning, its supposed antithesis (Garga, "Screen Personality Nawab," 45).

36. Evidence of such acting ability is already established for the viewer in the earlier song and dance sequence by Mohini, which takes place when Raj visits Mohini's *kotha.*

37. See Naremore, *Acting in the Cinema,* 69.

38. Gledhill, "Signs of Melodrama," 211; Vasudevan, "Melodramatic Mode," 49.

39. The film also directly incorporates music and dance styles popular in the United States at the time without first "Indianizing" them through Hindi versions.

40. Rajadhyaksha, "Neo-Traditionalism," 55. In its attempts at constructing an unmarked, generic Indian identity in the main characters, post-1960s Hindi cinema is not neutral, but usually privileges North Indian cultural norms. This is especially clear in films that give exaggerated, even stereotyped, regional mannerisms to comic or minor characters. In this respect, Hindi cinema is not so dif-

ferent from Hollywood, which "as a general rule . . . has required that supporting players, ethnic minorities, and women be more animated or broadly expressive than white male leads" (Naremore, *Acting in the Cinema,* 43).

41. In this context, it is no accident that the film sponsors "modern" Western medicine against "traditional" exorcism and makes the mother-in-law, the only other female character in the film, a bastion of superstition. In this respect, the mother-in-law exactly parallels Baruna's mother in her values. A similar split is present in *Mother India.* The film opens and closes with a celebratory inauguration of a modern dam, its mise-en-scène emphasizing mechanized progress. But the dam is inaugurated by the old mother (played by Nargis) precisely because her life and actions are a respected symbol of virtuous Indian womanhood, untouched by "modern" notions.

42. Dyer, *"A Star Is Born,"* 136; Gledhill, "Signs of Melodrama," 217.

7. *The Embodied Voice: Song Sequences and Stardom in Bombay Cinema*

1. Marre and Charlton, *Beats of the Heart,* 141. According to Alison Arnold, the numbers were only slightly different in the 1940s and 1950s: "record sales of film songs . . . represented an average seventy percent of a record store's business, while classical and non-classical records amounted to only thirty percent" ("Hindi Filmi Git," 258).

2. N. Sharma, "Half a Century of Song," 58.

3. *Antakshari* is an alphabetical game in which participants take turns to sing the opening line of a film song that begins with the last letter of the previous song.

4. As Alison Arnold notes, "in both urban and rural settings, the playing of film song cassettes is supplanting or displacing traditional folk and religious musical performance in many social and cultural contexts" ("Hindi Filmi Git," 34). For the impact of audio-cassette technology on the proliferation of nonfilm popular music in India, see Manuel, *Cassette Culture.* For more on the production, the national and international distribution, and the reception of Hindi film songs, see Morcom, *Hindi Film Songs and the Cinema*; Booth, *Behind the Curtain*; and Gopal and Moorti, eds., *Global Bollywood.*

5. In 1954 "talks between the Film Federation of India and the government fail over All-India Radio's policy of broadcasting film songs without crediting sources, driving producers into using Radio Ceylon" (Rajadhyaksha and Willemen, *Encyclopaedia of Indian Cinema,* 23).

6. All-India Radio's failing competition with Radio Ceylon is referenced in the opening sequence of *Chori Chori* (Anant Thakur, 1956), featuring Raj Kapoor, in which a radio playing in the background announces Radio Ceylon and plays another Raj Kapoor song.

7. *Times of India,* 15 October 1988 (rpt. in Subramaniam, *Flashback,* 269).

8. Ranade, "Extraordinary Importance of the Indian Film Song," 10; Arnold, "Popular Film Song in India," 186.

9. Dyer, "Entertainment and Utopia," 177; Thomas, "Indian Cinema—Pleasures

and Popularity," 124; Bhatia, "Stop the Action, Start the Song," 33; Ranade, "Extraordinary Importance of the Indian Film Song," 9.

10. In Trinidad, the greater popularity of Indian playback singers over stars "is indicated by 'camps' dedicated to the 50s and 60s playback singers" (Niranjana, *Mobilizing India,* 170).

11. The monopoly of playback singers is not really an aberration under the Indian star system. A similar monopoly can be found in other areas of specialization as well, such as that of dancing girl or villain.

12. Chandavarkar, "Now It's the Bombay Film Song," 22.

13. In this context, one would have to reverse Michel Chion's statement that "for a single body and a single face on the screen, thanks to synchresis, there are dozens of allowable voices" (*Audio-Vision,* 63).

14. Bharatan, *Lata Mangeshkar,* 69. Marsha Siefert discusses the Hollywood musical's matching of voice and body in "Image/Music/Voice."

15. Siefert, "Image/Music/Voice," 55; Feuer, *Hollywood Musical,* 46; Altman, *American Film Musical,* 258. This vocal substitution has taken on the aura of an apocryphal tale, especially since there are conflicting accounts of who dubbed Reynolds's voice (Siefert, "Image/Music/Voice," 56). Betty Noyes is most commonly given this credit.

16. Mark Larkin, "The Truth about Voice Doubling," *Photoplay,* July 1929 (rpt. in Griffith, *Talkies,* 208–9).

17. See Weidman, *Singing the Classical, Voicing the Modern,* for a discussion of the status of voice in Western thought and its impact on perceptions of Indian music.

18. Siefert, "Image/Music/Voice," 57.

19. See the entry on *Dhoop Chhaon* in the *Encyclopaedia of Indian Cinema* (Rajadhyaksha and Willemen, 262). In the playback technique, the song is recorded separately and played back when the sequence is being filmed. The singer may or may not be the same person as the actor lip-synching to the music.

20. Feuer, *Hollywood Musical,* 13–22. On Saigal, see, for example, Raghava Menon's biography, *K. L. Saigal.*

21. Siefert, "Image/Music/Voice," 46; Reuben, *Follywood Flashback, 16.* Such a mismatch is part of the critique of Devika Rani in V. Shantaram's parody of her *Achhut Kanya* song sequence in the filming scene in *Aadmi* (see chapter 3).

22. "The Editor's Mail," *filmindia,* January 1941, 15.

23. Zeenath Zahara, "College Girls and Glamour Boys," *filmindia,* November 1940, 24.

24. "The Editor's Mail," *filmindia,* December 1941, 13.

25. Quoted in Mitra, "O Indisputable and Indispensable Queen," 45.

26. Interestingly enough, the film has no trouble depicting Manju in an unspecified relationship with Bhulwa, with whom she makes her home.

27. An advertisement for *Khazanchi* in the December 1941 issue of *filmindia* was dominated by a large map of India with a *tanpura* across it. Although the film's narrative hardly stresses music at all, except in this radio scene, the ad explicitly acknowledges music as its primary appeal. The *Encyclopaedia of Indian Cinema* notes *Khazanchi's* historical importance as a "trend-setter of Hindi-Urdu film music, mainly through its adaptations of Punjabi folk music" (Rajadhyaksha and Willemen, *Encyclopaedia of Indian Cinema,* 290).

28. "The Editor's Mail," *filmindia,* December 1944, 29.

29. "Ghost Voices of the Screen," *filmindia,* January 1943, 11.

30. R. N. Prasad, "Woes and Echoes," in "Reader's Forum," *filmindia,* November 1946, 74.

31. See, for example, *Padosan* (Jyoti Swaroop, 1968).

32. The male playback singer, Kishore Kumar—who was the only playback singer with a brief acting career, primarily in comic roles—was known for his comic performance style on stage. In contrast, both Lata Mangeshkar and Asha Bhosle are known for the absence of visual frills in their performance.

33. Siefert, "Image/Music/Voice," 57. The moral status of anonymous voice dubbing in Hollywood becomes even more dubious in the context of the erasure of racialized bodies, as dramatized in Julie Dash's *Illusions* (1982).

34. Rosie Thomas, writing in 1985, describes the current odds against commercial success: "over 85 percent of films released in the last two years have not made profits." She cites the *Report of the Working Group on National Film Policy* for a similar statistic for the 1970s, "that only 10% of releases made . . . profits" ("Indian Cinema," 120).

35. Bhimani, *In Search of Lata Mangeshkar,* 154. Because of the sheer number of films that Lata Mangeshkar has worked in, the *Encyclopaedia of Indian Cinema* does not even try to provide a filmography for her as it does for other film personalities (Rajadhyaksha and Willemen, 144).

36. Bhimani, *In Search of Lata Mangeshkar,* 233; Manuel, *Cassette Culture,* 48; Gadgil, "Meet Lata Mangeshkar," 36.

37. "Editorial," *Rajatpat,* September 1948, 4–6.

38. "Setback for Playback," editorial, *Filmfare,* 19 September 1952, 5.

39. In the 1982 edition of the *Guinness Book of World Records,* Lata Mangeshkar had an entry as the most recorded voice in the world, having "reportedly recorded not less than 25,000 solo, duet and chorus-backed songs in 20 Indian languages." In a correspondence with the publishers of *Guinness,* Mohammed Rafi disputed this claim and was subsequently granted his own entry, in which he "claimed to have recorded 28,000 songs in 11 Indian languages between 1944 and April 1980." Rafi fans were upset over the *Guinness* editors' choice of words: "reportedly recorded" for Lata and "claimed to have recorded" for Rafi. The controversy does not end there, as Raju Bharatan details in his chapter, "The Guinness Empress that Never Was" (*Lata Mangeshkar,* 275–301), because Asha fans have been quick to point out that in the 1950s, despite Lata's greater vocal presence in the public imagination, Asha actually recorded more songs, 7,500 as opposed to Lata's 5,250. In Bharatan's view, Har Mandir Singh, the editor of the *Encyclopaedia of Hindi Film Songs,* has the final word when he "makes a passionate plea to all singers in India to think twice before claiming 20,000 and 30,000 songs. He points out how ridiculous the claim is in the context of the fact that, in 60 years of Hindustani talkie (1932–91), the total number of songs recorded is only 50,000 " (Bharatan, *Lata Mangeshkar,* 300). In response to the controversy, *Guinness* finally removed the category of most recorded voice, though, as far as public knowledge is concerned, Lata still has the *Guinness* pedigree of the most recorded voice in the world.

40. Mitra, "O Indisputable and Indispensable Queen," 42.

41. Quoted in Bhimani, *In Search of Lata Mangeshkar,* 211–12.

42. Quoted in Bhimani, *In Search of Lata Mangeshkar,* 235.
43. Thomas, "Indian Cinema," 126.
44. Thomas, "Sanctity and Scandal," 22.
45. Doane, "Voice in the Cinema," 378.
46. When arguing that she is not a star, Peter Manuel describes her as "portly and plain-looking" (*Cassette Culture,* 48).
47. Singh quoted in Bharatan, *Lata Mangeshkar,* 85. Gadgil, "Meet Lata Mangeshkar," 37.
48. Mitra, "O Indisputable and Indispensable Queen," 44.
49. P. Chatterjee, "Bit of Song and Dance," 213. This is the film critic, Partha Chatterjee, not the historian of the same name.
50. See, for example, Bunny Reuben's anecdotal chapter on Nargis, titled "The Woman in White," in *Follywood Flashback.* According to Raju Bharatan, "Lata in white was for Raj [Kapoor] a replica of Nargis in white, somewhere the Voice and the Vision merged" (*Lata Mangeshkar,* 92).
51. For example, an entry in a column of brief news items in *Sound* magazine stated: "LENDING: Her singing voice to such stars as Nargis, Kamini Kaushal, Geeta Bali, Nigar, etc., for hit songs like 'Meri Ladki'. . . frail, dark, freckled, 18-year-old-Winayak discovery Lata Mangeshkar, always heard but never seen" ("People," *Sound,* July 1949, 51).
52. Raj Kapoor explains his casting choice as follows: "When I took up the subject again, my concept of the heroine had changed. I wanted a woman with a beautiful voice and a beautiful body. I had Lata's voice as beautiful as ever. And Zeenat had the kind of body I wanted" (quoted in Bharatan, *Lata Mangeshkar,* 92).
53. Gadgil, "Meet Lata Mangeshkar," 37; P. Chatterjee, "When Melody Ruled the Day," 56.
54. "Melody Queen Pines for Classical Music," India Network News Digest 11.5, 22 March 1999. Archived at: http://listserv.indnet.org/cgi/wa?A1=ind9903&L=india-l.
55. Lata did not like singing songs in the nightclub genre and "felt inhibited" about songs with double entendres (Bharatan, *Lata Mangeshkar,* 158).
56. Bharatan, *Lata Mangeshkar,* 51. The word choice of *bazaar* (or marketplace) in this context is interesting. In his structural analysis of the space of the bazaar in Indian culture, Dipesh Chakrabarty notes its use "in a metaphorical way to represent an 'outside' to 'ghar-shangshar' (the way of the householder, i.e., domesticity); thus prostitutes are called . . . women of the bazaar . . . as opposed to women of the household" ("Of Garbage," 543). He also mentions the bazaar's significance as a space for the origin and dissemination of rumor or gossip ("Of Garbage," 544). Thus, the image of the bazaar, in Naushad's description of Asha's voice, may be said to invoke many of the negative connotations of female public performance in India.
57. Bharatan, *Lata Mangeshkar,* 344.
58. Rajeshwari Sundar Rajan observes that Indira Gandhi's identification with the nation through the slogan "Indira is India" worked to carefully invoke the "familiar equation of the nation with the mother, already a trope of nineteenth-century nationalist discourse" (*Real and Imagined Women,* 109).
59. According to Harish Bhimani, she is still "the only playback artiste who gets

royalty, over and above the remuneration paid per song (wherever a royalty exists between a producer and a recording company)" (*In Search of Lata Mangeshkar,* 196).

60. See note 39 above.

61. See Lelyveld, "Upon the Subdominant," on the administration of voices in radio programming. Weidman, *Singing the Classical, Voicing the Modern,* 18.

62. In the political realm, Lata's status as elder guru was confirmed in late 1999 when she was nominated as member of the Rajya Sabha, India's upper house of parliament.

63. Kavita Krishnamurty, one of the new playback singers who started as a "dubbing artiste," exemplifies this attitude in a 1996 interview: "As far as I'm concerned, I will be eternally indebted to Lataji. I started my career singing her songs which she would dub over later. . . . I owe everything to her" ("Crooning Glory," *Filmfare,* June 1996, 81–82).

64. I use the term *Bollywood* here loosely to mark and acknowledge the economic, institutional, and textual changes in Bombay cinema after the liberalization of India's economy in 1991.

65. Pinto, *Helen,* 17.

WORKS CITED

Abbas, K. A. *Mad, Mad, Mad World of Indian Films.* Delhi: Hind Pocket Books, 1972.

A. D. "America Abroad." *Cinema Vision India* 1.2 (April 1980): 91.

Alter, Joseph S. *The Wrestler's Body: Identity and Ideology in North India.* Berkeley: University of California Press, 1992.

Altman, Rick. *The American Film Musical.* Bloomington: Indiana University Press, 1987.

Amin, Shahid. "Gandhi as Mahatma: Gorakhpur District, Eastern UP, 1921–2." In *Subaltern Studies III: Writings on South Asian History and Society.* Ed. Ranajit Guha. New Delhi: Oxford University Press, 1984. 1–61.

Archer, W. G. *Bazaar Paintings of Calcutta.* Museum Monograph (Victoria and Albert Museum) No. 7. London: Her Majesty's Stationery Office, 1953.

Arnold, Alison. "Hindi Filmi Git: On the History of Commercial Indian Popular Music." Diss., University of Illinois at Urbana-Champaign, 1991.

———. "Popular Film Song in India—A Case of Mass Market Musical Eclecticism." *Popular Music* 7, no. 2 (May 1988): 177–88.

Arnold, David, and Stuart Blackburn. "Introduction: Life Histories in India." In *Telling Lives in India: Biography, Autobiography, and Life History.* Ed. David Arnold and Stuart Blackburn. Bloomington: Indiana University Press, 2004. 1–26.

Arora, Poonam. "'Imperiling the Prestige of the White Woman': Colonial Anxiety and Film Censorship in British India." *Visual Anthropology Review* 11.2 (Fall 1995). 36–50.

Assadullah, Syed. *Film in India.* Secunderabad: Osmania Printing Works, 1938.

Babington, Bruce. "Introduction: British Stars and Stardom." In *British Stars and Stardom: From Alma Taylor to Sean Connery.* Ed. Bruce Babington. Manchester: Manchester University Press, 2001. 1–28.

Bahadur, Satish, and Shyamala Vanarase. "The Personal and Professional Problems of a Woman Performer." *Cinema Vision India* 1.1 (January 1980): 22–25.

Balázs, Béla. "The Close-up." In *Film Theory and Criticism: Introductory Readings.* Ed. Gerald Mast and Marshall Cohen. 3d ed. New York: Oxford University Press, 1985. 255–64.

Bandopadhyay, Samik, ed. *Indian Cinema: Contemporary Perceptions from the Thirties.* Jamshedpur: Celluloid Chapter, 1993.

Banerjee, Sumanta. *The Parlour and the Streets: Elite and Popular Culture in Nineteenth Century Calcutta.* Calcutta: Seagull Books, 1989.

———. "Women's Popular Culture in Nineteenth Century Bengal." In *Recasting*

Women: Essays in Indian Colonial History. Ed. Kumkum Sangari and Suresh Vaid. New Brunswick, N.J.: Rutgers University Press, 1990. 127–79.

Bao, Weihong. "From Pearl White to White Rose Woo: Tracing the Vernacular Body of Nuxia in Chinese Silent Cinema, 1927–1931." *Camera Obscura* 60 (2005): 193–231.

Barlow, Tani E., Madeleine Yue Dong, Uta G. Poiger, Priti Ramamurthy, et al. "The Modern Girl around the World: A Research Agenda and Preliminary Finding." *Gender and History* 17.2 (August 2005): 245–94.

Bawa, Mohan. *Actors and Acting.* Bombay: India Book House, 1978.

Bean, Jennifer M. "Technologies of Early Stardom and the Extraordinary Body." In *A Feminist Reader in Early Cinema.* Ed. Jennifer M. Bean and Diane Negra. Durham, N.C.: Duke University Press, 2002. 404–43.

Bean, Jennifer M., and Diane Negra, eds. *Early Women Stars.* Special issue. *Camera Obscura* 48 (2001).

———. *A Feminist Reader in Early Cinema.* Durham, N.C.: Duke University Press, 2002.

Bear, Laura. "Traveling Modernity: Capitalism, Community and Nation in the Colonial Governance of the Indian Railways." Diss., University of Michigan, 1998.

Bhabha, Homi. *The Location of Culture.* London: Routledge, 1994, 2004.

Bharatan, Raju. *Lata Mangeshkar: A Biography.* New Delhi: UBS Publishers' Distribution Ltd., 1995.

Bhatia, Vanraj. "Stop the Action, Start the Song." *Cinema Vision India* 1.4 (1980): 31–36.

Bhattacharya, Neeladri. "Notes towards a Conception of the Colonial Public." In *Civil Society, Public Sphere and Citizenship: Dialogues and Perceptions.* Ed. Rajeev Bhargava and Helmut Reinfeld. New Delhi: Sage, 2005. 130–56.

Bhattacharya, Rimli. Introduction. In Binodini Dasi, *My Story and My Life as an Actress.* Trans. and ed. Rimli Bhattacharya. New Delhi: Kali for Women, 1998. 3–46.

———. "Notes on the Bengali Public Theatre." In Binodini Dasi, *My Story and My Life as an Actress.* Trans. and ed. Rimli Bhattacharya. New Delhi: Kali for Women, 1998. 160–85.

Bhattacharya, Rinki. "Nadia." *Filmfare,* 29 April–12 May 1977, 46–47.

Bhaumik, Kaushik. "The Emergence of the Bombay Film Industry, 1913–1936." Diss. Oxford University, 2001.

Bhimani, Harish. *In Search of Lata Mangeshkar.* New Delhi: HarperCollins, 1995.

Bhooch, Harish S., and Karing Doyle. *Star-Portrait: Intimate Life Stories of Famous Film Stars.* New rev. ed. Bombay: Lakhani Book Depot, 1962.

Binodini Dasi. *My Story and My Life as an Actress.* Trans. and ed. Rimli Bhattacharya. New Delhi: Kali for Women, 1998.

"Bodybuilding and Muscle Control in India." From "Sandow & the Golden Age of Iron Men: The Online Physical Culture Museum." http://www.sandowplus.co.uk/India/india.htm. Accessed on 12 April 2007.

Booth, Greg. *Behind the Curtain: Making Music in Mumbai's Film Studios.* New York: Oxford University Press, 2008.

Braudy, Leo. *The Frenzy of Renown: Fame and Its History.* 1986. Rpt., New York: Vintage, 1997.

Brigsby, C. W. E., ed. *Superculture: Europe, America, and the Cultural Debate.* Bowling Green, Ohio: Bowling Green State University Popular Press, 1975.
Bruno, Giuliana. *Streetwalking on a Ruined Map: Cultural Theory and the City Films of Elvira Notari.* Princeton, N.J.: Princeton University Press, 1993.
Chabria, Suresh, ed. *Light of Asia: Indian Silent Cinema 1912–1934.* New Delhi: Wiley Eastern, 1994.
Chakrabarty, Dipesh. "The Difference-Deferral of a Colonial Modernity: Public Debates on Domesticity in British Bengal." In *Subaltern Studies VIII: Essays in Honour of Ranajit Guha.* Ed. David Arnold and David Hardiman. New Delhi: Oxford University Press, 1994. 50–88.
———. "Nation and Imagination: The Training of the Eye in Bengali Modernity." *Topoi* 18 (1999): 29–47.
———. "Of Garbage, Modernity and the Citizen's Gaze." *Economic and Political Weekly*, 7–14 March 1992, 541–47.
———. "Postcoloniality and the Artifice of History: Who Speaks for 'Indian' Pasts?" In *The New Historicism Reader.* Ed. H. Aram Veeser. New York: Routledge, 1994. 342–69.
Chakravarty, Sumita. *National Identity in Indian Popular Cinema 1947–1987.* Austin: University of Texas Press, 1993.
Chandavarkar, Bhaskar. "Now It's the Bombay Film Song." *Cinema in India*, July–September 1989, 18–23.
Chang, Michael. "The Good, the Bad, and the Beautiful: Actresses and Public Discourse in Shanghai, 1920s–1930s." In *Cinema and Urban Culture in Shanghai, 1922–1943.* Ed. Yingjin Zhang. Stanford: Stanford University Press, 1999. 128–59.
Chapman, David L. *Sandow the Magnificent: Eugen Sandow and the Beginnings of Bodybuilding.* Urbana: University of Illinois Press, 1994.
Chatterjee, Gayatri. *Mother India.* London: BFI, 2002.
Chatterjee, Partha (1). "A Bit of Song and Dance." In *Frames of Mind.* Ed. Aruna Vasudev. New Delhi: UBSPD, 1995. 197–218.
———. "When Melody Ruled the Day." In *Frames of Mind.* Ed. Aruna Vasudev. New Delhi: UBSPD, 1995. 51–65.
Chatterjee, Partha (2). "The Nationalist Resolution of the Women's Question." In *Recasting Women: Essays in Indian Colonial History.* Ed. Kumkum Sangari and Suresh Vaid. New Brunswick, N.J.: Rutgers University Press, 1990. 233–53.
———. *The Nation and Its Fragments: Colonial and Postcolonial Histories.* New Delhi: Oxford University Press, 1995.
Chatterjee, Ratnabali. "Representation of Gender in Folk Paintings of Bengal." *Social Scientist* 28.3–4 (Mar–April 2000): 7–21.
Chatterjee, Sudipto. "The Colonial Stage(d): Hybridity, Woman, and the Nation in Nineteenth Century Bengali Theatre." Diss., New York University, 1998.
Chion, Michel. *Audio-Vision: Sound on Screen.* Ed. and trans. Claudia Gorbman. New York: Columbia University Press, 1990.
Chowdhry, Prem. *Colonial India and the Making of Empire Cinema: Image, Ideology, and Identity.* Manchester: Manchester University Press, 2000.
Dalvi, K. T. *A New Profession or Manual of Indian Talkies.* Bombay: K. T. Dalvi, 1931.

Dass, Manishita. "Outside the Unlettered City: Cinema, Modernity, and Nation in India." Diss., Stanford University, 2004.

deCordova, Richard. "The Emergence of the Star System in America." In *Stardom: Industry of Desire.* Ed. Christine Gledhill. London: Routledge, 1991. 17–29.

———. *Picture Personalities: The Emergence of the Star System in America.* Urbana: University of Illinois Press, 1990.

Dharamsay, Virchand. "Introduction: Indian Silent Cinema 1912–1934: A Filmography." In *Light of Asia: Indian Silent Cinema 1912–1934.* Ed. Suresh Chabria. New Delhi: Wiley Eastern, 1994. 69–71.

Doane, Mary Ann. "The Voice in the Cinema: The Articulation of Body and Space." *Yale French Studies* 60 (1980): 33–50. Rpt. in *Film Theory and Criticism.* Ed. Leo Braudy and Marshall Cohen. 6th ed. New York: Oxford University Press, 2004. 373–85.

Dwyer, Rachel, and Divia Patel. *Cinema India: The Visual Culture of Hindi Film.* New Brunswick, N.J.: Rutgers University Press, 2002.

Dyer, Richard. "Charisma." In *Stardom: Industry of Desire.* Ed. Christine Gledhill. London: Routledge, 1991. 57–59.

———. "Entertainment and Utopia." In *Genre: The Musical.* Ed. Rick Altman. London: Routledge & Kegan Paul, 1981. 175–89.

———. *Heavenly Bodies: Film Stars and Society.* 2d ed. London: Routledge, 2004.

———. "*A Star Is Born* and the Construction of Authenticity." In *Stardom: Industry of Desire.* Ed. Christine Gledhill. London: Routledge, 1991. 132–40.

———. *Stars.* London: BFI, 1979.

———. *Stars.* With a supplementary chapter and bibliography by Paul McDonald. London: BFI, 1998.

———. *White.* London: Routledge, 1997.

Eco, Umberto. "The Myth of Superman." Trans. Natalie Chilton. In *The Role of the Reader.* Bloomington: Indiana University Press, 1979. 107–24.

Ellis, John. "Stars as Cinematic Phenomenon." In *Visible Fictions: Cinema: Television: Video.* 1982. Rev. ed. London: Routledge, 1992. 91–108.

Fazalbhoy, Y. A. *The Indian Film: A Review.* Bombay: Bombay Radio Press, 1939.

Fearless: The Hunterwali Story. Dir. Riyad Vinci Wadia. 1993.

Feuer, Jane. *The Hollywood Musical.* Bloomington: Indiana University Press, 1984.

Fischer, Lucy. "Greta Garbo and Silent Cinema: The Actress as Art Deco Icon." In *A Feminist Reader in Early Cinema.* Ed. Jennifer M. Bean and Diana Negra. Durham, N.C.: Duke University Press, 2002. 476–98.

Fuller, Kathryn H. *At the Picture Show: Small-Town Audiences and the Creation of Movie Fan Culture.* 1996. Rpt., Charlottesville: University of Virginia Press, 2001.

———. "*Motion Picture Story Magazine* and the Gendered Construction of the Movie Fan." In *In the Eye of the Beholder: Critical Perspectives in Popular Film and Television.* Ed. Gary R. Edgerton, Michael T. Marsden, and Jack Nachbar. Bowling Green, Ohio: Bowling Green State University Popular Press, 1997. 97–112.

Gadgil, Gangadhar. "Meet Lata Mangeshkar." *Illustrated Weekly of India,* 30 April 1967, 36.

Gandhy, Behroze, and Rosie Thomas. "Three Indian Film Stars." In *Stardom: Industry of Desire.* Ed. Christine Gledhill. London: Routledge, 1991. 107–31.

Gardner, William O. "New Perceptions: Kinugasa Teinosuke's Films and Japanese Modernism." *Cinema Journal* 43.3 (Spring 2004): 59–78.

Garga, B. D. *The Art of Cinema: An Insider's Journey through Fifty Years of Film History.* New Delhi: Viking, 2005.

———. "A New Look at an Old Report." *Cinema Vision India* 1.1 (January 1980): 67–70.

———. "Screen Personality Nawab: An Appreciation of a Great and Versatile Character Actor." *Sound,* August 1949, 43, 45.

Gargi, Balwant. *Folk Theatre of India.* Seattle: University of Washington Press, 1966.

George, T. J. S. *The Life and Times of Nargis.* New Delhi: Indus, 1994.

Gledhill, Christine. "The Screen Actress from Silence to Sound." In *The Cambridge Companion to the Actress.* Ed. Maggie B. Gale and John Stokes. Cambridge, U.K.: Cambridge University Press, 2007. 193–214.

———. "Signs of Melodrama." In *Stardom: Industry of Desire.* Ed. Christine Gledhill. London: Routledge, 1991. 207–29.

Gopal, Sangita, and Sujata Moorti, eds. *Global Bollywood: Travels of Hindi Song and Dance.* Minneapolis: University of Minnesota Press, 2008.

Gopalan, Lalitha. *Cinema of Interruptions: Action Genres in Contemporary Indian Cinema.* London: BFI, 2002.

Griffith, Richard. *The Talkies: Articles and Illustrations from a Great Fan Magazine 1928–1940.* New York: Dover, 1971.

Guha, Ranajit. *Dominance without Hegemony: History and Power in Colonial India.* Cambridge, Mass.: Harvard University Press, 1997.

———. *Elementary Aspects of Peasant Insurgency in Colonial India.* New Delhi: Oxford University Press, 1983.

Guha-Thakurta, Tapati. *The Making of a New "Indian" Art: Artists, Aesthetics and Nationalism in Bengal, c. 1850–1920.* Cambridge, U.K.: Cambridge University Press, 1992.

Gunning, Tom. "The Cinema of Attractions: Early Film, Its Spectator and the Avant-Garde." In *Early Cinema: Space Frame Narrative.* Ed. Thomas Elsaesser. London: BFI, 1990. 56–62.

Gupt, Somnath. *The Parsi Theatre: Its Origins and Development.* Ed. and trans. Kathryn Hansen. Calcutta: Seagull Books, 2005.

Gupta, Charu. *Sexuality, Obscenity, Community: Women, Muslims, and the Hindu Public in Colonial India.* New Delhi: Permanent Black, 2001. New York: Palgrave, 2002.

Gutman, Judith Mara. *Through Indian Eyes: Nineteenth and Early Twentieth Century Photography from India.* New York: Oxford University Press International Center of Photography, 1982.

Hansen, Kathryn. "A Different Desire, a Different Femininity: Theatrical Transvestism in the Parsi, Gujarati, and Marathi Theaters, 1850–1940." In *Queering India: Same-Sex Love and Eroticism in Indian Culture and Society.* Ed. Ruth Vanita. New York: Routledge, 2002. 163–80.

———. *Grounds for Play: The Nautanki Theatre of North India.* Berkeley: University of California Press, 1992.

———."Making Women Visible: Gender and Race Cross-Dressing in the Parsi Theatre." *Theatre Journal* 51 (1999): 127–47.

———. "The Virangana in North Indian History, Myth and Popular Culture." *Economic and Political Weekly* 23.18 (30 April 1988): 25–33.

Hansen, Miriam. "Adventures of Goldilocks: Spectatorship, Consumerism, and Public Life." *Camera Obscura* 22 (1990): 51–72.

———. "Early Cinema, Late Cinema: Permutations of the Public Sphere." *Screen* 34.3 (Autumn 1993): 197–210. Rpt. in *Viewing Positions.* Ed. Linda Williams. New Brunswick, N.J.: Rutgers University Press, 1995. 134–52.

———. "Early Silent Cinema: Whose Public Sphere?" *New German Critique* 29 (Spring–Summer 1983): 147–84.

———. "Falling Women, Rising Stars, New Horizons: Shanghai Silent Film as Vernacular Modernism." *Film Quarterly* 54.1 (2000): 10–22.

———. "The Mass Production of the Senses: Classical Cinema as Vernacular Modernism." *Modernism/Modernity* 6.2 (1999): 59–77. Rpt. in *Reinventing Film Studies.* Ed. Christine Gledhill and Linda Williams. London: Arnold, 2000. 332–50.

Hastie, Amelie. *Cupboards of Curiosity: Women, Recollection, and Film History.* Durham, N.C.: Duke University Press, 2007.

Heckel, Angelika. "*Rasa*: The Audience and the Stage." *Journal of Arts & Ideas* 17–18 (June 1989): 33–42.

Hughes, Stephen Putnam. "Is There Anyone Out There? Exhibition and the Formation of Silent Film Audiences in South India." Diss., University of Chicago, 1996.

Huyssen, Andreas. *After the Great Divide: Modernism, Mass Culture, Postmodernism.* Bloomington: Indiana University Press, 1986.

Indian Cinematograph Committee. *Indian Cinematograph Committee 1927–1928: Evidence.* Calcutta: Central Publication Branch, 1928.

———. *Report of the Indian Cinematograph Committee 1927–1928.* Calcutta: Central Publication Branch, 1928.

Jaikumar, Priya. *Cinema at the End of Empire: A Politics of Transition in Britain and India.* Durham, N.C.: Duke University Press, 2006.

Jain, Kajri. "Figures of Locality and Tradition: Commercial Cinema and the Networks of Visual Print Capitalism in Maharashtra." In *Bollyworld: Popular Indian Cinema through a Transnational Lens.* Ed. Rajinder Kaur and Ajay J. Sinha. New Delhi: Sage, 2005. 70–89.

Jenkins, Henry. *Textual Poachers: Television Fans and Participatory Culture.* New York: Routledge, 1992.

Joshi, Priya. *In Another Country: Colonialism, Culture, and the English Novel in India.* New York: Columbia University Press, 2002.

Joshi, Sanjay. *Fractured Modernity: Making of a Middle Class in Colonial North India.* New Delhi: Oxford University Press, 2001.

Kak, Siddharth. "The Colossus and the Little Flower from India." *Cinema Vision India* 1.3 (April 1980): 71–75.

———. Editorial. *Cinema Vision India* 1.1 (January 1980): 1.

Kapur, Anuradha. "The Representation of Gods and Heroes: Parsi Mythological Drama of the Early Twentieth Century." *Journal of Arts and Ideas* 23–24 (1993): 85–107.

Kapur, Geeta. "Mythic Material in Indian Cinema." *Journal of Arts & Ideas* 14–15 (July–December 1987): 79–108.

———. "Ravi Varma: Representational Dilemmas of a Nineteenth Century Indian Painter." *Journal of Arts & Ideas* 17–18 (June 1989): 59–80.

———. "Revelation and Doubt: *Sant Tukaram* and *Devi*." In *Interrogating Modernity: Culture and Colonialism in India*. Ed. Tejaswini Niranjana and Vivek Dhareshwar. Calcutta: Seagull Books, 1993. 19–46.

Karnad, Girish. "Glorious Gohar." *Cinema Vision India* 1.1 (January 1980): 74–79.

———. "This One Is for Nadia." *Cinema Vision India* 1.2 (April 1980): 84–90.

Kaul, Gautam. *Cinema and the Indian Freedom Struggle*. New Delhi: Sterling, 1998.

Kaur, Raminder. *Bollyworld: Popular Indian Cinema through a Transnational Lens*. New Delhi: Sage, 2005.

Kaviraj, Sudipto. "The Invention of Private Life: A Reading of Sibnath Sastri's *Autobiography*." In *Telling Lives in India: Biography, Autobiography, and Life History*. Ed. David Arnold and Stuart Blackburn. Bloomington: Indiana University Press, 2004. 83–115.

Kazim, Lubna, ed. *A Woman of Substance: The Memoirs of Begum Khurshid Mirza (1918–1989)*. New Delhi: Zubaan, 2005.

Kesavan, Mukul. "Urdu, Awadh and the Tawaif: The Islamicate Roots of Hindi Cinema." In *Forging Identities: Gender, Communities and the State in India*. Ed. Zoya Hasan. Boulder: Westview Press, 1994. 244–57.

Khote, Durga. *I, Durga Khote*. Trans. Shanta Gokhale. New Delhi: Oxford University Press, 2006.

Kinkar, Shashikant. "Lasting Lady, Khurshid-Saraswati." *Cinema Vision India* 2.2 (1983): 70–72.

Klinger, Barbara. "To Infinity and Beyond: The Web Short, Parody, and Remediation." In *Beyond the Multiplex: Cinema, New Technologies, and the Home*. Berkeley: University of California Press, 2006. 191–238.

Knight, Arthur. "Star Dances: African-American Constructions of Stardom, 1925–1960." In *Classic Hollywood, Classic Whiteness*. Ed. Daniel Bernardi. Minneapolis: University of Minnesota Press, 2001. 386–414.

Knizkova, Hana. *The Drawings of the Kalighat Style: Secular Themes*. Prague: National Museum Prague, 1975.

Kuhn, Annette. *Cinema, Censorship and Sexuality, 1909–1925*. London: Routledge, 1988.

Lelyveld, David. "Upon the Subdominant: Administering Music on All-India Radio." *Social Text* 39 (Summer 1994): 111–27.

Macnab, Geoffrey. *Searching for Stars: Stardom and Screen Acting in British Cinema*. London: Cassell, 2000.

Majumdar, Neepa. "Film Fragments, Documentary History, and Colonial Indian Cinema." *Canadian Journal of Film Studies* 16.1 (Spring 2007): 63–79.

Manto, Saadat Hasan. *Stars from Another Sky: The Bombay Film World of the 1940s*. Trans. Khalid Hasan. New Delhi: Penguin, 1998.

Manuel, Peter. *Cassette Culture: Popular Music and Technology in North India*. Chicago: University of Chicago Press, 1993.

Marre, Jeremy, and Hannah Charlton. *Beats of the Heart: Popular Music of the World*. New York: Pantheon, 1985.

Mazumdar, Ranjani. *Bombay Cinema: An Archive of the City.* Minneapolis: University of Minnesota Press, 2007.

———. "From Subjectification to Schizophrenia: The 'Angry' Man and the 'Psychotic' Hero of Bombay Cinema." In *Making Meaning in Indian Cinema.* Ed. Ravi Vasudevan. New Delhi: Oxford University Press, 2000. 215–37.

"Melody Queen Pines for Classical Music." *India Network News Digest* 11.5, 22 March 1999. Archived at: http://listserv.indnet.org/cgi/wa?A1=ind9903&L=india-l.

Menon, Raghava. *K. L. Saigal: The Pilgrim of the Swara.* Delhi: Clarion Books, 1978.

Mishra, Vijay. *Bollywood Cinema: Temples of Desire.* New York: Routledge, 2002.

———. "Decentering History: Some Versions of Bombay Cinema." *East-West Film Journal* 6.1 (1992): 111–55.

Mishra, Vijay, Peter Jeffery, and Brian Shoesmith. "The Actor as Parallel Text in Bombay Cinema." *Quarterly Review of Film and Video* 11.3 (October 1989): 49–67.

Mitra, Sumit. "O Indisputable and Indispensable Queen." *Cinema Vision India* 2.2 (1983): 38–45.

Morcom, Anna. *Hindi Film Songs and the Cinema.* Farnham, Surrey, U.K.: Ashgate, 2007.

Mujumdar, D. C. *Encyclopedia of Indian Physical Culture.* Baroda: Good Companions, 1950.

Nadkarni, Mohan. *Bal Gandharva, the Nonpareil Thespian.* New Delhi: National Book Trust, 1988.

Nandy, Ashis. "The Double in Hindi Cinema." *Times of India,* 14 October 1979, 8.

———. "The Popular Hindi Film: Ideology and First Principles." *India International Centre Quarterly* 8.1 (March 1980): 89–96.

Naremore, James. *Acting in the Cinema.* Berkeley: University of California Press, 1988.

Nargis. Interview. In *Indian Cinema Superbazaar.* Ed. Aruna Vasudev and Philippe Lenglet. New Delhi: Vikas, 1983. 252–61.

Niranjana, Tejaswini. *Mobilizing India: Women, Music, and Migration between India and Trinidad.* Durham, N.C.: Duke University Press, 2006.

Niranjana, Tejaswini, and Vivek Dhareshwar, eds. *Interrogating Modernity: Culture and Colonialism in India.* Calcutta: Seagull Books, 1993.

Ojha, Rajendra, ed. *75 Glorious Years of Indian Cinema: Complete Filmography of All Films (Silent and Hindi) Produced between 1913 and 1988.* Bombay: Screen World Publication, 1988.

Orr, John. *Cinema and Modernity.* Cambridge, U.K.: Polity Press, 1993.

Orsini, Francesca. *The Hindi Public Sphere, 1920–1949: Language and Literature in the Age of Nationalism.* London: Oxford University Press, 2002.

———. "Reading a Social Romance: *Cand hasinom ke khutut.*" In *Narrative Strategies: Essays on South Asian Literature and Film.* Ed. Vasudha Dalmia and Theo Damsteegt. New Delhi: Oxford University Press, 1998. 185–210.

———. "The Reticent Autobiographer: Mahadevi Varma's Writings." In *Telling Lives in India: Biography, Autobiography, and Life History.* Ed. David Arnold and Stuart Blackburn. Bloomington: Indiana University Press, 2004. 54–81.

Patel, Baburao. "I Was the Only Paper That Counted." *Cinema Vision India* 1.2 (April 1980): 66–69.

Pearson, Roberta. *Eloquent Gestures: The Transformation of Performance Style in the Griffith Biograph Films.* Berkeley: University of California Press, 1992.

Pfleiderer, Beatrix, and Lothar Lutze, eds. *The Hindi Film: Agent and Re-agent of Cultural Change.* Delhi: Manohar Press, 1984.

Phalke, D. G. "Indian Cinema—I." In *Phalke Centenary Souvenir.* Ed. Firoze Rangoonwala. Bombay: Phalke Centenary Celebrations Committee, 1978. 88–94.

Pinney, Christopher. "Indian Magical Realism: Notes on Popular Visual Culture." In *Subaltern Studies X: Writings on South Asian History and Society.* New Delhi: Oxford University Press, 1999. 201–33.

———. "The Indian Work of Art in the Age of Mechanical Reproduction: Or, What Happens When Peasants 'Get Hold' of Images." In *Media Worlds: Anthropology on New Terrain.* Ed. Faye D. Ginsburg, Lila Abu-Lughod, and Brian Larkin. Berkeley: University of California Press, 2002. 355–69.

———. "The Nation (Un)Pictured? Chromolithography and 'Popular' Politics in India." *Critical Inquiry* 23.4 (Summer 1997): 834–67.

———. *Photos of the Gods: The Printed Image and Political Struggle.* London: Reaktion, 2004.

Pinto, Jerry. *Helen: The Life and Times of an H-Bomb.* New Delhi: Penguin, 2006.

Prasad, Madhava. *Ideology of the Hindi Film: A Historical Construction.* New Delhi: Oxford University Press, 1998.

———. "This Thing Called Bollywood." *Seminar* 525 (May 2003): 17–20. Archived at http://www.india-seminar.com/2003/525/525%20madhava%20prasad.htm.

Purohit, Vinayak. *Profile of the Hindi Hit Movie, 1951–1985.* Bombay: Indian Institute of Social Research, 1985. Rpt. in *Some Aspects of Sociology of Indian Films and Profile of the Hindi Hit Movie, 1951–1985.* Bombay: Indian Institute of Social Research, 1990.

Rajadhyaksha, Ashish. "The 'Bollywoodization' of Indian Cinema: Cultural Nationalism in a Global Arena." *Inter-Asia Cultural Studies* 4.1 (2003): 25–39. Rpt. in *City Flicks: Indian Cinema and the Urban Experience.* Ed. Preben Kaarsholm. Calcutta: Seagull Press, 2005. 113–39.

———. "India's Silent Cinema: A 'Viewer's View.'" In *Light of Asia: India's Silent Cinema 1912–1934.* Ed. Suresh Chabria. New Delhi: Wiley Eastern, 1994. 25–40.

———. "Neo-Traditionalism: Film as Popular Art in India." *Framework* 32–33 (1986): 20–67.

———. "The Phalke Era: Conflict of Traditional Form and Modern Technology." In *Interrogating Modernity: Culture and Colonialism in India.* Ed. Tejaswini Niranjana and Vivek Dhareshwar. Calcutta: Seagull Books, 1993. 47–82.

Rajadhyaksha, Ashish, and Paul Willemen, eds. *Encyclopaedia of Indian Cinema.* New rev. ed. London: BFI and Oxford University Press, 1999.

Rajan, Rajeshwari Sundar. *Real and Imagined Women: Gender, Culture and Postcoloniality.* London: Routledge, 1993.

Ranade, Ashok. "The Extraordinary Importance of the Indian Film Song." *Cinema Vision India* 1.4 (1980): 4–11.

Ray, Bharati. "Calcutta Women in the Swadesh Movement (1903–1910): The Nature and Implications of Participation." In *The Urban Experience Calcutta: Essay in Honour of Professor Nisith R. Ray.* Ed. Pradip Sinha. Calcutta: Riddhi-India, 1987.

Reuben, Bunny. *Follywood Flashback: A Collection of Movie Memories.* New Delhi: Indus, 1993.

———. "Hindi Screen Acting: An Assessment of Three Generations." *Star and Style* 3.4 (1970): 16–17.

———. *Raj Kapoor the Fabulous Showman.* New Delhi: Indus, 1995.

Roselli, John. "The Self-Image of Effeteness: Physical Education and Nationalism in Nineteenth-Century Bengal." *Past and Present* 86 (February 1980): 121–48.

Roy, Parama. *Indian Traffic: Identities in Question in Colonial and Postcolonial India.* Berkeley: University of California Press, 1998.

Russell, Catherine. "Naruse Mikio's Silent Films: Gender and the Discourse of Everyday Life in Interwar Japan." *Camera Obscura* 60 (2005): 57–89.

Russell, Catherine, ed. *New Women of the Silent Screen: China, Japan, Hollywood.* Special issue. *Camera Obscura* 60 (2005).

Sarkar, Tanika. *Hindu Wife, Hindu Nation: Community, Religion and Cultural Nationalism.* New Delhi: Permanent Black, 2000.

———. "Scandal in High Places: Discourses on the Chaste Hindu Woman in Late Nineteenth Century Bengal." In *Embodiment: Essays on Gender and Identity.* Ed. Meenakshi Thapan. New Delhi: Oxford University Press, 1997. 35–73.

Saunders, Thomas J. *Hollywood in Berlin: American Cinema and Weimar Germany.* Berkeley: University of California Press, 1994.

Schechner, Richard. *Performative Circumstances: From the Avant Garde to Ramlila.* Calcutta: Seagull Books, 1983.

Sengupta, Shuddhabrata. "Reflected Readings in Available Light: Cameramen in the Shadows of Hindi Cinema." In *Bollyworld: Popular Indian Cinema through a Transnational Lens.* Ed. Rajinder Kaur and Ajay J. Sinha. New Delhi: Sage, 2005. 118–40.

Shah, Panna. *The Indian Film.* Bombay: Motion Picture Society of India, 1950. Westport, Conn.: Greenwood Press, 1981.

Sharma, Ashwini. "Blood Sweat and Tears: Amitabh Bhachchan, Urban Demi-God." In *You Tarzan: Masculinity, Movies and Men.* Ed. Pat Kirkham and Janet Thumim. New York: St. Martin's Press, 1993. 167–80.

Sharma, Narendra. "Half a Century of Song." *Cinema Vision India* 1.4 (1980): 56–61.

Shefrin, Elana. "*Lord of the Rings, Star Wars,* and Participatory Fandom: Mapping New Congruencies between the Internet and Media Entertainment Culture." *Critical Studies in Media Communication* 21.3 (September 2004): 261–81.

Shoesmith, Brian. "The Problem of Film: A Reassessment of the Significance of the Indian Cinematograph Committee, 1927–1928." *Continuum* (December 1984): 74–89.

Siefert, Marsha. "Image/Music/Voice: Song Dubbing in Hollywood Musicals." *Journal of Communication* 45.2 (Spring 1995): 44–64.

Singer, Ben. *Melodrama and Modernity: Early Sensational Cinema and Its Contexts.* New York: Columbia University Press, 2001.

Singh, Har Mandir, ed. *Hindi Film Geet Kosh 1931–70.* 4 vols. Kanpur: Satinder Kaur, 1980–88.

Sinha, Mrinalini. *Colonial Masculinity: The 'Manly Englishman' and the 'Effeminate Bengali' in the Late Nineteenth Century.* Manchester: Manchester University Press, 1995.

———. "Giving Masculinity a History: Some Contributions from the Historiography of Colonial India." *Gender & History* 11.3 (November 1999): 445–60.

———. "Nationalism and Respectable Sexuality in India." In *Genders 21: Forming and Reforming Identity.* Ed. Carol Siegel and Ann Kibbey. New York: New York University Press, 1995. 30–57.

———. "Reading *Mother India:* Empire, Nation, and the Female Voice." *Journal of Women's History* 6.2 (1994): 6–44.

Slide, Anthony. *Lois Weber: The Director Who Lost Her Way in History.* Westport, Conn.: Greenwood Press, 1996.

Solomon, Rakesh. "Culture, Imperialism, and Nationalist Resistance: Performance in Colonial India." *Theatre Journal* 46 (1994): 323–47.

Somaaya, Bhawana. *The Story So Far.* Bombay: Indian Express Group, 2005.

Staiger, Janet. "Seeing Stars." In *Stardom: Industry of Desire.* Ed. Christine Gledhill. London: Routledge, 1991. 3–16.

Studlar, Gaylyn. *This Mad Masquerade: Stardom and Masculinity in the Jazz Age.* New York: Columbia University Press, 1996.

Subramaniam, K. N., with Ratnakar Tripathy, eds. *Flashback: Cinema in the* Times of India. Bombay: Times of India, 1990.

Tharu, Susie, and K. Lalitha, eds. *Women Writing in India: 600 B.C. to the Early Twentieth Century.* New York: Feminist Press, 1991.

Thomas, Rosie. "Indian Cinema—Pleasures and Popularity." *Screen* 26.3–4 (1985): 116–32.

———. "Not Quite (Pearl) White: Fearless Nadia, Queen of the Stunts." In *Bollyworld: Popular Indian Cinema through a Transnational Lens.* Ed. Raminder Kaur and Ajay J. Sinha. New Delhi: Sage, 2005. 35–69.

———. "Sanctity and Scandal: The Mythologization of Mother India." *Quarterly Review of Film and Video* 11.3 (1989): 11–30.

Tsivian, Yuri. "New Notes on Russian Film Culture between 1908 and 1919." In *The Silent Cinema Reader.* Ed. Lee Grieveson and Peter Krämer. London: Routledge, 2004. 339–48.

Vasudev, Aruna, and Phillippe Lenglet, eds. *Indian Cinema Superbazaar.* New Delhi: Vikas, 1983.

Vasudevan, Ravi. "Addressing the Spectator of a 'Third World' National Cinema: The Bombay 'Social' Film of the 1940s and 1950s." *Screen* 36.4 (Winter 1995): 305–24.

———. "Cinema and Citizenship in the 'Third World.'" The Van Zelst Lecture in Communication. School of Speech, Northwestern University, Evanston, Ill. 4 May 1996.

———. "The Melodramatic Mode and the Commercial Hindi Cinema: Notes on Film History, Narrative and Performance in the 1950s." *Screen* 3.3 (1989): 29–50.

———. "Sexuality and the Film Apparatus: Continuity, Non-continuity, Discontinuity in Bombay Cinema." In *A Question of Silence? The Sexual Econo-*

mies of Modern India. Ed. Mary E. John and Janaki Nair. New Delhi: Kali for Women, 1998. 192–215.

———. "Shifting Codes, Dissolving Identities: The Hindi Social Film of the 1950s as Popular Culture." *Journal of Arts & Ideas* 23–24 (January 1993): 51–84.

Vincendeau, Ginette. *Stars and Stardom in French Cinema.* London: Continuum, 2000.

Virdi, Jyotika. *The Cinematic ImagiNation: Indian Popular Films as Social History.* New Brunswick, N.J.: Rutgers University Press, 2003.

Viswanathan, Gauri. *Masks of Conquest: Literary Study and British Rule in India.* New York: Columbia University Press, 1989.

Wada-Marciano, Mitsuyo. "Imaging Modern Girls in the Japanese Women's Film." *Camera Obscura* 60 (2005): 15–55.

Wadia, JBH. "Those Were the Days, Parts One and Two." Unpublished manuscript. Portions of this manuscript published as: Wadia, JBH. "Those Were the Days." *Cinema Vision India* 1.1 (January 1980): 91–99; Wadia, JBH. "JBH in Talkieland." *Cinema Vision India* 1.2 (April 1980): 82–83.

Weidman, Amanda J. *Singing the Classical, Voicing the Modern: The Postcolonial Politics of Music in South India.* Durham, N.C.: Duke University Press, 2006.

Wenner, Dorothee. *Fearless Nadia: The True Story of Bollywood's Original Stunt Queen.* New Delhi: Penguin, 1999.

Wollen, Peter. "Cinema/Americanism/The Robot." In *Modernity and Mass Culture.* Ed. James Naremore and Patrick Brantlinger. Bloomington: Indiana University Press, 1991. 46–69.

Zahara, Zeenath. "College Girls and Glamour Boys." *filmindia,* November 1940, 21–24.

Zhang, Zhen. *An Amorous History of the Silver Screen: Shanghai Cinema, 1896–1937.* Chicago: University of Chicago Press, 2005.

Zutshi, Somnath. "Women, Nation and the Outsider in Contemporary Hindi Cinema." In *Interrogating Modernity: Culture and Colonialism in India.* Ed. Tejaswini Niranjana and Vivek Dhareshwar. Calcutta: Seagull Books, 1993. 83–142.

Magazines and Newspapers

The Bombay Chronicle (newspaper)

The Cinema (English-language monthly. Started in 1931, became bimonthly in 1932. Published from Lahore; editor, B. R. Oberoi.)

Cinema Sansar (Hindi weekly from Bombay, started in 1932. "Edited by Radhakrishna Sharma and featuring screenplays, lyrics, stories and film news" [*Encyclopaedia of Indian Cinema,* 20].)

Chitrapat (Hindi film periodical from Delhi, started in 1934; edited by Hrishamcharan Jain. Published "scripts, fiction serials, poetry and news about international cinema" [*Encyclopaedia of Indian Cinema,* 20].)

Filmfare (English film weekly started in 1952. "The first serious effort in film journalism in India" ["Introducing Ourselves," *Filmfare,* 7 March 1952 (first issue), 3]).

filmindia (English monthly published from Bombay, 1935–61. Editor, Baburao Patel.)
Filmland (English weekly from Calcutta, started in 1932.)
The Mirror (English weekly)
Moving Picture Monthly (English)
PicturPost ("The National Guide to Picturegoers." English monthly, published from Madras; started in 1943.)
Rajatpat (Hindi monthly, started in September 1948.)
Rangbhoomi ("The Illustrated Hindi Weekly," published from Delhi, started in 1932.)
Sound (English monthly started in 1942; editor, Zabak. "Featuring politics, fiction, reviews and essays on Indian film" [*Encyclopaedia of Indian Cinema*, 21].)
The Times of India (newspaper)
Varieties Weekly (English weekly, published from Calcutta.)

INDEX

NEEPA MAJUMDAR is an associate professor of English and film at the University of Pittsburgh.

The University of Illinois Press
is a founding member of the
Association of American University Presses.

Composed in 9.5/12.5 Trump Mediaeval
by Jim Proefrock
at the University of Illinois Press
Manufactured by Cushing-Malloy, Inc.

University of Illinois Press
1325 South Oak Street
Champaign, IL 61820-6903
www.press.uillinois.edu